**POSITION OF WOMEN
ON THE LABOUR MARKET
IN THE EUROPEAN COMMUNITY**

Position of Women
on the Labour Market
in the European Community

DANIÈLE MEULDERS
ROBERT PLASMAN
VALÉRIE VANDER STRICHT

Department of Applied Economics
of the Free University of Brussels

Dartmouth
Aldershot · Brookfield USA · Hong Kong · Singapore · Sydney

Published by
Dartmouth Publishing Company Limited
Gower House
Croft Road
Aldershot
Hants GU11 3HR
England

Dartmouth Publishing Company
Old Post Road
Brookfield
Vermont 05036
USA

British Library Cataloguing in Publication Data
Meulders, Danièle
   Position of Women on the Labour Market
   in the European Community
   I. Title
   331.4094

Library of Congress Cataloging-in-Publication Data
Meulders, Danièle.
   Position of women on the labour market in the European Community /
   Danièle Meulders, Robert Plasman, Valérie Vander Stricht.
      p.   cm.
   Includes bibliographical references.
   ISBN 1-85521-419-9
   1. Women--Employment--European Economic Community countries.
   I. Plasman, Robert. II. Vander Stricht, Valérie. III. Title.
   HD6134.5..M48 1993
   331.4'12'094--dc20   93-26641
                                                                     CIP

ISBN 1 85521 419 9

Printed and bound in Great Britain by
Hartnolls Limited, Bodmin, Cornwall

Contents

List of tables

List of figures

Preface

The European network of experts on the Situation of Women in the Labour Market researches into women's employment for the Equal Opportunities Unit of the Directorate General, 'Employment, Industrial Relations and Social Affairs' of the European Communities.

In 1991 the network investigated the evolution of the position of women on the labour market during the 1980s, and the results are published in this book, drawing on twelve unpublished national surveys produced by the following experts :

D. Meulders and V. Vander Stricht	:	Belgium
R. Knudsen	:	Denmark
K. Figge, S. Quack and K. Schäfgen	:	Germany
M. Cavouriaris	:	Greece
M.P. Alcobendas Tirado	:	Spain
A. Gauvin and R. Silvera	:	France
U. Barry	:	Ireland
G. Altieri and P. Villa	:	Italy
O. Plasman and R. Plasman	:	Luxembourg
J. Plantenga	:	Netherlands
M. Chagas Lopes, C. Ferreira and H. Perista	:	Portugal
J. Humphries and J. Rubery	:	United Kingdom

This study was financed by the Equal Opportunities Unit of the Directorate General, 'Employment, Industrial Relations and Social Affairs' of the European Communities. However, this publication does not necessarily reflect the opinion of the Commission of the European Communities.

The first report produced by the network was a document by Bouillaguet-Bernard, Gauvin and Prokovas, published in 1985, synthesizing and analysing developments in women's employment and activity in the European Economic Community during the 1970s and 1980s.

Changes taking place in the labour market over recent years - particularly the increased flexibility and tertiarization of employment - have caused the network to take further stock of the position of women on the labour market since 1983. Most of the statistics utilized are taken from the Eurostat's Labour Force Surveys and have the advantage of not having undergone modifications to their definitions since 1983 and so of being comparable from one European country to another.

This book contains the results of this survey. Its authors would like to thank Pauline Jackson and Els Van Winckel of the Commission for their support. The Statistical Office of the European Communities has been a source of rapid and efficient assistance and, in this respect, our thanks go to Neil Bain, Hildegard Fürst, Bettina Knauth and Bernard Langevin in particular. The typesetting of the book was undertaken by Renée Vanwinkel of the Department of Applied Economics of the Free University of Brussels (ULB) and the translation by John Lamb of the Institute of Phonetics of ULB.

Introduction

The 1980s were marked by profound changes on the labour market. While during the first half of the decade the recession continued apace, an improvement in the economic situation after 1985 led to the creation of several million new jobs in Europe (Commission of the European Communities, 1990, p. 3). However, 85 per cent of these new jobs were taken up by new arrivals on the labour market and unemployment consequently dropped only slightly and still remains in excess of 8 per cent of the active population. The structure of the labour market has also undergone modification, with tertiarization increasing and flexibility growing. Such is the context of this study, which looks at the position of women on the labour market of the 1980s and thus continues the study carried out by the European network of experts on the Situation of Women in the Labour Market in 1985 (see Bouillaguet-Bernard, Gauvin and Prokovas, 1985).

This research begins with a study of the supply side of female labour, which forms the subject of the first chapter. This chapter deals with the development of activity rates according to age, family situation and levels of educational attainment.

Supply does not generate its own demand on the labour market and even if women's employment has increased, it is still concentrated in some sectors of activity, and often it does not have the same quality as men's employment. Chapter 2 looks at the development of employment, and its sectoral distribution, and particular reference is made to employment in the public sector and agriculture, a feature which has brought about the integration of considerable numbers of women on the labour market. Besides the differences between the various countries, regional disparities can be noted.

Chapter 3 deals with the quality of women's employment and analyses developments in the occupational status of women and their presence in atypical forms of employment such as part-time, temporary and flexible hour working.

The suppression of direct and indirect pay discrimination was the first directive proposed by the Commission and adopted by the Council, serving, in a manner of speaking, to spark off equal opportunity policies throughout the Community. It is therefore vitally important to check to what extent directives and national legislation on equal pay are being implemented. This is the purpose behind Chapter 4.

Chapter 5 looks at unemployment with a view to ascertaining whether developments are the same for both sexes not only by region, but also in terms of age and levels of educational attainment. The circumstances behind entry into unemployment and the periods covered by unemployment benefits are also analysed. In addition, a section is devoted to the very recent unemployment in the five new *Länder* of Germany.

Lastly, since this study coincides with the end of the second Community equal opportunities programme (*Bulletin des Communautés Européennes*, 1986) and the beginning of the third (*Bulletin des Communautés Européennes*, 1990), it seems to us to be important to include in Chapter 6 an evaluation of women's participation in general unemployment policies and the effect of measures taken towards equal opportunities.

1 An increase in the supply of female labour

This chapter is devoted to the development of labour supply in the 1980s and also to the factors determining it. The first section looks at demographic aspects - birth rate, longevity and migration - all of which determine the potentially active population in each of the countries. The second section is devoted to developments in women's activity rates. Even if the upward trend in these rates remained constant throughout the period, there are still some serious differences from one country to another; these are analysed in section three. The final two sections - also devoted to activity rates - contain correlations between activity and life cycles, between activity and the presence and number of children, and between activity and levels of educational attainment.

1. Population changes do not seem to be responsible for the tensions on the European labour market

Birth rate, longevity and migration constitute the three factors which determine the development of a country's population. In general, the countries of Europe are characterized by falling birth rates (with the exception of Denmark, [1] where fertility has been on the increase since 1983, particularly in the 25-40 age group) and an increase in longevity, both of which have combined to bring about an ageing of the population which is reflected in the Community's age pyramid which is now showing signs of inversion, with the apex becoming broader than the base (see figure 1.1). In 1990 Ireland had the youngest population (27 per cent of which was aged between zero and fourteen), while Germany (before the reunification) had the oldest (15.1 per cent between zero and fourteen).

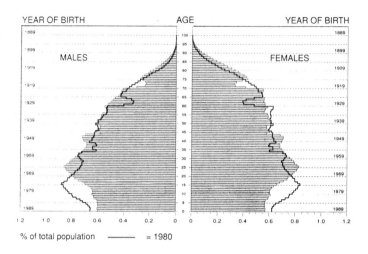

Percentage of total population : ——— = 1980.

Figure 1.1   The Community's age pyramid - a comparison between 1980
and 1990

Source : Eurostat (1991c), *Demographic Statistics*, p. XXII.

The rate of natural population growth was positive, if feeble, in all the
countries except Germany, where it was negative; the countries with the
highest growth rates were Ireland, France and the Netherlands.

In this context, net migration had a decisive effect on population developments, with the generally positive balance undergoing a considerable increase
in 1989 :

> In 1989, the Community population rose by 1,647,000 persons, with two-thirds of
> this increase being due to net migration and only one-third (or 581,000 persons) to a
> surplus of births over deaths. This exceptional situation resulted from the upheavals in
> eastern Europe in 1989. Net migration into the Community was higher than ever
> before, and for the first time, too, net migration was the main component of popula-
> tion growth (Eurostat, 1991c, p. XXI).

Germany was particularly affected by this growth, which accounted for the
overall rise in the country's population. There was a high rate of immigration
into Luxembourg where, as we will see, immigration compensates for the lack
of local labour. In contrast, in the case of Ireland there was a high level of
emigration that led to a drop in the overall population after 1987. Between
1983 and 1990 the overall population rates were positive in all the countries
with the exception of Ireland and the ex-German Democratic Republic. The
highest average growth rates per annum (in excess of 3 per cent) were recorded in Portugal, the Netherlands, Luxembourg and France. In Italy, there
was a marked difference in developments between the North and the South,
where developments between 1983 and 1989 constituted a 'synthesis of two

divergent lines of development, with an increase in the South of 748,000 persons and a limited decrease in the Centre-North (139,000 persons)' (Altieri and Villa, 1991, p. 1).

To grasp the influence of demographic factors on labour supply, we must study developments in the potentially active population, i.e. the whole population aged between fifteen and sixty-four. Between 1983 and 1990 the active population increased slightly in all the countries of the Community, but there is now a tendency for growth to level off in a number of them. Thus, demographic features do not seem to be responsible for the tensions on the European labour market; quite the contrary, a low birth rate and the ageing of the population are likely to encourage a slackening off in the supply of labour.

As far as the future is concerned, forecasts obviously depend on assumptions concerning birth rate, longevity and, in particular, migration which, in the short term, will be the principal demographic factor likely to affect labour supply in the European Community. Relatively well qualified emigrants from eastern Europe could cause new tensions on the labour market and enter into competition with the supply of female labour in the Community countries.

2. An increase in the activity rates for women between twenty-five and forty-nine is visible throughout the Community

Trends observed in the 1970s (Bouillaguet-Bernard, Gauvin and Prokovas, 1985, p. 11) were confirmed and corroborated, with women's activity rates rising and men's either falling (in the ex-German Democratic Republic, Belgium, Spain, France, the United Kingdom, Greece, Ireland, Italy and Portugal), or increasing less rapidly than women's (Germany, Denmark, Luxembourg and the Netherlands).

The only exception was Ireland, where women's activity rates remained stagnant despite 'changes in social and demographic patterns and the legislation on equality passed in the seventies' (Barry, 1991).

Changes in men's activity rates can be explained by a drop in their activity at either end of the age spectrum. At one end of the scale there was an increase in the requirement for education either voluntarily, or as the result of government measures; in France, 'the difficult integration of young people caused the government to take steps to encourage them to continue in education' (Gauvin and Silvera, 1991, p. 3), while in Belgium, the law of 29 June 1983 increased the school leaving age from fourteen to eighteen. At the other, people in the 50-64 age group in a number of the countries (Belgium, the Netherlands, France, Denmark, the United Kingdom and Italy) tended to turn their backs on the labour market, often encouraged by provisions for early retirement and greater use of workers' sickness and disability coverage in the Netherlands (Plantenga, 1991, p. 9) and, in Belgium (Meulders and Vander Stricht, 1991, p. 105), the collective agreement (no. 17 of 19 December 1974) on early retirement, the royal decree of 28 August 1986 and early retirement pensions for male employees (royal decree no. 95 of 28 September 1982).

These phenomena also affected women. The increase in their activity rates is mainly due to the activity of women in the 25-49 age group. Even in Ireland, the activity rate increased for this age group (by 18 per cent between 1983 and 1989 according to the Eurostat data), with the overall stability find-

3

ing its explanation in the lower activity rate for young women (to be found with increasingly greater frequency in secondary education) and in the decline in the activity rate for women between fifty-five and sixty-four linked to the sharp reduction in jobs in agriculture (Barry, 1991).

If we focus our attention on the activity rates for the 25-49 age group which, happily, remain untainted by the influence of institutional phenomena such as the age of compulsory schooling and retirement formulae, we will see that, in 1989, Ireland had the lowest activity rate (45 per cent), followed by Spain (47.9 per cent), Luxembourg (51.6 per cent), Greece (54.3 per cent), Italy (55.8 per cent) and the Netherlands (58.2 per cent). At the other end of the scale there were rates of 87.9 per cent for Denmark, 73.2 per cent for France, 69.9 per cent for Portugal, 65.5 per cent for Belgium and 63.4 per cent for Germany (see table 1.1). The five new *Länder* had extremely high activity rates, close to those for Denmark in fact; in 1989, 85 per cent of women between fifteen and sixty were economically active.

Table 1.1
Activity rates for women between twenty-five and forty-nine

Country	Activity rate in 1989	Annual growth rate between 1983 and 1989 (in percentage points)	Forecast for the year 2000 [b]
Ireland	45.0	2.77	60.8
Spain [a]	47.9	7.74	94.8
Luxembourg	51.6	2.42	67.1
Greece	54.3	3.14	76.3
Italy	55.8	2.43	72.7
Netherlands	58.2	4.23	91.8
Germany	63.4	1.44	74.2
Belgium	65.5	1.81	79.8
Portugal [a]	69.9	2.61	92.8
United Kingdom	72.7	2.39	94.3
France	73.2	1.14	82.9
Denmark	87.9	0.29	90.7
Europe 12 [a]	63.7	2.30	81.8
Europe 10	65.5	1.99	81.4

a. 1986 and 1989.
b. Forecast based on annual average growth rate.

Source : Eurostat (1983c, 1986c and 1989c), *Labour Force Survey*.

In the German Democratic Republic the high employment rate for women was the result of an active policy pursued by the government since the country's inception. Alongside the right to work enshrined in the constitution, there was also a moral 'obligation' to work. In the seventies, when the birth rate was falling, a number of social policies were applied in an attempt to resolve the dilemma of squaring economic activity with motherhood, and of arresting the falling birth rate through the granting of numerous privileges to working mothers. Special provisions were made under labour legislation with a view to modifying the legal conditions of employment. These provisions included the protection against dismissal of pregnant women, of mothers with children under one year of age, and of lone mothers with children under three. At the time of childbirth, women were entitled to six weeks' pre- and twenty weeks' post-natal leave of absence (with a net wage corresponding to the average). During their child's first year they could have themselves released from work (with a maternity grant of as much as 90 per cent of the net average wage). For mothers with at least two children under sixteen and working full time, the weekly work load of forty-three and a quarter hours was reduced to forty hours. In the ex-German Democratic Republic free and unregulated family planning was available to women. In contrast to the German Federal Republic, child care facilities were developed in the eighties to care for children between 6 a.m. and 6 p.m. These facilities were heavily subsidized by the government and contributed to the high proportion of working women. Ideological purposes apart, the level of employment can also be explained on the one hand by a relatively low productive capacity coupled with a high labour requirement, and on the other by structural modifications inside the German Democratic Republic economy itself.

Thus, in a certain number of sectors, persons made available as the result of rationalization were needed to enable a switch to a shift system to take place, while others were trained to develop underdeveloped sectors such as the services. Furthermore, women's wages were necessary in view of the low overall income level if a comparatively high standard of living was to be attained (Figge, Quack and Schäfgen, 1991, p. 9).

Knudsen (1991, p. 24) explains women's high activity rates in Denmark, Finland and Sweden by :

> ... a long-standing tradition of women's independence and equality that led to women acquiring political and economic rights at an early date in the Nordic countries. Neither their family circumstances nor any domestic help that they might receive explains Nordic women's extremely high activity rates. They marry and have children like women elsewhere. Domestic servants and the availability of mutual help within the family disappeared more rapidly from Nordic households than in the countries of southern Europe.

The relatively high rate of activity on the part of Portuguese women in relation to the other countries of southern Europe can perhaps be explained by the events that took place after the 1960s :

> It was particularly after the sixties with the colonial war and the massive wave of emigration involving the departure of several thousand active men that the need to integrate women on the labour market was finally acknowledged. With the advent of 25 April 1974, the political, economic, social and even cultural changes had repercussions on the position of women in that they created the conditions for an increase in their rate of activity (Chagas Lopes, Ferreira and Perista, 1991, p. 7).

The relatively low rate of activity in the Netherlands in relation to the other countries of northern Europe can be explained by the Netherlands government's initiatives in support of the family, which provided women with nothing in the way of financial incentives to work. The paucity of public child care facilities also acted as a brake on women's activity. In 1988, only 3 per cent of children between zero and four were cared for in a manner that enabled both of their parents to undertake paid work. Whereas, with the exceptions of

5

Portugal and the Netherlands, the difference between the north and south of Europe seems to be fairly clearcut, an analysis of growth rates between 1983 and 1989 suggest an eventual blurring of this divide.

Thus, the highest average annual growth rates were recorded in Spain (7.74 per cent between 1986 and 1989), the Netherlands [2] (4.23 per cent), Greece (3.14 per cent), Ireland (2.77 per cent) and Portugal (2.61 per cent). The taking up of economic slack, a falling off in the feeling of discouragement, changes in women's traditional role and steps taken since 1984 to develop employment are some of the reasons for the spectacular increase in the economically active population in Spain over recent years (Alcobendas Tirado, 1991).

A simple projection of this growth rate up to the threshold of the year 2000 produces a totally different picture, with the women's rate in Spain catching up with the men's (94.8 per cent); the United Kingdom, Portugal, the Netherlands and Denmark appear to be over 90 per cent while Ireland (60 per cent) and Luxembourg (67.1 per cent) seem to fall short of the 70 per cent mark.

While the 1989 analysis of women's activity rates still evidenced a dichotomy between the countries of the North and South of Europe, it seems improbable that such a difference will survive in the future given the dynamic nature of the growth in activity rates in certain countries of the south.

3. Activity rates by age : differentiated profiles

An analysis of women's activity rates by age produces three types of curve (Plantenga, 1991, pp. 9-10) : [3]

- A left-hand peak between twenty and twenty-four :

- Two peaks separated by a trough at about thirty :

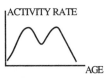

- A broad plateau :

The left hand peak pattern may be generated in societies where most women either withdraw permanently from paid employment after marriage or child-bearing, or confine their subsequent paid employment to intermittent episodes. The relatively high participation rates of unmarried women in their early twenties produces the left-hand peak.

The second pattern, that of two peaks, may be generated where the presence of young children, rather than marriage, is the major barrier to labour force participation. The second peak in the age profile reflects married women returning to employment as their children get older. There is a valley around age thirty, the predominant age band for mothers of young children.

The third pattern, with no mid-life valley, represents a situation where employment is combined with rearing young children sufficiently often for there to be no major distinction between the participation rates of women at different stages of family building (OECD, 1988, p. 134).

In this latter model, women remain economically active even when they have children.

What we have here is mainly a cross-section of activity rates by age since diachronic data are not available in all the countries. This means that it is not always possible to establish a distinction between the effects of age and generation.

3.1 Differentiated profiles

The curve takes the shape of an inverted U in the cases of Denmark, the ex-German Democratic Republic (ex-GDR) and France, countries with extremely high women's activity rates [4] (see figure 1.2).

On the other hand, the curve includes a left-hand peak in the cases of countries with very low women's activity rates (Ireland, Spain and Luxembourg) (see figure 1.3).

Generally speaking, between these two extremes there are two types of curves associated with countries with relatively higher activity rates. In the cases of Germany, the Netherlands and the United Kingdom the curve is M shaped (see figure 1.4), while it is flat topped in the cases of Greece, Italy, Portugal and Belgium (see figure 1.5).

The transition from the traditional unimodal model to the inverted U model, does not necessarily pass by the M shaped model; rather, an alternative intermediary phase might be the flat topped model.

3.2 Developments in the direction of the Danish model

Between 1983 and 1989 the activity rates for women aged between twenty-five and forty-nine increased throughout the European Community. In addition to a drop in the activity rate for the youngest age group (14-19 age group) due to an increase in the school leaving age for girls, in a number of the countries (Ireland, Luxembourg, Belgium, Italy, Greece, Portugal, Germany and France) there was a more marked desire to work after leaving education - a phenomenon which is reflected in the peaking of women's activity rates around the age of twenty-five (Gauvin and Silvera, 1991, p. 4).

In the United Kingdom, the configuration showed signs of flattening out, with the 'kiddies' trough' being less marked. What changed most sharply in

7

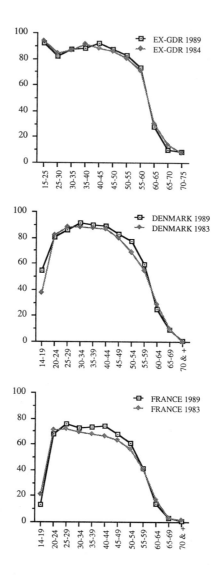

Figure 1.2   Activity rates by age in the ex-German Democratic Republic,
              Denmark and France

Sources : Ex-German Democratic Republic : Figge, Quack and Schäfgen,
          1991, table 1.26.
          Denmark and France : Eurostat (1983c and 1989c), *Labour Force
          Survey*.
          Graphs by the Department of Applied Economics of the Free Uni-
          versity of Brussels (DULBEA).

8

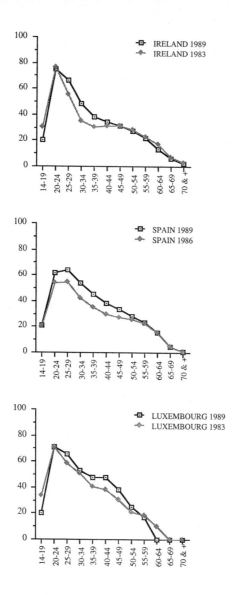

Figure 1.3   Activity rates by age in Ireland, Spain and Luxembourg

Sources : Eurostat (1983c, 1986c and 1989c), *Labour Force Survey*.
Graphs by DULBEA.

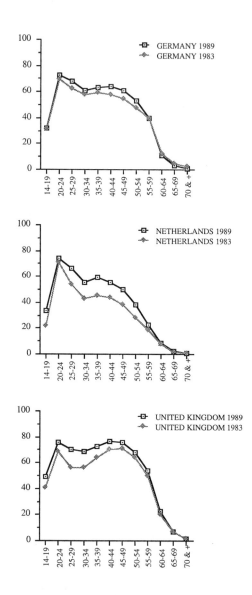

Figure 1.4   Activity rates by age in Germany, the Netherlands and the United Kingdom

Sources : Eurostat (1983c and 1989c), *Labour Force Survey*.
          Graphs by DULBEA.

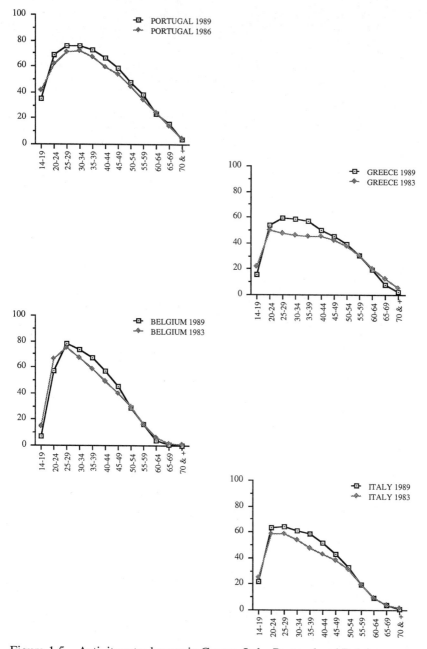

Figure 1.5   Activity rates by age in Greece, Italy, Portugal and Belgium

Sources : Eurostat (1983c, 1986c and 1989c), *Labour Force Survey.*
          Graphs by DULBEA.

11

the United Kingdom was the activity rate for married women. 'The increased activity rates of women in the main child-bearing/rearing age groups reflect the increase in the participation of women with young children' (Humphries and Rubery, 1991, p. 11).

On the other hand, in France there was the reappearance of a slight bimodal curve which had disappeared in 1983. The French experts interpreted this as follows :

> It would, however, be exaggerated to interpret these observations as a return to a hiatus in women's activity. To begin with, the activity rates for women of thirty-five remain at an extremely high - indeed, unprecedented - level. It is thus nearer the mark to speak of a threshold in thirty-five year old women's participation in economic activity rather than of any real change in their activity patterns. Our assumption is therefore that in view of their family circumstances, the 71 per cent activity rate for thirty-five year old women corresponds to a maximum levelling-off point. This age group is perhaps the most sensitive of all to the problems of compatibility between work and domestic life (it is in the 35-39 age group that the number of small children is often greatest) (Gauvin and Silvera, 1991, p. 10).

In the case of Germany, the M remains clearly delineated despite the increase in activity rates. This might be explained by the leave of absence for parenthood which has been in existence since 30 June 1986. Paradoxical though it may be, while this leave of absence facilitates a return to working life, it also encourages women to turn their backs on it (Landenberger, 1990; quoted by Figge, Quack and Schäfgen, 1991, p. 48).

Between 1985 and 1989 the rise in activity rates for women between twenty-five and forty-nine was paralleled in all the countries by the development of the curves towards a model in the shape of an inverted U.

4. Explanatory factors : to be sought within the context of labour supply and demand

'Far from being undifferentiated, female labour supply is determined first and foremost within the family. Hence the weight of social and family constraints upon careers, which vary according to family category' (Bouillaguet-Bernard, Gauvin and Prokovas, 1985, p. 28).

A number of variables likely to influence the level and development of women's careers have been analysed by Bouillaguet-Bernard, Gauvin and Prokovas (1985, op. cit. p. 28) : marital status, family responsibilities, social environment, levels of training, family income, status of their partner's activity.

> Economic theory predicts that households allocate time between paid work, household production and leisure according to market rates of wages, the shadow price of leisure and home production and productivity in home production. Family obligations appear in this model as an influence on the shadow price of home production rather than as a constraint, and it is difficult to generate a gender division of labour from the model without a priori assumptions about productivity in domestic work (Humphries and Rubery, 1991, pp. 11-12).

> Both women's activity rates and the hours that they work vary more than men's. This

greater variation seems to reflect the greater family responsibilities of women and the changes occurring in the burden of this responsibility over the life cycle. These relationships vary between societies and depend on the particular systems of social reproduction, labour market regulation and social organization (Rubery, 1988, quoted by Humphries and Rubery, 1991, p. 12).

In addition to factors associated with labour supply, there are also factors more associated with labour demand. Altieri and Villa emphasize that in Italy the explanation for the increase in women's activity in the 1980s had been a matter of debate.

Whereas on the one hand economists attached particular importance to the state of the labour market, to tertiarization and to family wage and income levels, on the other the representatives of other disciplines (particularly demographers and sociologists) placed emphasis on factors of change such as the drop in women's fertility rates, changes in the structure of the family unit (the decrease in family size, the rising instability of marriage, etc.), and the enormous increase in the numbers of women in education, all of which were alleged to have contributed to the modification of women's behaviour patterns (Altieri and Villa, 1991, p. 16).

In this section we will limit ourselves to two factors connected with labour supply; on the one hand there are family responsibilities which 'of all the factors weighing most on the levels and structure by age of women's activity, this is certainly the one that weighs most heavily on women's activity patterns' (Bouillaguet-Bernard, Gauvin and Prokovas, 1985, p. 42) while on the other, there are educational attainments. Other factors more specific to each country will then be dealt with. Changes in labour demand (regional and sectoral distribution, etc.) are examined in the following chapter.

4.1 A falling off in the influence of family responsibilities [5]

'Whatever her age, a woman's activity is in inverse proportion both to the size of her family and to whether her youngest child is of school age' (Bouillaguet-Bernard, Gauvin and Prokovas, 1985, p. 42). This equation, applicable to all the member states during the 1970s, retained its validity during the 1980s in all cases except Denmark.

It should be noted that the link between fertility and women's activity rates can be interpreted in two ways : on the one hand, the drop in their fertility has eased their entry and continued presence on the labour market; on the other, their increased activity seems to be one of the reasons for this drop in fertility (Desplanques, Raton and Thave, 1991, quoted by Gauvin and Silvera, 1991, p. 10).

Ideally, an analysis of women's activity rates in function of the numbers and ages of their children should be carried out diachronically, but in the absence of appropriate data, it is essential to know the women's ages. In fact, an analysis of overall activity rates in function of children's numbers and ages masks the generation effect. Thus, in Belgium and France, for instance, the activity rates for women forming part of couples without children are below those for couples in Belgium with one, two or even three children (Institut National de Statistique, 1990, quoted by Meulders and Vander Stricht, 1991, p. 16). This stems from the fact that the average age of couples without children is considerably higher than that of those with children because couples are included whose children have left home. These generation-bound differences also explain why, in certain of the countries (Belgium, etc.), overall activity rates decrease in proportion to children's ages.

Influence of the presence of children. In Denmark, the fact of having children no longer seems to influence their mothers' activity rates. In fact, 'a study of the daily lives of households with children carried out by the Institute of Social Research in November and December 1989 shows that women with children aged between zero and two are as economically active as childless women between twenty and forty-nine and women with children between the ages of three and fourteen' (Andersen, 1991, quoted by Knudsen, 1991, p. 26).

Although there are no statistics for the ex-German Democratic Republic that deal with activity rates in function of numbers and ages of children, it can nevertheless be assumed that their presence has an influence on women's activity rates. In fact, the slight dip in women's activity rates in the 25-35 age group can be explained by the possibility for women to be exempted from work for a year after childbirth while still drawing pay.

In the Netherlands and Ireland, the arrival of a first child is the cause of a heavy decline in women's activity rates. In fact, in Ireland (see Appendix 1.2, table A1.1.3), 'the activity level of women in the 20-24 and 25-34 age groups with one dependent child is half that of women without children' (Barry, 1991), while in the Netherlands (see Appendix 1.1, table A1.1.4), the 1988 activity rates for childless women between eighteen and thirty-seven was 74 per cent, with this figure falling to 34 per cent in the case of women with one child and 30 per cent for those with one child or more. According to the Dutch expert, 'the number of children plays a relatively limited role in behaviour on the labour market. What counts is whether there is a child or not' (Plantenga, 1991, p. 13).

In France (see Appendix 1.1, table A1.1.2), 'whereas divergences in activity rates between zero and one child and between one and two children are comparatively slight, there is an enormous gap in the rates between two and three children. Thus, for 1989, the activity rate for the 39-45 age group was 85 per cent for childless women, 81 per cent for women with one child, 75 per cent for those with two children and 45 per cent for those with three'. So, while the threshold of incompatibility between work and family life coincides in France with the birth of a third child, the activity rates for Irish and Dutch women drop at the time of the first birth.

> However, it must not be concluded that the advent of a third child equates to a withdrawal from economic activity. In fact, in our case, it was not the same women who had one, two, or three children. To arrive at any such conclusion, the starting point would have to be a series of longitudinal studies of women's activity subsequent to their last child. Now, in this particular case, the results are not so clear and are even inverted. In the case of older women who have had all their children - certain of which are no long dependent - the change from the second to the third child is accompanied by a markedly less abrupt decrease in activity than the change from the first to the second one (Gauvin and Silvera, 1991, pp. 11-12).

A decreasing influence with age. The presence of children on the activity rates

14

for women in their thirties seems to be less important than on the rates for younger women. In the Netherlands,

> ... whatever the age of the youngest child, women's activity rates are more marked in the older age groups than in the younger ones. Thus, while in 1982 only 7 per cent of women in the 18-24 age group with one child under three were active, the figure was 21 per cent in the 35-37 age group. In 1988, the same phenomenon was observed, with the data for women whose youngest child was in the 4-12 age group following the same tendency. In this case, the explanatory variables may well lie in the direction of levels of training and the work experience acquired. Many women in the 35-37 age group with one child aged between zero and three will have different training and work experience from women in the 18-24 age group whose youngest child is between zero and three. This means that women in the latter group in particular will endeavour to remain in employment (Plantenga, 1991, p. 13).

An analysis of the data for Germany (see Appendix 1.1, table A1.1.1) also shows that, whatever their children's ages, the activity rates for women between thirty-five and forty-five are higher than those for women under thirty-five (15-25 and 25-35 age groups).

In Ireland and France (see Appendix 1.1, tables A1.1.3 and A1.1.2), for a given number of children, the employment rates for women in their thirties are higher than for younger women. In Ireland, for example, 'the rate of participation for women in the 25-34 and 35-44 age groups with two dependent children is almost double that for women in the 20-24 age group with two dependent children' (Barry, 1991).

It can be concluded that in the Netherlands and Germany, women choosing to have their children later more frequently remain in employment. As the Dutch expert emphasizes, this is probably also connected with the mothers' training. The interpretation of the French and Irish data is less clearcut since the children of women in their thirties are very likely to be older than those of women aged twenty.

The pursuit of economic activity, but on a part-time basis. It seems that despite the development of child care facilities in the ex-German Democratic Republic women had difficulty in reconciling their family responsibilities with full-time work. In fact,

> ... almost 30 per cent of women were on reduced hours. Since this was only possible with the employer's agreement and under exceptional circumstances subject to annual review (heavy family responsibilities or responsibility for handicapped children or others), it can be assumed that it was mainly mothers who had recourse to part-time work; part-time work was more or less out of the question for men because the government's (and consequently the employers') attitude was based on compatibility between work and motherhood (Figge, Quack and Schäfgen, 1991, p. 10).

The difficulty in reconciling full-time work and children is also existent, for example, in the cases of the Netherlands, Germany and the United Kingdom, Humphries and Rubery (1991, p.17) underline that 'women are less likely to work full time the more children they have, whereas the pattern of part-time working by number of children appears more variable'.

Child care facilities. 'Levels of provision vary substantially between countries (see table 1.2). Denmark has, by far, the highest overall levels of provision, and has gone further than any other country (with the possible exception of East Germany) in developing a comprehensive system of services for children of all ages ... . Some way behind come France and Belgium. At the other extreme, lowest levels overall are in Ireland, the Netherlands and the United Kingdom' (Moss, 1990, p. 11).

This table lists the percentage of places in facilities financed by the government in relation to the numbers of children involved. The percentage of children attending a facility financed by the government may be higher because some places are occupied on a part-time basis. The figures for the Netherlands do not take account of playgroups despite the fact that 10 per cent of children under three and four attend these facilities, which draw on public funds. The hours of attendance (five or six per week) are so low in relation to the other facilities that it would be difficult and perhaps misleading to include them on the same footing. They should not, however, be neglected in the study of government-financed facilities in the Netherlands.

The large-scale development of child care facilities in the ex-German Democratic Republic and Denmark seems to be associated with women's high activity rates. However, it cannot be concluded that well developed child care facilities imply high activity rates (the rate in Belgium is relatively low despite a relatively significant infrastructure) nor, indeed, that women's activity rates are low in countries where child care facilities are few and far between (in the United Kingdom, women's activity rates are significantly high despite the shortage of child care facilities).

Cohabiting or married women. In the case of cohabiting women, the influence of the presence of children (ages and numbers) is not the same as for married women. In the United Kingdom, activity rates follow a different pattern for married and for cohabiting women (a recently defined category). An analysis of the 1989 data reveals that :

> ... cohabiting women have relatively low participation rates when their children are aged 0-4, although rates which are above those of never married women and divorced mothers of preschool children. But cohabiting mothers of older children exhibit high activity rates. In fact, for women with children aged 11-15, they have the highest activity rates. Perhaps cohabiting women with very young children fall into the welfare trap that appears to affect lone mothers, or perhaps they are less likely than married mothers to be able to rely on other family members (mainly male partners) to provide assistance with child care. Cohabiting women with older children may be less able to rely on the income of partners and so are more likely to work. On the other hand, for mothers of 11-15 year olds, cohabiting may be correlated with occupation and income group and so with relatively high participation. Although caution should be exercised in putting a life cycle interpretation onto an observation from a cross-section, the implied exaggerated life cycles for cohabiting women are important given the likely growth of cohabitation as a form of marital status (Humphries and Rubery, 1991, pp. 17-18).

A greater increase in mothers' activity rates between 1983 and 1989. An analysis of the developments in women's activity rates from 1983 to 1989 shows a greater increase in the activity rates of mothers, and particularly of mothers with young children.

Table 1.2

Places of publicly funded child care services as percentage of all children in the age group

	Date to which data refer	For children under three	For children from three to compulsory school age	Age when compulsory schooling begins	Length of school day (including midday break)	Outside school hours care for primary school children
Germany	1987	3 %	65-70 %	6-7 years	4-5 hours [a]	4 %
France	1988	20 %	95 % +	6 years	8 hours	?
Italy	1986	5 %	85 % +	6 years	4 hours	?
Netherlands	1989	2 %	50-55 %	5 years	6-7 hours	1 %
Belgium	1988	20 %	95 % +	6 years	7 hours	?
Luxembourg	1989	2 %	55-60 %	5 years	4-8 hours [a]	1 %
United Kingdom	1988	2 %	35-40 %	5 years	6½ hours	(-)
Ireland	1988	2 %	55 %	6 years	4½-6½ hours [b]	(-)
Denmark	1989	48 %	85 %	7 years	3-5½ hours [a,b]	29 %
Greece	1988	4 %	65-70 %	5½ years	4-5 hours [b]	(-)
Portugal	1988	6 %	35 %	6 years	6½ hours	6 %
Spain	1988	?	65-70 %	6 years	8 hours	(-)

NB. This table should be read in conjunction with the national reports, which contain important qualifications and explanations. The table shows the number of places in publicly funded services as a percentage of the child population; the percentage of children attending may be higher because some places are used on a part-time basis. Provision at playgroups in the Netherlands has not been included, although 10 per cent of children under three and 25 per cent of children aged between three and four attend and most playgroups receive public funds. Average hours of attendance - 5-6 hours per week - are so much shorter than for other services, that it would be difficult and potentially misleading to include them on the same basis as other services; however, playgroups should not be forgotten when considering publicly funded provision in the Netherlands.

Key : ? = no information; (-) = less than 0.5 per cent; (a) = school hours vary from day to day; (b) = school hours increase as children get older.

Source : Moss, 1990, p. 10.

In Ireland,

> ... the figures show a considerable increase in the number of working women of all ages, and particularly the 20-24s and the 25-35s, with one or two dependent children. The activity rates for women with three dependent children show greater variations. For example the number of women in the 20-24 age group with three dependent children and active in the official economy declined heavily, i.e. from 8.7 per cent to 5.3 per cent, between 1983 and 1987, while the number increased for women in the 25-34 and 35-44 age groups with three dependent children (Barry, 1991).

In France, the activity rates for mothers increased in all the age groups, and particularly in the case of women aged between thirty and forty-four with three or more children.

In the Netherlands, the activity rate for women in the 18-37 age group with children under three went from 17 per cent to 27 per cent in the period 1982-88, while the activity rate for women with children aged between four and twelve remained static.

In the United Kingdom, the increase in the activity rates from 1983 to 1988 was greater in the case of women with dependent children (46 per cent to 56 per cent) than for women without (65 per cent to 72 per cent) (Humphries and Rubery, 1991, p. 14). 'The trend increase in the percentage of mothers who work has been most marked for the mothers of 0-4 year olds, and this increase has been concentrated in the years since 1983' (Humphries and Rubery, 1991, p. 16).

The appearance of the poverty trap for lone mothers. In the United Kingdom,

> ... over the longer period 1973-88 the key change was an increase in the percentage of women with dependent children who were working which was due mainly to an increase in part-time work. The trend for lone mothers was markedly different. Throughout the seventies and eighties lone mothers were less likely than married women with dependent children to be working. The proportion of lone mothers working has remained stable since 1983 and the trend is downward if calculations are based on 1981-83, with the decline particularly marked in full-time work. In contrast, the proportions of married women working both part time and full time has increased. An explanation of the distinctive behaviour of lone mothers and the opposite trends in their activity compared with married women with children should be sought in the nature of the welfare benefits available for such women which trap them into uneconomic activity and perhaps in the increasing youth of lone mothers (Humphries and Rubery, 1991, pp. 15-16).

In Greece, most lone mothers with children under twelve hold temporary jobs (Cavouriaris, 1991a, p. 5).

It seems that what we have here is the poverty trap; 'a situation in which a person - employed or otherwise - experiences no financial incentive to increase his working hours if he is employed, or to enter the labour market if he is not. In fact, if such a person decided to work more, he would see his net income stagnate or even decline' (Demazy, 1991, p. 5).

This phenomenon, which also seems to affect lone mothers in Belgium, deserves more detailed study (see also below).

4.2 *Levels of educational attainment : the deciding factor for the participation of women in the labour market* [6]

Improvements in the levels of women's training. In 1989, the number of young women under thirty-five with a higher education exceeded that of young men (Belgium and Germany). If the whole of the female population of working age is taken into account, their level of training remains below men's (France, Belgium and Germany). In Denmark, 1988 saw the numbers of men and women with a higher education draw level.

In Portugal, 1983 saw women constituting 47 per cent of the total of those in higher education; in 1987, they ran to more than 50 per cent, while 65 per cent of all postgraduate students were women.

'In Greece, the number of students increased by 22.0 per cent between 1982-83 and 1986-87 while the number of women in university education increased by 34.9 per cent. The number of qualified women increased by 6.5 per cent, but the number of female graduates in higher education increased by 22.2 per cent' (Cavouriaris, 1991, p. 6).

However, as the Danish expert (Knudsen, 1991, p. 44) emphasizes, women's steps are still directed towards areas such as the services and caring activities in the case of short- and medium-length training, and to the arts, medicine and psychology at tertiary level. There has been such a craze amongst women for these types of training that the number of those qualified is in excess of the number of jobs available.

'In Greece too, women are in the majority in arts and in a number of social sciences departments. On the other hand, they are underrepresented in the sciences' (Cavouriaris, 1991, p. 6).

During the forty years of its existence, much was done in the ex-German Democratic Republic to enable women to qualify. The standardization of the educational system and the establishment of the same entrance criteria for technical and vocational training colleges and the universities placed men and women on the same formal footing in the acquisition of qualifications. The gap between the degrees of qualification for men and women was narrowed, but not eliminated. At this point we must bear in mind the distinctive nature of conditions in the ex-German Democratic Republic based as they were on a planned economy. In theory there were apprenticeships available for school-leavers and places at university for those with the *Abitur* (general certificate of education). But since apprenticeships and university places were quota-based according to the needs of society, it was a struggle to obtain one, and the outcome often depended on a student's sex. The formal level of women's degrees did not serve as grounds for occupational discrimination against them, but gender-based assignments in certain occupations and areas of employment involving lower average wages and poorer prospects went part of the way towards cancelling out the formal equality of their qualifications.

Activity rates - levels of qualification : a more marked relationship in the case of women. In the case of women there is a much more marked relationship between activity rates and employment than in the case of men. Highly qualified women are much more likely to be economically active than less qualified ones.

According to the OECD (1989, pp. 70 and 79-80), differences in activity rates as a function of educational attainments seem to be somewhat lower in the case of men, probably because they can draw upon unbroken work experience and, at least to a certain extent, can fall back on this experience to compensate for their qualification levels.

Qualification levels also have an effect on activity cycles. Highly qualified women more often pursue an uninterrupted career and, should an interruption occur, they more frequently take up the reins again. This is shown by a study of women's careers in the Netherlands (Dessens *et al.*, 1990, p. 76, quoted by Plantenga, 1991, p. 14). In Germany young women with the *Abitur* or the *Realschulabschluss* (high school leaving certificate) put off marriage and children and, once married, are more likely to continue working than women of the same age with the *Hauptschulabschluss* (junior high school leaving certificate) (Tölke, 1989, quoted by Figge, Quack and Schäfgen, 1991, p. 8). So far, there are no confirmed empirical results as to whether, in the case of childbirth, career interruptions would be less frequent on their part. What is known is that, after a career break, they return to active life more often and earlier than *Hauptschulabschluss* holders (Huinink and Lauterbach, 1990, quoted by Figge, Quack and Schäfgen, 1991, p. 8).

In the United Kingdom,

> ... activity rates among well qualified women were over 80 per cent except for women with preschool children. But although the activity rate of well qualified mothers of preschoolers was sharply lower (61 per cent), it was reduced less than the activity rates of mothers of preschoolers with lower educational attainments. This difference can be explained by the lower proportional burden of child care expenses on higher earnings, and by the greater likelihood that well qualified women are on career ladders for which time out of the labour market would have adverse effects. There are fewer unemployed women among the well qualified (Humphries and Rubery, 1991, pp. 19-20).

It seems that in the countries of southern Europe (Spain and southern Italy), where activity rates are relatively low, the differences in terms of qualifications are greater. This means that the activity rates for women with a higher level of education exhibit fewer differences from country to country than in the case of poorly educated women.

In Italy, 'the activity rate for women graduates in the South is 86.4 per cent as opposed to 78.8 per cent for women in the Centre-North, while for school dropouts the activity rate is only 17.2 per cent in the South and 18.6 per cent in the Centre-North' (Altieri and Villa, 1991, p. 18).

4.3 Other factors

The development of the tertiary sector. The development of tertiary employment in Italy has encouraged women's integration on the labour market in many respects. One worthy of emphasis is the part played by the tertiary sector in encouraging modifications to the age structure of the female labour force or, in other words, a switch from a predominance of young women of pre-marriage age to a situation characterized by a marked tendency to continue in employment on the part of adult women with probable family responsibilities (Altieri and Villa, 1991, p. 18).

Low wages and family status. British experts went into much greater detail about the poverty trap already referred to in the analysis of mothers' activity rates. In the United Kingdom,

> ... lower pay is a disincentive to participate. Social security, which takes family income as the basis for entitlement, has the same effect. Child care expenses provide yet another disincentive to participate and reduce the hours women work, which in turn limits job choice. The accumulation of human capital, employers' attitudes to working time which discourages the participation of women who only want to work part time, barriers to training and dependencies other than children, reinforce the constraints outlined above. Constraints associated with low pay and social security operate to discourage the participation of lone mothers. Many constraints are interrelated and stem firstly from women's role as mothers, and secondly from employers' tendency to treat lifelong full-time work as the norm. As Metcalf concludes, these factors form a vicious circle : 'returning women face a poor job choice and so participation and commitment fall, confirming the employers' view' (Metcalf and Leighton, 1989, quoted by Humphries and Rubery, 1991, p. 14).

Spouses' economic status may also influence wives' labour market decisions. Economic theory is ambiguous about the effects of the employment status of husbands on that of wives. Spouses' unemployment might create 'added worker' effects which raise the activity rate of wives. Alternatively, the benefits trap may operate to stymie such added worker effects. Moreover, the unemployment status of husbands is not independent of the job prospects of wives or their qualification levels. In female labour supply models, husbands' income is usually taken as analogous to property income, and if leisure is a normal good, higher income associated with employment implies a reduced likelihood of activity. But husbands' employment status is not independent of wives' potential earnings, and so own wage substitution effects may cancel out negative income effects.

Empirically, in the United Kingdom in 1990, among couples without children, both partners had a job in 65 per cent of cases, with full-time working common amongst wives (General Household Survey, 1988, pp. 212-13, quoted by Humphries and Rubery, 1991, p. 18). 25 per cent of couples with children reported the husband working and the wife looking after the home and family, but only 7 per cent of couples without children. About 7 per cent of couples with children reported neither partner in employment and in half these cases the wife was looking after the family and the husband was unemployed. In only 4 per cent of couples was the wife in employment and the husband unemployed or inactive. These female breadwinners represented only 7 per cent of working wives.

Of unemployed and economically inactive wives, 24 per cent had unemployed or inactive husbands compared with 6.8 per cent for wives in employment; inactive or unemployed wives are more likely to have inactive or unemployed husbands than are employed wives. Similarly, unemployed husbands are more likely to have unemployed and inactive wives than are employed husbands (Humphries and Rubery, 1991, pp. 18-19).

5. Conclusions

Demographic factors do not explain the tensions on the labour market. In all the countries of the Community the 1980s witnessed a firm resolve on the part of adult women to participate in the labour market. This resolve was evident in all the countries, and the dynamic nature of the growth in the countries of the South suggests that, in terms of women's activity rates, they will draw level with the countries of the North and even leave them behind.

Even if family responsibilities remain onerous, their full weight is becoming attenuated. Mothers' participation in economic activity is on the increase and its cessation for child-rearing is no longer the dominant model.

Education has a decisive influence and its correlation with activity rates is high. The more advanced a woman's education, the more she will want to pursue an occupational activity. Inversely, the poverty trap may affect women in a difficult situation, such as lone mothers and the wives of the unemployed. The latter women are penalized by the tax and transfer system if they enter the labour market.

Notes

1. It should, however, be remembered that the 1988 fertility rate for Denmark was below that for Spain, France, Ireland and the United Kingdom and equal to that for the Netherlands and Belgium. What is interesting is that this slight increase in the case of the 25-40 age group holds good for the other Nordic countries and that Denmark does not stand out as an exception in their company.

Total fertility rate

	1980	1989
Belgium	1.67	1.58 *
Denmark	1.55	1.62
Germany	1.45	1.39
Greece	2.23	1.50 *
Spain	2.22	1.39 *
France	1.95	1.81
Ireland	3.23	2.11 *
Italy	1.69	1.29 *
Luxembourg	1.50	1.52
The Netherlands	1.60	1.55
Portugal	2.19	1.50
United Kingdom	1.89	1.81

* Provisional data.

Source : Eurostat (1991), *Demographic Statistics.*

2. However, Plantenga (1991) mentions the effect of the 1987 change in definition; unlike previous years, a large female labour force employed for only a few hours per week was classified in the new census as part of the economically active (i.e. working) population. Even if we assume that (possible) developments between 1983 and 1985 and between 1987 and 1989 were less marked than (possible) developments between 1983 and

22

1989, we can still say that there was a net increase in women's activity during the 1983-89 period.
3. For further details see Plantenga, Schippers and Siegers, 1990, pp. 337-54.
4. In the case of the ex-German Democratic Republic, girls still in education are included as part of the active population; this accounts for the high activity rate in the 15-25 age group.
5. See Appendix A1.1.
6. See Appendix A1.2.

Appendix 1.1 : Link between activity rates and children's numbers and ages - national data

Germany

Table A1.1.1
Employed women aged fifteen and above according to own age,
children's ages and family circumstances; 1982 and 1988
(in percentage points of women of the same age
and in the same family circumstances)

Aged between ... and at least ...	Total		Married		Single		Non-married	
	1982	1988	1982	1988	1982	1988	1982	1988
Childless women *								
15-24	50.2	56.4	80.4	77.6	47.5	54.9	47.5	54.7
25-35	81.6	81.6	83.9	83.3	79.7	80.6	79.7	80.6
35-45	77.7	78.6	72.6	74.0	84.2	83.1	86.9	85.7
45-55	57.1	59.0	49.3	53.0	74.6	72.5	85.1	82.4
55-65	24.8	21.0	20.4	18.3	31.9	26.0	50.5	39.7
65 and over	2.2	1.6	2.4	2.0	2.1	1.4	4.5	3.2
Total	34.5	36.7	34.6	34.2	34.5	38.1	50.4	57.0
Women with children aged between zero and at least three								
15-25	34.2	28.0	33.9	27.4	36.9	31.4	42.6	34.2
25-35	34.3	31.2	33.8	30.7	43.4	38.8	52.9	45.9
35-45	32.0	38.2	31.3	37.2	42.5	48.9	-	-
45-55	-	-	-	-	-	-	-	-
55-65	-	-	-	-	-	-	-	-
65 and over	-	-	-	-	-	-	-	-
Total	34.0	31.5	33.6	30.9	40.5	37.6	48.3	42.7
Women with children aged between zero and at least six								
15-25	36.2	30.5	35.5	29.6	41.6	34.8	46.3	37.3
25-35	36.9	35.0	36.3	34.2	47.3	44.2	54.6	50.1
35-45	34.8	39.2	33.9	37.9	47.9	53.5	-	69.8
45-55	34.0	34.3	31.5	32.2	-	-	-	-
55-65	-	-	-	-	-	-	-	-
65 and over	-	-	-	-	-	-	-	-
Total	36.4	35.2	35.7	34.3	45.5	43.4	52.5	47.3
Women with children aged between zero and at least eighteen								
15-25	37.0	31.2	36.1	29.9	44.1	36.9	47.5	39.9
25-35	43.4	40.5	41.7	38.6	61.3	54.7	63.8	58.0
35-45	47.9	49.4	45.8	47.1	68.8	68.0	86.4	76.5
45-55	41.8	44.8	40.1	42.5	56.2	61.6	73.4	91.4
55-65	30.0	27.4	28.8	27.3	35.1	27.8	-	-
65 and over	-	-	-	-	-	-	-	-
Total	44.1	43.7	42.4	41.7	59.7	57.5	64.2	57.4

* Non-married children in the woman's household.

Source : Statistiches Bundesamt (ed.) (1982 and 1988), PS 1, Reihe 3, quoted by Figge, Quack and Schäfgen, 1991.

France

Table A1.1.2
Women's activity rates by age and number of children
(in per cent)

	1983				1989			
	Zero	One	Two	Three and over	Zero	One	Two	Three and over
15-24	81.7	62.2	37.0	15.1	81.8	65.5	40.7	11.0
25-29	87.7	78.0	57.2	23.1	89.1	78.1	63.1	22.0
30-34	83.8	82.0	68.3	33.7	85.7	83.1	73.6	37.5
35-39	78.0	77.8	67.9	41.4	85.1	81.5	75.1	44.9
40-44	76.1	70.8	57.9	40.2	77.5	76.3	68.5	48.1
45-54	59.6	43.8	45.4	28.1	63.7	60.8	52.4	32.9
55 and over	17.9	35.8	24.0	21.9	16.3	32.7	29.6	0.0
Aggregate	41.3	69.4	61.5	35.0	42.4	73.7	61.9	39.5

Source : Employment Survey, quoted by Gauvin and Silvera, 1991.

Ireland

Table A1.1.3
Married women's activity rates in function
of numbers of dependent children (in per cent)

Age group	Number of children under fifteen	1983	1987
20-24	Zero	77.1	79.0
	One	31.0	38.8
	Two	11.7	19.4
	Three and over	8.7	5.3
25-35	Zero	72.8	81.8
	One	36.4	47.6
	Two	17.5	28.5
	Three and over	9.8	13.2
35-44	Zero	39.8	49.6
	One	23.9	31.4
	Two	18.9	25.5
	Three and over	13.6	16.9
45-49	Zero	27.2	31.1
	One	18.6	21.9
	Two	16.8	20.6
	Three and over	15.2	18.7

Source : Blackwell (1986 and 1989), quoted by Barry, 1991.

Netherlands

Table A1.1.4
Women in the 18-37 age group by age, type of activity, the age of the youngest child, and numbers of children

	Childless women				Women whose youngest child is aged between zero and three				Women whose youngest child is aged between four and twelve				Total number of women
	No paid work	Part-time work	Full-time work	Total (absolute = 100 %)	No paid work	Part-time work	Full-time work	Total (absolute = 100 %)	No paid work	Part-time work	Full-time work	Total (absolute = 100 %)	
18-24													
1982	34	8	57	2143	92	7	0	245	x	x	x	18	2406
1988	33	15	51	1921	82	15	2	182	x	x	x	9	2112
25-29													
1982	22	15	62	787	82	14	3	649	71	23	5	193	1630
1988	17	15	67	867	78	18	4	562	70	21	8	94	1523
30-34													
1982	26	17	56	320	79	16	3	546	66	26	6	729	1626
1988	15	18	66	389	66	28	5	551	64	31	5	461	1427
35-37													
1982	23	24	51	118	76	18	3	126	58	33	8	551	878
1988	25	13	61	126	66	27	6	144	63	30	7	400	753
Total (18-37)													
1982	30	11	58	3368	82	14	3	1566	64	28	6	1491	6540
1988	26	16	58	3303	73	22	5	1437	64	29	6	964	5815

	Childless women				Women with one child				Women with two or more children				Total number of women
	No paid work	Part-time employment	Full-time employment	Total (absolute = 100 %)	No paid work	Part-time employment	Full-time employment	Total (absolute = 100 %)	No paid work	Part-time employment	Full-time employment	Total (absolute = 100 %)	
1982	30	11	58	3368	71	22	7	994	73	22	5	2178	6540
1988	26	16	58	3303	66	26	8	821	70	25	4	1691	5815

Deriving, as they do, from the survey by the Central Statistics Office of the make-up of the family, these tables give information on women's employment position while bringing in details such as numbers of children and the age of the youngest. To interpret the data, we must bear in mind that they do not cover the whole active female population, but are based on a sample in the 18-37 age group. In comparison with the data from the other sources, these have the great advantage of not being affected by the far-reaching changes to the census system.

Source : Onderzoek Gezinsvorming (1982 and 1988), quoted by Plantenga, 1991.

Table A1.1.5
Economic activity rates of women aged between sixteen
and fifty-nine by youngest child's age (in per cent)

	1983	1988
Youngest child aged between zero and four		
Full-time	5	11
Part-time	18	25
Total employment	24	36
Youngest child aged between five and nine		
Full-time	13	18
Part-time	40	47
Total employment	54	65
Youngest child aged ten and above		
Full-time	25	30
Part-time	42	43
Total employment	66	73
Total with (a) dependent child(ren)		
Full-time	14	19
Part-time	32	37
Total employment	46	56

Source : General Household Survey, quoted by Humphries and Rubery,
1991.

Table A1.1.6
Full-time activity rates, part-time activity rates and unemployment
rates for women between sixteen and fifty-nine with children (in per cent)

	Economically active women with dependent children				
	Working full-time	Working part-time	All working	Unemployed	Economical-ly active
Youngest child aged between zero and four					
One child	17	20	37	10	48
Two children	8	29	37	5	41
Three or more children	6	24	30	3	34
Total	11	24	36	6	42
Youngest child aged between five and nine					
One child	20	40	60	4	65
Two children	14	52	66	4	71
Three or more children	17	44	61	4	65
Total	16	47	64	4	68
Youngest child aged ten or over					
One child	31	41	73	3	75
Two children	27	49	76	3	80
Three or more children	22	43	65	3	68
Total	29	44	74	3	76
Total with (a) dependent child(ren)					
One child	24	33	58	6	63
Two children	15	42	58	4	62
Three or more children	11	32	44	3	47
Total	18	37	55	5	60

Source : General Household Survey, quoted by Humphries and Rubery,
1991.

Appendix 1.2 : Link between women's activity and their levels of educational attainment

Belgium

Table A1.2.1

Employment rates by gender according to level of educational attainment, 1989 (in per cent)

	Primary	Lower secondary	Upper secondary	Teacher training	Tertiary non-university		University
					Short type	Long type	
Over fourteen							
Men	33.97	60.83	67.63	85.51	84.67	80.39	83.33
Women	12.25	30.41	47.14	74.36	75.59	74.07	73.52
25-34							
Men	73.67	92.78	90.76	95.90	96.90	91.12	89.81
Women	38.61	55.99	72.96	88.92	85.13	88.17	82.65

Source : Institut National de Statistique, quoted by Meulders and Vander Stricht, 1991.

Germany

Table A1.2.2

Activity rates by gender, age and trade/professional training, 1989 (in per cent)

Age	Total	Apprentice-ships	Master craftsmen and technicians	Engineers and business specialists	University graduates	Unqualified
Women						
15-20	38.4	93.1	-	-	-	33.0
20-25	74.1	89.0	88.9	92.6	88.9	51.3
25-30	69.3	74.7	79.7	85.4	84.1	48.5
30-40	63.6	64.4	71.7	75.0	79.3	53.0
40-50	63.2	65.4	74.3	77.8	83.5	54.0
50-60	48.4	54.5	63.2	54.5	74.7	41.4
60-65	11.2	11.4	20.1	-	33.6	10.1
65 and over	1.7	1.9	5.4	-	-	1.5
Total	37.1	54.2	62.3	67.4	74.1	21.0
15-64	43.0	54.2	61.7	66.9	73.5	28.1
Men						
15-20	43.1	96.7	-	-	-	38.3
20-25	79.6	93.3	92.9	79.6	79.6	59.0
25-30	87.0	94.2	96.5	95.7	92.0	62.2
30-40	96.7	97.9	98.4	98.1	98.3	88.5
40-50	97.0	97.2	98.6	97.0	98.0	94.6
50-60	86.7	86.0	91.9	93.2	95.9	82.2
60-65	34.2	29.4	47.6	46.3	66.6	30.5
65 and over	4.5	2.8	7.1	6.8	16.0	4.6
Total	60.4	76.2	78.7	83.5	87.8	32.5
15-64	71.6	76.3	78.7	84.0	86.6	54.8

Source : Bundesminister für Bilding und Wissenschaft (ed.), Grund- und Strukturdaten 1990-91, quoted by Figge, Quack and Schäfgen, 1991.

Spain

Table A1.2.3
Activity rate in function of level of educational attainment (in per cent)

	1983		1990	
	Men	Women	Men	Women
Illiterate / no schooling	13.3	50.3	13.4	42.3
Primary schooling	25.1	78.3	26.9	71.6
Secondary schooling	-	-	47.6	69.9
Vocational training	46.1	65.7	68.6	77.0
Tertiary	-	-	65.7	71.5
University level studies	77.2	83.7	80.7	83.6

Source : Alcobendas Tirado (1991).

France

Table A1.2.4
Population over fifteen and the active population by gender and qualification level (in per cent)

	1983				1989			
	Men		Women		Men		Women	
	Total	Active	Total	Active	Total	Active	Total	Active
Level VI	53.5	45.1	61.2	44.9	47.6	37.4	55.1	37.1
Level V	28.0	32.4	22.3	29.4	31.6	37.1	25.4	32.9
Level IV	8.3	9.0	7.8	10.6	9.0	9.7	9.0	12.2
Level III	3.7	4.3	5.6	8.4	4.6	5.6	6.4	9.6
Level I and II	6.5	7.2	3.1	4.8	7.2	8.1	4.1	6.3
Studies under way	0.0	2.0	0.0	1.9	0.0	2.1	0.0	1.9
Total	100.0	100.0	100.0	100.0	100.0	100.0	100.0	100.0

Source : Enquête Emploi, quoted by Gauvin and Silvera, 1991.

Italy

Table A1.2.5
Activity rates by level of educational attainment
and by major region (in per cent)

	Centre-North			South			Italy		
	Men	Women	Women + men	Men	Women	Women + men	Men	Women	Women + men
1989									
Primary	49.85	18.65	31.89	54.48	17.20	33.53	51.51	18.16	32.48
Lower secondary	70.69	46.84	59.33	70.46	33.18	52.97	70.60	42.23	57.17
Upper secondary	76.34	63.96	70.27	76.70	60.01	68.35	76.46	62.65	69.64
University	84.24	78.78	82.04	87.93	86.43	87.29	85.25	81.93	83.90
1983									
Primary	60.12	22.27	38.81	64.63	20.15	39.84	61.71	21.54	39.17
Lower secondary	71.76	45.51	59.19	67.94	28.54	49.32	70.54	40.07	56.00
Upper secondary	77.26	61.89	69.99	72.40	56.62	64.82	75.66	60.12	68.27
University	87.17	80.06	84.59	90.94	89.23	90.28	88.44	83.39	86.57

Source : Istat.

Netherlands

Table A1.2.6
Activity rates by level of educational attainment (in per cent)

	Men		Women	
	1983	1989	1983	1989
Primary	79.5	73.5	28.3	29.8
Junior general secondary education	90.8	91.6	47.8	54.4
Junior secondary vocational training	92.3	90.3	41.2	47.7
Senior general secondary education	95.3	94.3	66.1	68.7
Senior secondary vocational training	94.3	91.7	59.1	66.4
Higher vocational education	95.8	92.8	73.2	77.6
University degree	97.3	94.9	84.1	87.2
Unknown	87.9	95.8	49.0	46.7
Student (school/university)	8.1	31.8	8.8	30.5

Source : Recensement de la Main-d'Oeuvre (1983) and Enquêtes sur la Population Active (1989), quoted by Plantenga, 1991.

United Kingdom

Table A1.2.7

Economic activity of women of working age : percentage working full-time, working part-time; and unemployed by highest education qualification and age of youngest dependent child, 1987 and 1988 combined

Age of youngest dependent child and economic activity	Highest educational qualification							
	Degree of equivalent	Higher education below degree level	CCE 'A' level or equivalent	GCE 'O' level or equivalent CSE grade 1	CSE other grades / commercial / apprenticeship	Foreign / other qualifications	No qualifications	Total [a]
With dependent children working								
Full-time	34	34	17	18	16	23	13	18
Part-time	33	37	33	37	39	34	37	37
All working [b]	68 } 73	72 } 75	50 } 55	56 } 62	55 } 60	57 } 61	51 } 55	55 } 60
Unemployed	5	3	5	6	5	4	4	5
Base = 100 %	296	579	395	1588	905	173	2368	6428
Without dependent children working								
Full-time	76	69	62	63	58	36	29	50
Part-time	11	16	14	17	19	23	31	21
All working [b]	87 } 92	86 } 88	76 } 82	80 } 85	77 } 84	62 } 69	60 } 66	72 } 77
Unemployed	5	2	6	5	7	7	6	5
Base = 100 %	486	650	695	2006	982	189	3156	8534
Total [c] working								
Full-time	60	53	46	43	38	31	23	36
Part-time	19	26	21	26	28	28	34	28
All working	80 } 85	79 } 82	67 } 72	69 } 75	66 } 72	59 } 65	56 } 61	65 } 70
Unemployed	5	3	5	5	6	6	5	5
Base = 100 %	783	1231	1090	3600	1894	362	5553	15007

a. Total includes no answers to educational qualifications and proxy interviews.
b. Including a few women whose hours of work were not known.
c. Total is not equal to the sum of totals with and without dependent children because the dependency of some children could not be established.

Source : General Household Survey, quoted by Humphries and Rubery, 1991.

2 Growth and segregation in female employment

Between 1980 and 1984 the burgeoning supply of female labour found itself facing a fall in demand. Between 1985 and 1990 demand picked up again, only to fall in 1991.

The purpose of this chapter is to ascertain how female employment patterns behaved during this period of contrast. To this end we will firstly study their overall development and the distribution of newly created jobs amongst new arrivals on the labour market, women returners and the unemployed. We will then focus on the sectoral distribution of female employment, which remains concentrated in certain specific sectors.

The third section is devoted to agriculture which, in Europe, is on the wane, and the fourth looks at regional disparities. The final section deals with women in the public sector.

1. The increase in female employment between 1983 and 1989

Between 1985 and 1990 (Commission of the European Communities, 1991, pp. 9-10), the net increase in employment in the Community was 1.5 per cent per annum. 70 per cent of these jobs went either to young people reaching working age or to persons obtaining access to the labour market after having been looked upon as not forming part of the active population. Only 30 per cent went to the registered unemployed. Of all the new jobs, two-thirds were taken by women and 30 per cent were part-time.

Where job increases occurred it was in the tertiary sector and industry, with little in the way of growth being noted in building and construction. Agriculture was on the wane and there were considerable differences between regions. If we focus our attention on female employment, we will see that the situation was better than in the case of male employment. Between 1983 and 1989 female employment increased throughout the Community while male employment decreased in Ireland, Italy and France (see table 2.1). Growth was most sustained in the Netherlands, France, Spain, Portugal and the United Kingdom. However, as we will see in the next chapter, these points must be relativized due to different developments in part-time working.

Table 2.1
Annual growth rate of employment between 1983 and 1989 (in per cent)

Country	Women	Men
Ireland	0.81	-0.88
Spain *	6.28	3.07
Luxembourg	1.67	0.51
Greece	1.93	0.16
Italy	1.24	-0.33
Netherlands	5.30	2.29
Germany	1.10	0.80
Belgium	2.00	0.16
Portugal *	4.14	1.63
United Kingdom	2.39	1.59
France	3.12	-0.16
Denmark	1.62	1.42
Europe 12 *	1.83	0.58
Europe 10	1.19	0.55

* 1986 and 1989.

Source : Eurostat (1983 and 1989), *Labour Force Survey.*

If we look at the contribution to the net increase in female employment in the various member states (see figure 2.1), stemming from net variations in the population of working age, activity rates and unemployment, what emerges is that net job creation between 1983 and 1989 was not reflected in any concomitant drop in female unemployment.

In fact, on an average, the contribution stemming from a decrease in unemployment and directed towards the creation of jobs in the Community (10) was negative (-0.7 per cent) as far as women were concerned. 84.5 per cent of the new jobs were taken up by women returners and 14.8 per cent by young women arriving on the labour market. This average stems from the fact that in Italy, France, and Greece the increase in female employment was accompanied by an increase in unemployment. In the other countries, the process of job creation benefited unemployed women, but only marginally in the majority of the cases.

2. The concentration of female employment in the tertiary sector [1]

The growth in employment (see Appendix 2.1, table A2.1.1) has been mainly

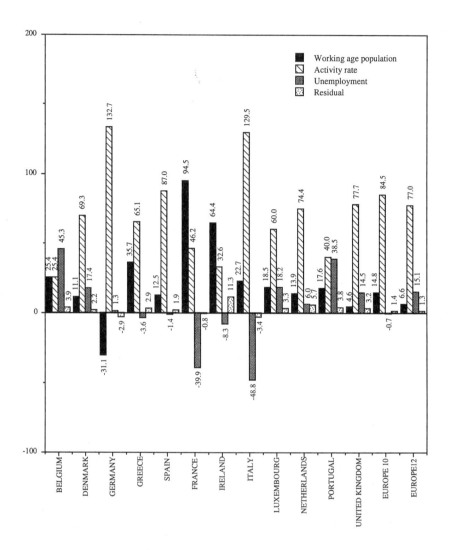

Figure 2.1 Contribution to the net increase in female employment, in the European Community member states, stemming from net variations in the population of working age (14-64 years), activity rates, and unemployment (in percentage of net employment variations from 1983 * to 1989)

* 1986 for Spain, Portugal and Europe 12.

Sources : Eurostat (1983c, 1986c and 1989c), *Labour Force Survey.* Graph by DULBEA.

34

due to the growth in employment in the tertiary sector and, more particularly, in the employment of women in banking and finance, business services and renting (NACE 8 [2]) as well as in 'other services' (NACE 9).

> The development of the services is due to two things, namely :
> - the development of new activities in the services;
> - the transfer of activities from the manufacturing to the tertiary sector by the handing over of services previously catered for in-house. By way of an example, industrial cleaning and canteen management are now dealt with by outside contractors. This transfer of activity from one sector to another has meant a decline in industrial employment and an increase in mainly women's jobs in the services (Hecq and Meulders, 1990, p. 21).

The pre-eminent role played by the services in women's employment and its growth over the decade must not hide the fact that, in industry too, women's employment has either increased or has diminished less dramatically than men's. Except in France and Italy, women's employment has increased in almost every sector (NACE 2), and what is remarkable is that this has also taken place in sectors in the throes of contraction. [3] As the United Kingdom report suggests, the presence or otherwise of an increase in women's participation does not seem to be directly affected by sectoral behaviour patterns. This said, account must be taken of sectoral employment structures. In the case of a sector such as the coal industry which is in the throes of reconstruction, most job losses have occurred amongst the miners - mainly men - while the administrative staff - mainly women - has hardly been affected. And another contributory factor to the increase in the employment of women is the overall development in industry towards a reduction in the number of manual, as opposed to white collar, workers. This is emphasized with respect to Italy by Altieri and Villa (1991, p. 61), who also show that women have been better at holding their ground even amongst manual workers, a factor that seems to attest to changes in the patterns of female labour supply which has become more resistant than previously. The developments in the employment of women result from the union of several factors including the overall development of employment, the relative weights of the sectors, and the rate of feminization by sector. Humphries and Rubery (1991, pp. 23-4) have worked out the effect of each of these factors for the United Kingdom. Usually in times of recession women's employment is less affected than men's since job losses are essentially in industry and have little in the way of repercussions on the services, but boom periods are relatively unfavourable to women's employment because the services react relatively less rapidly to cyclical fluctuations. The good show put up by women's employment in comparison with men's over the 1983-89 period in the United Kingdom seems to have resulted from continued long-term restructuring of industry dominating the effects from the cyclical upturn.

'Other services' remains the most highly feminized sector (see Appendix 2.1, table A2.1.3); taken over all the European countries, it accounts for more than 50 per cent of women and represents between 19 per cent (Greece) and 46 per cent (the Netherlands) of all female employment (see Appendix 2.1, table A2.1.2). In most of the countries (Germany, Belgium, Spain, France, United Kingdom, Greece, the Netherlands and Portugal) there was a high level of feminization between 1983 and 1989. In all the countries women

35

remain concentrated in certain sectors such as 'other services' (NACE 9) which includes education, health, hotels and catering and the distributive trades (NACE 8); in the South, they congregate in the sectors of the remaining manufacturing industries including footwear and clothing, i.e. the sectors close to the tasks traditionally allocated to women (making clothes, bringing up children, caring for the sick, cooking, cleaning, etc.).

Even in the ex-German Democratic Republic, where women's penetration of the labour market was encouraged, there was the same concentration of women in commerce and non-productive activities (health, social affairs, training, education and research).

> The reasons for the unequal distribution of male and female workers over the various sectors and branches of activity had their roots in both tradition and training policies. Thus, there were thirty skilled trades which, for reasons of industrial health and safety reasons, were not recommended for young women, and this was in fact tantamount to a legally imposed limitation on the range of jobs from which young women could choose. In addition, there were no balanced apprenticeship quotas, and this enabled the training centres to cut back on the number of women apprentices. This reflected the opinion that women dropped out during pregnancy and that the mothers of young children were less efficient and so constituted an economic risk whilst, in fact, absences from work on the part of women between twenty and thirty with two children or more either because of their own indisposition or that of their children were hardly in excess of the average number of absences from work on the part of older men and women. An analysis of the apprenticeship register shows that within the structure of planned gender bound job allocation, young women were continuously channeled towards skilled trades with a high proportion of women. Another reason for the unequal distribution of men and women over the various sectors of the economy lay in girls' and women's tradition based leanings and job choices. This led to women's and girls' job preferences being centred upon a small number of careers and areas of study. Thus, in 1989 for example, the proportion of women apprentices in skilled occupations such as secretarial work was 99.8 per cent; for textile workers the figure was 99.4 per cent and for semi-skilled saleswomen 95.6 per cent; on the other hand, the figures were 5.8 per cent for mechanics, 5.2 per cent for toolmakers and only 4 per cent for electricians (Winkler, 1990b, quoted by Figge, Quack and Schäfgen, 1991, pp. 18-19).

This latter phenomenon is not limited to the women in the five new German *Länder*. Figge, Quack and Schäfgen (1991) also mention it with respect to the old Germany, as does Plantenga (1991, p. 20) in her examination of the factors determining horizontal segregation in employment from the point of view of female labour supply. However, it seems that horizontal segregation has decreased due to the dynamism of female employment in the innovative and advanced technology sectors (Altieri and Villa, 1991, p. 37).

We turned to a 'dissimilarity index' [4] in order to see to what extent the increase in women's employment is reflected in a convergence in the distribution of jobs between men and women (see figure 2.2).

> The dissimilarity index has the property that it takes the value one (or 100 per cent) if the distribution for men and women is so dissimilar that they are never found together in the same employment category. It takes the value zero if the proportion of women in each category is the same as the proportion of women in employment as a whole. This can happen only when, relative to their overall proportions in employment, the

36

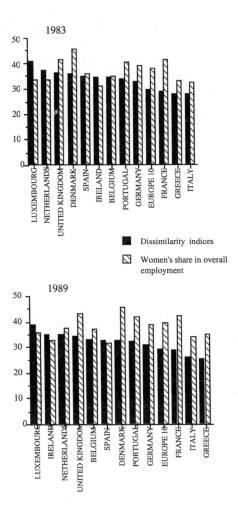

Figure 2.2   Dissimilarity indexes and women's share in overall employment (countries classified according to the descending value of the dissimilarity index) *

* 1986 for Portugal, see also table 2A1.2 in appendix 1 to chapter 2.

Sources : Eurostat (1983c, 1986c and 1989c), *Labour Force Survey*.
            Spain 1983 : Alcobendas Tirado (1991).
            Graphs by DULBEA on the basis of NACE 1 data per sector.

distribution of women across employment categories is the same as that of men (OECD, 1988, p. 210).

It should be noted that there is no negative correlation between the dissimilarity index and women's share in employment in the various countries of the European Community. A higher women's share in employment does not mean that the distribution by sector is any closer to men's. In Denmark, the United Kingdom and Portugal, where women's share in employment is high (respectively 45.4 per cent, 43.1 per cent and 41.7 per cent) (Eurostat (1989), *Labour Force Survey*), the dissimilarity index is high too. It is highest in Luxembourg.

The dissimilarity index decreased slightly for all the countries except Ireland, where it rose, and France, where it remained static (see figure 2.3). The sectoral concentration of female employment is thus confirmed. At the beginning of the 1980s, women's employment was relatively safe due to the fact that it was concentrated in the tertiary sector, which was still productive of jobs. But, more recently, firms have no longer been giving priority to the employment of women. The rate of increase of women's employment has now drawn closer to men's; hitherto, it had a distinct edge over it. The increase in the employment of women - albeit at a slower rate - is still a feature of the tertiary sector; job losses in industry are higher for women and even surpass men's, particularly in the traditional sectors (see Meulders and Plasman, 1991). In addition, there is confirmation of job losses in those services which had recruited large numbers of women in the seventies (see Jortay, Meulders and Plasman, 1990).

Even if the horizontal segregation between sectors has declined slightly, in most of the countries the national experts were more guarded about vertical segregation with its inequalities in corporate hierarchies and matters pertaining to qualifications in both the sectors and the firms themselves. The survey undertaken by the 'Women in employment' network on the impact of the implementation of the single market in textiles, clothing and banking has highlighted this vertical segregation, particularly in banking which, as we pointed out above, was one of the prime movers of the increase in women's employment in recent years (Meulders and Plasman, 1991 and Jortay, Meulders and Plasman, 1990). Hierarchical and job segregation are not studied systematically in this survey. Figge, Quack and Schäfgen (1991), Plantenga (1991), and Humphries and Rubery (1991) nevertheless deal with this aspect in their surveys. In the United Kingdom there has been an increase in the number of women in executive and managerial posts, and the same applies to office jobs. Similar observations are made by Figge, Quack and Schäfgen (1991, p. 14); female employment has increased in skilled jobs in the tertiary sector at the expense of less skilled jobs, though this phenomenon has not brought about any basic modification to the concentration of women's jobs in certain trades and professions. In Italy, the process of tertiarization/bureaucratization has given rise to a redistribution in the demand for labour to the advantage of the best educated job seekers (Altieri and Villa, 1991, p. 62). Women in the services sector in Italy are not only better educated on average than other women employed in agriculture and industry, but also than men in the services. This higher educational level does not necessarily mean that vertical segregation has decreased; it has been demonstrated that women are often more qualified for any given job and, indeed, that they are even overqualified

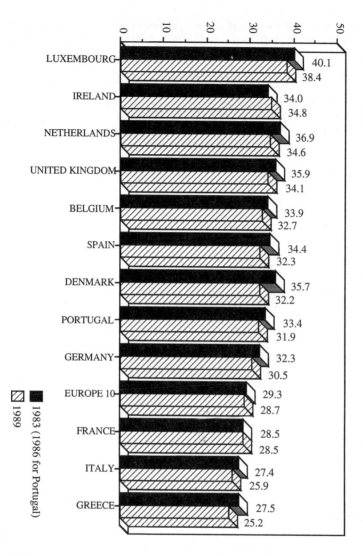

Figure 2.3   1989-83 dissimilarity indexes classified in descending order
from the 1989 index

Sources : Eurostat (1983c, 1986c and 1989c), *Labour Force Survey*.
Spain 1983 : Alcobendas Tirado (1991).

to the extent that we can speak of the underemployment of female labour (Jortay, Meulders and Plasman, 1990). As the German experts suggest, this underemployment goes back - at least in part - to the selection of training. In 1989, 40 per cent of girls in Germany trained as hairdressers, saleswomen, businesswomen, medical auxiliaries and trade representatives in industry, while only 26 per cent of boys chose typically men's training. What is very important is that once their training is complete, many more women than men are affected by the devaluation of their qualifications. Men's and women's career distributions thus contain the germ of hierarchical segregation. Furthermore, even young women completing their training in typically masculine trades experience great difficulty in getting started in these types of jobs and, unlike their male counterparts, often end up in less skilled jobs in their particular fields. Although limited to Germany, these observations are very important because they show that the problem of segregation is linked not only to job choice and training or, in other words, to female labour supply patterns. The demand patterns stemming from public and private concerns seem to be at least as important from the vertical segregation point of view. Apart from the level at which recruitment takes place, vertical segregation is governed by in-house promotion prospects. A survey carried out in 1986 in the Netherlands (Weggelaar *et al.*, 1986, quoted by Plantenga, 1991, p. 23) perceives three factors which apparently lie behind the differences in men's and women's possible career development, namely structural barriers like the opposition to part-time working in posts of responsibility, cultural barriers involving preconceived ideas on the nature of women, and psychological barriers. Over and above this, it seems that the legislation on equal opportunities is badly understood and is accorded little in the way of priority since there is no external supervision to back it up.

3. The decline of employment in agriculture

In the countries of the South, agriculture is still one of the main sectors allowing women to enter the labour market (see table 2.2). The proportion of women employed in agriculture is particularly high in Greece and Portugal (respectively 32.3 per cent and 22.8 per cent of working women were employed in agriculture in 1989 as opposed to 21.6 per cent and 16.9 per cent of men). The rates are also high in Spain and Italy (respectively 11.2 per cent and 9.2 per cent of working women in 1989), but in these latter two countries the percentages of employment in agriculture in relation to overall male employment are almost equal. Employment in agriculture is also considerable in Ireland, but mainly with respect to men.

However, as the Irish expert (Barry, 1991) comments,

> ... the statistics traditionally underestimate the number of women working in agriculture due to the idea of the 'family holding', where the husband is acknowledged as the head of the family and so as the 'active' farmer. Despite the existence of the 'family worker' category, a considerable amount of women's (often unpaid) labour tends to be overlooked.

The Italian experts (Altieri and Villa, 1991, p. 39) also emphasize the difficulties inherent in establishing proper distinctions between various classes of

Table 2.2
Women in agriculture (in per cent)

	Growth rate of women's employment in agriculture	Percentage of employment in agriculture in the overall employment of women		Percentage of women employed in agriculture	
	1983-89	1983	1989	1983	1989
Germany	-36.4	7.4	4.4 ↓	49.9	44.8 ↓
Ex-GDR	-4.1 a	8.5 a	6.7 a ↓	40.0 a	37.4 a ↓
Belgium	-3.0	2.8	2.4 ↓	28.9	26.7 c ↓
Denmark	-16.7	3.9	3.0 ↓	23.9	23.3 ↓
Spain	-24.6 a	16.1 a	11.2 ↓	26.3 a	26.7 ↑
France	-19.1	7.5	5.7 ↓	36.2	34.9 ↓
United Kingdom	-4.2	1.3	1.0 ↓	20.5	19.4 ↓
Greece	-9.0	39.8	32.3 ↓	43.4	44.6 ↑
Ireland	-38.5	7.6	4.5 ↓	13.3	9.5 ↓
Italy	-25.1	13.3	9.2 ↓	35.5	34.3 ↓
Luxembourg	0.0	4.3	3.6 ↓	28.6	33.3 ↑
Netherlands	+29.6	3.3	3.1 ↓	19.7	24.5 ↑
Portugal	-15.5	29.4 a, b	22.8 ↓	50.9 a, b	49.1 ↓

a. Source : National reports.
b. Fishing not included.
c. There is a rising tendency according to the data from the Belgian Ministry
   of Labour and Employment.

Source : Eurostat (1983 and 1989), *Labour Force Survey.*

workers (self-employed, family workers and employees) since cases of workers classified as self-employed also working for others are extremely common.

Most women working in agriculture do so as family workers except in the United Kingdom, where they are mostly wage earners, and in Portugal, where they are mainly employers or self-employed; in Spain and Italy, more than 50 per cent of the women working in agriculture fall into no particular category.

However, it cannot be concluded that the Portuguese, Spanish and Italian women enjoy a more favourable status. In fact the Italian experts (Altieri and Villa, 1991, p. 39) emphasize that in Italy it is frequent for the person running a family holding to be the wife rather than the husband for tax reasons (statistically, this places her in the 'self-employed and employer' category).

Furthermore, employment in agriculture is closely tied to the seasons and is characterized by 'extremely flexible work patterns, a high degree of uncertainty, an extremely fragmented return on labour and conditions of employment with little in the way of guarantees and all too frequently of an irregular nature' (Altieri and Villa, 1991, p. 38).

Temporary employment (see Appendix 2.1, table A2.1.4) is highly developed in those countries where employment in agriculture is considerable, and this is particularly so in the case of women. In 1989, 77.7 per cent of those employed in Spanish agriculture were in temporary jobs; in Greece, the percentage was 73.4 per cent, in Portugal 49.4 per cent, in Italy 40.3 per cent and in Ireland 30 per cent. Between 1983 and 1989 there was a downward trend in temporary employment (in the countries for which figures are available) with the exception of Greece and Ireland, where there was a rise.

Part-time working (see Appendix 2.1, table A2.1.4) is also more developed in agriculture than in any other sector of the economy. This is particularly the case in Ireland (where the proportion of part-time working in relation to overall female employment is 16.5 per cent and 35.1 per cent for women working in agriculture) and in Italy (10.8 per cent and 24.5 per cent respectively). Developments between 1983 and 1989 indicate a downward turn in the proportion of part-time employment.

Male and female employment in agriculture, hunting, forestry and fishing has declined in all the countries of the Community except the Netherlands.[5]

> Certain surveys highlight the fact that whenever agricultural output - and particularly the fruit harvest - declines, the possibility of finding work in the sector is reduced. Finding the route into other sectors barred either through the non-availability of work elsewhere or as the result of their training, the casual workforce, i.e. a certain number of women and older male workers, becomes discouraged at the prospect of remaining on the agricultural labour market. In fact, since they are mainly in an almost permanent state of underemployment, they tend to shade in with non-active elements such as pensioners and women who have returned to the home. However, when things pick up, these same workers feel encouraged to take up the reins again. From a more general angle, what emerges is that agricultural workers are in a position where the lines separating unemployment, underemployment and a lack of employment are very finely drawn indeed (Barbero and Marotta, 1987, p. 77, quoted by Altieri and Villa, 1991, pp. 41-2).

The decline in employment in agriculture in the countries of the South may lead to the elimination from employment, and so from the labour market, of certain women, particularly those who are not regular wage earners.

4. The accentuation of regional disparities

An analysis of activity rates by region (see Appendix 2.1, table A2.1.5) reveals some fairly large disparities (see figure 2.4).

> It may be thought that in addition to the regional disparities common to either sex (structures by age and the varying extents of compulsory schooling according to region), there are also disparities related to women's activity which are linked to demographic, socio-economic and cultural factors such as marriage patterns, family responsibilities, trade and professional categories and the types of jobs offered. However, as the French experts emphasize, 'taken singly, none of these criteria provides a satisfactory explanation. However, taken together, they provide a relatively good explanation for the regional disparities in women's activity' (Gauvin and Silvera, 1991, p. 16).

An analysis of sectoral distributions shows a concentration of women in the

42

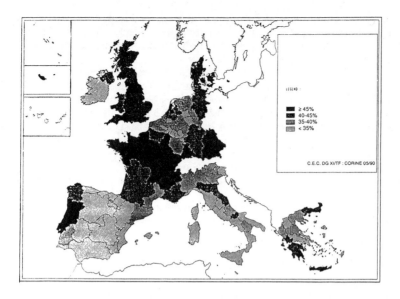

Figure 2.4   1988 activity rates for women of fourteen and over

Source : Eurostat (1990a), 'Rapid Reports', *Regions*.

tertiary sector and agriculture in the countries of the South (Greece, Portugal, Spain and southern Italy). So, higher activity rates can be expected in the countries of the South both in those regions where the services sector is more developed and in those where agriculture predominates. And the activity rates for women are highest in the regions where the tertiary sector is the most developed. Thus, in Germany, women's activity rates are higher in Berlin and Hamburg, two areas where the tertiary sector is more developed than in the rest of the country (see Appendix 2.1, table A2.1.6) and where there is an above average proportion of lone women (Figge, Quack and Schäfgen, 1991, p. 17). In France (Gauvin and Silvera, 1991, p. 17), the activity rate is highest in the *Ile-de-France*, which is the region with the largest tertiary sector. In this region there is also a large number of lone women and the percentage of manual workers in the male population is low, as is the age of the female working population. In the Mediterranean region, however, the proportion of employment in the tertiary sector is even greater, and it is in this region that the activity rate is the lowest in the whole of France. This can no doubt be explained by the weight of the more traditional model existing in southern France. In the United Kingdom, women's activity rates are higher in the South (according to the British experts' figures, the differences are greater in comparison with the North than according to the labour force survey data), and it is also in the South that the amount of employment in private services is highest. In Belgium, the tertiary segment of women's employment is higher in Wallonia and Greater-Brussels, and it is in these regions that activity rates are highest. Also in the Netherlands women's activity rate is highest in the West,

43

the region where the tertiary sector is most developed. However, in the Utrecht area the very high rate of activity which pushes up the average for the West can be explained by the mainly tertiary sector-oriented structure of employment (Plantenga, 1991, p. 28).

Generally speaking, women's activity rates are relatively higher in countries' agricultural regions. In Bavaria, where the services sector is well developed but where agriculture has lost none of its importance, there is a very high women's activity rate, and this is particularly so since the industrial core consists of heavily labour-intensive industries (clothing and textiles) (Figge, Quack and Schäfgen, 1991, p. 17). In north-west France women often live with a spouse and have considerable numbers of children, and the percentage of manual workers in the male population is relatively high. A low women's activity level could be expected as a consequence. However, the structure of activity is favourable to women (family-based agriculture, consumer goods and agro-alimentary concerns), and this explains the high rate of activity recorded for these regions (Gauvin and Silvera, 1991, p. 17). 'In Greece, the female activity rate is higher in agricultural regions (eastern Macedonia and Trace, western Greece, Crete). On the other hand, the region of Attica, where Athens is located, has the lowest activity rate of all' (Cavouriaris, 1991b, appendix : table 2).

> The 1990 women's activity rate for Spain was 33.3 per cent, with lower rates for Extramadura (26.7 per cent), Castille La Mancha (25.7 per cent), Rioja (26.1 per cent) and Andalusia (29.3 per cent). The rates were higher in the cases of Galicia (39.4 per cent), Catalonia (37.5 per cent) and the Balearic Islands (38 per cent). These regional differences are even more pronounced if the 1990 women's employment rates are analysed. The national average was 25.3 per cent, with Galicia (33.8 per cent), the Balearic Islands (32 per cent), Catalonia (29.8 per cent) and Madrid (27.5 per cent) showing higher rates. These were lower for Extramadura (16.5 per cent), Castille La Mancha (19.6 per cent) and Andalusia (18.6 per cent) (Alcobendas Tirado, 1991).

In the more industrial areas, women's activity rates are generally lower. In Germany, the two laggards - the Saar and North-Rhine Westphalia - are old industrial areas with as yet underdeveloped tertiary sectors and relatively few part-time jobs (Figge, Quack and Schäfgen, 1991, p. 17). In north-eastern France, women live relatively frequently with a spouse and, on average, have a considerable number of children per head; the proportion of manual workers in the male population is relatively high and the jobs available on the labour market are more for men (semi-finished goods, engineering and power). Even though the female population of working age is relatively young, it is hardly surprising that there is a relatively low level of women's activity. In Italy, the distribution by major sector is not sensitive enough to explain regional differences.

Whereas the sectoral distribution of regional employment offers an incomplete account of activity rate levels, it does provide a better explanation of certain developments. In general, women's activity rates have developed more rapidly in regions with large tertiary sectors than in industrial and agricultural zones.

In the United Kingdom, manufacturing employment fell dramatically between 1979 and 1981, but the impact of the decline was felt disproportionately in the North as opposed to the more diversified South, which is more oriented towards private services and which has suffered much less from the decline in employment in manufacturing.

> The private services were the dominant source of new jobs in the eighties and the extent to which they counteracted the decline in manufacturing varied across the regions, which were thus differentially integrated into the process of economic restructuring. The South-East was from the outset best placed to take advantage of the potential of private services to generate new jobs, and its position has been enhanced so that the South entered the nineties with a large advantage in employment that its early experience of the current recession has not eroded. The North lost far more jobs in the early eighties and subsequently gained much less in the boom of the late eighties. The divergence in employment growth has promoted much higher levels of unemployment and consequently a widening gap in income per head. Spending power has been increasingly concentrated in the South, which has reinforced the differential economic trends with higher consumption expenditure boosting southern employment, especially in population based services such as distribution. High participation rates have boosted employment through demands for services such as child care. Better employment prospects in the South have attracted in-migration. The credit boom of 1986-89 added to the regional disparity given the concentration of financial and business services in the South (Humphries and Rubery, 1991, pp. 27-8).

Whereas female employment has increased throughout the United Kingdom, it has done so much more rapidly in the South. This increase may stem from either a decline in unemployment, or a natural increase in regional populations, or in-migration, or increased participation (Humphries and Rubery, 1991, pp. 27-8). In all the regions of the United Kingdom, the growth in women's employment has been accompanied by a growth in activity rates. Women's activity rates have increased sharply in the South-east, the very region where men's rates remain static, in response to the pressures of the labour market. At all events, the regional dimension is essential for the United Kingdom since, according to Humphries and Rubery (1991), the excess labour demand in the South-east will be absorbed by increasing activity rates either in the region itself or in contiguous ones. Thus, it seems that the old industrial North will only benefit marginally from this excess labour demand. A more precise breakdown by area is doubtless necessary. This is what emerges from a spatial analysis of the growth poles and the probable effects on the United Kingdom of the final implementation of the single market (Green, 1991, quoted by Humphries and Rubery, 1991, pp. 30-1). The North-South divide remains the primary axis, but the winning regions seem to consist of medium-sized towns situated in a band stretching along the northern edge of the South-eastern development area. Women located in these growth poles share in their growth and job opportunities, particularly if they possess a qualification. On the other hand women - and particularly unqualified women - located in underprivileged areas such as the large industrial conurbations of the North will find themselves facing reduced job prospects, particularly since migrating or commuting to areas in expansion is more difficult for married women. In Germany too, women's activity rates have been particularly enhanced in the Saar- and Bremen-Land, the two regions that have experienced the large-scale expansion of their tertiary sectors.

In Italy, the reduced amount of dynamism in women's employment in the South is due a dramatic decline in jobs in agriculture which, in itself, still accounts for an extremely large share of female employment in the South (Altieri and Villa, 1991, p. 48). Moreover, unlike in the Centre-North, women in the South did not display much resistance to job cuts in industry. In the South, the services sector seems to suffer from a considerable degree of backwardness and inefficiency due to the survival of a large segment of a traditional tertiary sector with a low level of productivity. Amongst other things, this sector serves as a refuge for sections of the labour force - particularly women and young people - otherwise condemned to unemployment. In addition, the weakness of the industrial structure hampers the development of services more directly linked to production - services of the type that constitute the more dynamic part of employment in the rest of the country. An overview of the public services with their no less pressing need for modernization is anything but optimistic (Papo, 1989, pp. 93-115, quoted by Altieri and Villa, 1991, p. 51).

The incidence of female employment in the tertiary sector in the various regions is obviously connected with local production structures. The regions where female employment in the tertiary sector has increased most are Lombardy and Venezia. In these regions there has also been a relatively greater increase in employment in the services due to the tertiarization of industrial employment.

Women's activity rates have increased in a similar manner in all the regions of Italy, both North and South, though employment has grown less rapidly in the South. This is reflected in the southern regions by a worsening of female unemployment; indeed, in certain regions like Calabria, Campania Basilicata and Sicily, the rate has almost doubled. The increase in tertiary sector employment in the North has largely contributed to bringing the unemployment rate down. In contrast, the considerable increase in tertiary sector growth is not reflected in a reduction in unemployment in any of the regions of the South. These divergences stem from the nature of the labour supply which, in the South, is characterized by a surplus of agricultural workers who can be employed in the least efficient and innovative subsectors of the services sector, but not in the advanced technology areas of the tertiary sector. Another cause of divergence lies in the reaction to labour requirements in the South : 'It would seem that, faced with a demand that is insufficient to absorb the labour available, the labour market in the South more than anywhere else has been inclined to pass over the young in favour of more adult workers' (Altieri and Villa, 1991, p. 52). In fact, while the number of tertiary jobs is increasing in the South, the employment of young women in the tertiary sector has declined by 7.5 per cent in favour of the older age groups. The mechanisms excluding women with minimal educational attainments from employment, and even from the labour market, are particularly important in the South. The effects of discouragement are concentrated in this part of labour supply and partly explain the increase in the percentage of women remaining at home. Regional differences are thus well delineated with respect to female participation on the labour market. Apart from the differences in the rates of participation, employment and unemployment, what are worrying are the types of development that we have been able to identify with respect to the United Kingdom and Italy since the trends observed indicate divergent rather than convergent lines of development, and these are increasing the disparities in the female labour force (and not only there). Humphries and Rubery are quite right in this respect when they emphasize that 'the presumption that workers should pursue jobs rather than that there should be an active regional policy has particularly problematic implications for women' (Humphries and Rubery, 1991, p. 32). The situation in Germany is, of course, quite unique due to the inclusion of the five new *Länder*, where the labour market operated in a basically different way from that of the other regions. The problems of convergence and divergence arise in a totally different manner since what is involved is the integration of these regions into the rest of the country.

5. The bad example of the public sector [6]

It is not easy to obtain employment statistics for the public sector and the data that are available are frequently incomplete and cannot be compared across the Community. NACE 91 (public administration, [7] national defence, and compulsory social security) can be used as an approximation, but NACE 91 only represents a small section of the public sector (hospitals, schools, the postal service and the public corporations are not taken into account). We will not, therefore, give any figures in this section.

In the 1960s and 1970s the number of civil service posts increased considerably in almost all the countries. Since the beginning of the 1980s, almost all the governments have been forced to devote a large part of their budgets to servicing their national debts, and this has led to a considerable slowdown in public sector employment (according to the International Labour Office, 1989, pp. 43 and 49). Public sector employment has grown less sharply than private sector employment, particularly in Germany; it has remained static in Belgium, and has dropped in the United Kingdom due to privatization. But there has been an increase in the number of women employed in the public sector in almost all the countries (particularly in Spain, where 83.5 per cent of the new recruits to the public sector are women), and their relative percentage has increased in all the countries (the Netherlands, Germany, etc.). This percentage varies widely from country to country, with women accounting for 65.5 per cent of the jobs in the public sector in France in 1989, while in the United Kingdom most public sector employees are men (52 per cent in 1989). In Denmark, almost half of the women in employment are in the public sector, as opposed to a fifth of men employees. 'In Greece, the proportion of men decreased between 1983 and 1989. However, their participation rate in 1989 was 69 per cent' (Cavouriaris, 1991a, p. 7).

Although in most of the countries (Germany, Belgium, Denmark, Spain, France, Italy and Portugal) the public sector is relatively more feminized than the private sector, the degree to which it segregates men and women seems to be just as great. In Italy, there is a tendency for women to find themselves pursuing, medium- to low-level careers with pay levels below men's (Altieri and Villa, 1991, p. 31). Women rarely obtain executive posts. What emerged from a survey of senior male and female civil servants in a ministry in the Netherlands (Plantenga, 1991, p. 18) was that the men blamed this phenomenon on the women's lack of individual investment; this reason was also put forward by the women, but they placed more emphasis on their unpleasant working environment ('the men gang up against the women'). The government's post-1976 equal opportunities policy and the positive steps that it has

47

taken since 1988 are hardly known if, indeed, they are known at all. In Denmark (Knudsen, 1991, p. 50), the percentage of women amongst senior managers and others in positions of authority increased rapidly between 1984 and 1988. In Germany, 'jobs have been created in typically women's areas of interest' (part-time jobs in education, health, social affairs and public administration), although the number of women has also increased in other areas of the public service. It seems that women have been given relatively more frequent consideration in recruiting campaigns, even for posts requiring both highly and very highly qualified personnel. It is probable that, in addition to demographic developments, the measures adopted in many government departments in the 1980s in favour of women have led to the more extensive recruitment of younger and better qualified women. Thus, the proportion of women employed in the public service passed from 40.1 per cent in 1983 to 41.7 per cent in 1988. It was possible for the number of women civil servants to rise from 25 per cent to 27.1 per cent, with the figures for the middling grades indicating an increase from 38.1 per cent to 39.6 per cent and those for the senior grades one from 22.6 per cent to 23.8 per cent. Women nevertheless continue to be heavily underrepresented in these groups (Figge, Quack and Schäfgen, 1991, pp. 12-13). At the same time, it must also be emphasized that the jobs created in the public sector mainly to benefit women are mostly temporary or part-time.

5.1 Part-time working

In Germany, there has been an above-average development of part-time working in the civil service. Certain full-time posts have been converted into part-time ones, and new posts are mainly on a part-time basis. Calculations relative to education (Breidenstein, 1990, quoted by Figge, Quack and Schäfgen, 1991, p. 12) show that while the volume of part-time work carried out by women remains largely unchanged, the number of women employed is on the increase. In Denmark (Knudsen, 1991, p. 38), 'long-term' and 'short-term' part-time working is much more frequent in the public than in the private sector. In Ireland, 'there is a greater proportion of women among the temporary part-timers in the 'public administration and national defence' category than in the rest of the economy' (Barry, 1991). In Belgium, an increase in the number of part-time posts accounts for the lion's share of the growth in civil service employment (Meulders and Vander Stricht, 1991, p. 27).

5.2 Temporary working

In Germany, the percentage of fixed-term civil service posts occupied by both male and female blue and white collar workers rose from 6.8 per cent to 9.6 per cent in 1988, i.e. a markedly higher rate than in the private sector (Figge, Quack and Schäfgen, 1991, p. 13, and Büchtemann and Höland, 1989, quoted by Figge, Quack and Schäfgen, 1991, p. 13). The Büchtemann and Höland survey (1989) concludes that over the period May 1987-April 1988, more than one of every two cases of recruitment to the civil service involved a fixed-term contract. Since the middle of the 1980s, the imposition of fixed-term contracts - particularly in the universities - when male as well as female employees are at the beginning of their careers has been facilitated by changes to the legislation (Lörcher, 1982, quoted by Figge, Quack and Schäfgen, 1991, p. 13). This partly accounts for the fact that between 1983 and 1988, the proportion of employees with fixed-term contracts increased more in the case of men than in that of women. In Spain, of the 291,000 jobs created in the public sector since 1987, 51 per cent have been on the basis of temporary contracts (Alcobendas Tirado, 1991). In Belgium, more than 90 per cent of men are established in government departments and public institutions as opposed to an approximately 70 per cent of women. Moreover, the proportion of established posts is on the decline, and particularly where women are concerned (Meulders and Vander Stricht, 1991, p. 28). In France (Gauvin and Silvera, 1991, p. 20),[8] 11.2 per cent of women civil servants were not established in 1989 (as opposed to 4.5 per cent of men). This is the form of employment that has increased the most.

Taking the European Community as a whole, the public sector has thus made a positive contribution to the increase in women's employment. This said, women's employment has not escaped the modifications to the general conditions of employment in the public sector that resulted from changes to most of the European governments' economic policies during the 1980s. Whereas variations in public employment still formed part of contracyclical policy in the 1970s, in the 1980s these variations in employment and the associated direct and indirect financial rewards were used to reduce public expenditure and budget deficits. Hence the slowdown, the stagnation and even the regression in public employment, the prolongation of the temporary contracts of persons occupying posts on an unestablished basis or awaiting appointment as established civil servants, and the generalization of part-time appointments.... Moreover, while all the governments have been obliged to enact equal opportunities legislation, the segregation of men and women - particularly from the career distribution point of view - does not differ to any great extent from what obtains in the private sector. And, in this connection, the Netherlands report concludes that the lead justifiably expected from government exists more on paper than in reality.

6. Conclusions

Between 1983 and 1989 female employment increased in all the countries of the Community, where it followed a more favourable pattern than men's. This increase was not reflected in any concomitant drop in unemployment because the new jobs were taken up by young people arriving on the labour market and by women returners. Female employment remains concentrated in certain specific sectors and its growth stems from the increase in employment in the tertiary sector and particularly in banking and insurance, services to industry, renting and other services. In parallel to this horizontal segregation vertical segregation persists, with all its inequalities in corporate hierarchies and matters pertaining to qualifications.

The employment of women in agriculture is widespread in Greece, Portugal, Spain and Italy, and its decline could easily mean the exclusion from the labour market of certain categories of women, particularly those who are not wage earners.

Pronounced regional disparities characterize the development of female employment. Generally speaking, female activity rates have increased more rapidly in those regions where the tertiary sector is predominant than in agricultural or industrial regions, and the development of the various sectors presages diverging lines of regional development which will accentuate the inequalities between women.

Lastly, the public sector has not acted as an example in the way that certain women had expected. It incorporates the same forms of hierarchical and occupational segregation as the private sector.

Notes

1. The figures given in this section are taken from the Eurostat (1983, 1986 and 1989), *Labour Force Survey*. See also tables A2.1.1, A2.1.2 and A2.1.3 in Appendix 2.1.
2. NACE is a code of the general industrial classification of economic activities within the European Community (see detailed classification pp. 127-8).
3. There has also been a marked increase in the employment of women (cf. table 2.1) in building and civil engineering (NACE 5) in Denmark, the United Kingdom, the Netherlands and Italy (+35.7 per cent, +40.5 per cent, +43.5 per cent and +13.8 per cent). In Ireland too, the employment of women in industry has increased by 20 per cent in the extraction and processing of non-energy producing minerals and derived products, in the chemical industry (NACE 2) and by 29.4 per cent in metal manufacture, mechanical, electrical and instrument engineering (NACE 3). These dramatic increases can be explained by the low initial rate of feminization in these sectors.
4. Using the following notation : the respective numbers of men, women and people in general in professional and trade categories $i = 1, ..., k$, are $NM_1, ..., NM_k$; $NF_1, ..., NF_k$; and $N_1, ..., N_k$; since the totals are NM, NF and N respectively, the dissimilarity index (DI) is given by :

$$DI = \sum_i \left| \frac{NM_i}{NM} - \frac{NF_i}{NF} \right| / 2$$

5. However Plantenga's (1991) analysis in the Netherlands report shows that the increase in employment in agriculture in the Netherlands is mainly due to an increase in part-time employment which might stem, at least in part, from the 1987 switch from a labour force census (AKT) to a survey of the active population (EBB). The number of persons with a weekly work load of under twenty hours is much greater according to the EBB than according to the AKT.
6. The statistics given in this section are from the national reports.
7. Data are listed in the tables by sector (tables A2.1.1, A2.1.2 and A2.1.3 in Appendix 2.1).
8. The French experts list any government employee as 'unestablished' who did not provide precise details of his/her status, and this has led to some heavily inflated results (almost half of those listed as 'unestablished' are involved). This said, it seemed more logical to them to assume that such

persons were not 'real civil servants' in view of their hesitation in detailing their status.

Table A2.1.1
1983-89 employment growth rates by sector and sex

	Germany	Belgium	Denmark
Men : 1983-89 growth rates			
Agriculture	-21.8%	8.6%	-14.2%
Energy and water	-6.8%	-32.2%	57.1%
Extraction of minerals; chemical industry	2.6%	-12.2%	25.0%
Metal manufacture; electrical and instrument engineering	9.5%	8.7%	-8.1%
Other manufacturing industries	0.1%	-3.3%	1.3%
Building and civil engineering	-6.5%	5.1%	18.4%
Industry : total	2.2%	-1.8%	6.0%
Distributive trades, hotels and catering	4.1%	-2.0%	16.2%
Transport and communication	4.7%	-5.1%	4.4%
Banking, finance and insurance	21.1%	21.4%	60.5%
Public administration	0.9%	-0.4%	10.8%
Other services	34.0%	7.3%	3.8%
Services : total	10.8%	2.5%	15.5%
Total (where a sector is declared)	4.9%	0.9%	8.8%
Women : 1983-89 growth rates			
Agriculture	-36.4%	-3.0%	-16.7%
Energy and water	-5.3%	50.0%	-100.0%
Extraction of minerals; chemical industry	7.6%	13.0%	13.3%
Metal manufacture; electrical and instrument engineering	19.3%	0.0%	2.4%
Other manufacturing industries	-4.3%	-4.6%	17.4%
Building and civil engineering	3.6%	10.0%	35.7%
Industry : total	5.6%	0.0%	12.7%
Distributive trades, hotels and catering	1.7%	5.1%	0.5%
Transport and communication	25.7%	0.0%	20.9%
Banking, finance and insurance	23.5%	33.3%	68.6%
Public administration	-4.0%	42.4%	44.6%
Other services	22.5%	15.8%	1.8%
Services : total	12.0%	16.2%	11.1%
Total (where a sector is declared)	6.8%	12.7%	10.2%

continued

	France	United Kingdom	Greece

Men : 1983-89 growth rates

Agriculture	-14.4%	2.6%	-13.4%
Energy and water	-1.7%	-24.6%	13.5%
Extraction of minerals; chemical industry	-17.9%	-5.6%	-14.1%
Metal manufacture; electrical and instrument engineering	-11.2%	-2.8%	-1.9%
Other manufacturing industries	-2.9%	6.2%	4.3%
Building and civil engineering	-3.0%	20.1%	-12.2%
Industry : total	-7.4%	2.5%	-4.1%
Distributive trades, hotels and catering	-1.7%	19.0%	13.8%
Transport and communication	0.5%	6.5%	-4.5%
Banking, finance and insurance	17.8%	48.2%	30.4%
Public administration	13.6%	3.0%	28.8%
Other services	11.6%	12.9%	15.6%
Services : total	6.6%	17.5%	13.3%
Total (where a sector is declared)	-1.2%	9.9%	1.0%

Women : 1983-89 growth rates

Agriculture	-19.1%	-4.2%	-9.0%
Energy and water	3.8%	-14.6%	20.0%
Extraction of minerals; chemical industry	-5.1%	2.6%	0.0%
Metal manufacture; electrical and instrument engineering	-11.9%	8.9%	0.0%
Other manufacturing industries	-8.6%	6.2%	16.0%
Building and civil engineering	-2.2%	40.5%	-100.0%
Industry : total	-8.3%	7.8%	11.6%
Distributive trades, hotels and catering	3.1%	13.4%	28.1%
Transport and communication	6.6%	37.9%	8.0%
Banking, finance and insurance	18.2%	55.9%	53.5%
Public administration	11.4%	12.0%	58.3%
Other services	16.3%	24.2%	26.0%
Services : total	12.0%	23.9%	31.4%
Total (where a sector is declared)	5.6%	20.4%	11.9%

continued

	Ireland	Italy	Netherlands
Men : 1983-89 growth rates			
Agriculture	-9.5%	-21.0%	-1.8%
Energy and water	-13.3%	3.2%	-3.4%
Extraction of minerals; chemical industry	-12.1%	1.2%	17.4%
Metal manufacture; electrical and instrument engineering	8.5%	-14.2%	8.2%
Other manufacturing industries	-12.4%	-8.3%	12.4%
Building and civil engineering	-22.3%	-17.4%	10.9%
Industry : total	-12.2%	-11.6%	10.6%
Distributive trades, hotels and catering	0.8%	3.0%	17.2%
Transport and communication	2.1%	-0.7%	9.7%
Banking, finance and insurance	8.7%	22.1%	49.6%
Public administration	-6.4%	8.8%	3.3%
Other services	7.4%	30.6%	20.2%
Services : total	2.4%	10.6%	19.7%
Total (where a sector is declared)	-5.4%	-2.0%	14.9%
Women : 1983-89 growth rates			
Agriculture	-38.5%	-25.1%	29.6%
Energy and water	-	11.1%	33.3%
Extraction of minerals; chemical industry	20.0%	11.2%	38.9%
Metal manufacture; electrical and instrument engineering	29.4%	-15.0%	33.3%
Other manufacturing industries	2.7%	-6.0%	18.1%
Building and civil engineering	-25.0%	13.8%	43.5%
Industry : total	9.5%	-5.2%	26.1%
Distributive trades, hotels and catering	9.1%	15.2%	38.8%
Transport and communication	-7.7%	29.6%	51.1%
Banking, finance and insurance	11.4%	61.2%	60.8%
Public administration	-15.0%	0.6%	43.0%
Other services	12.1%	25.2%	33.6%
Services : total	7.9%	20.6%	38.9%
Total (where a sector is declared)	4.7%	7.7%	37.0%

Source : Eurostat (1983c and 1989c), *Labour Force Survey*.
Calculations DULBEA.

Table A2.1.2
Sectoral distribution of employment in 1989 and the disparity index for 1983 and 1989

	Germany	Ex-GDR	Belgium	Denmark
Men's share by sector, 1989				
Agriculture	3.5%	-	3.9%	8.1%
Energy and water	2.7%	-	1.8%	1.5%
Extraction of minerals; chemical industry	6.8%	-	7.0%	2.5%
Metal manufacture; mechanical, electrical and instrument engineering	20.6%	-	12.2%	10.3%
Other manufacturing industries	9.8%	-	10.2%	11.0%
Building and civil engineering	10.1%	-	9.1%	11.7%
Industry : total	50.0%	-	40.3%	37.0%
Distributive trades, hotels and catering	13.0%	-	15.4%	15.6%
Transport and communication	7.1%	-	9.8%	10.0%
Banking, finance and insurance	7.2%	-	7.8%	9.7%
Public administration	9.9%	-	9.8%	6.4%
Other services	9.4%	-	13.0%	13.2%
Services : total	46.5%	-	55.8%	54.9%
Total (where a sector is declared)	100.0%	-	100.0%	100.0%
Women's share by sector, 1989				
Agriculture	4.4%	6.7%	2.4%	3.0%
Energy and water [a]	0.5%	25.6%	0.5%	0.0%
Extraction of minerals; chemical industry [b]	3.3%	1.9%	2.0%	1.4%
Metal manufacture; mechanical, electrical and instrument engineering	9.3%	-	3.6%	3.5%
Other manufacturing industries	9.9%	2.8%	9.4%	9.1%
Building and civil engineering	1.9%	1.9%	0.8%	1.6%
Industry : total	24.8%	-	16.2%	15.7%
Distributive trades, hotels and catering	22.3%	12.3%	22.0%	15.4%
Transport and communication	3.7%	4.5%	2.7%	4.4%
Banking, finance and insurance	9.5%	-	8.5%	10.0%
Public administration	8.0%	-	9.9%	7.9%
Other services [c]	27.2%	44.2%	38.3%	43.6%
Services : total	70.7%	-	81.4%	81.4%
Total (where a sector is declared)	100.0%	-	100.0%	100.0%
1983 dissimilarity index	32.3%	-	33.9%	35.7%
Women's share in employment	38.6%	-	34.3%	45.1%
1989 dissimilarity index	30.5%	-	32.7%	32.2%
Women's share in employment	39.0%	-	36.8%	45.4%

continued

	Spain	France	United Kingdom
Men's share by sector, 1989			
Agriculture	14.0%	7.8%	3.2%
Energy and water	1.6%	1.8%	3.3%
Extraction of minerals; chemical industry	4.5%	4.1%	4.1%
Metal manufacture; mechanical, electrical and instrument engineering	9.5%	12.5%	13.4%
Other manufacturing industries	11.5%	9.3%	10.2%
Building and civil engineering	12.8%	12.0%	12.9%
Industry : total	39.8%	39.8%	44.0%
Distributive trades, hotels and catering	19.9%	16.0%	17.0%
Transport and communication	7.4%	7.7%	8.5%
Banking, finance and insurance	5.5%	7.9%	9.6%
Public administration	5.5%	8.7%	6.3%
Other services	7.9%	12.1%	11.5%
Services : total	46.2%	52.4%	52.9%
Total (where a sector is declared)	100.0%	100.0%	100.0%
Women's share by sector, 1989			
Agriculture	11.2%	5.7%	1.0%
Energy and water [a]	0.3%	0.6%	0.8%
Extraction of minerals; chemical industry [b]	1.5%	1.8%	1.8%
Metal manufacture; mechanical, electrical and instrument engineering	2.4%	4.8%	5.1%
Other manufacturing industries	12.1%	8.7%	8.4%
Building and civil engineering	0.7%	1.5%	1.6%
Industry : total	17.0%	17.4%	17.6%
Distributive trades, hotels and catering	26.6%	18.3%	25.3%
Transport and communication	2.1%	3.7%	3.5%
Banking, finance and insurance	4.9%	10.1%	12.1%
Public administration	5.2%	10.2%	5.7%
Other services [c]	32.8%	34.5%	34.9%
Services : total	71.8%	76.9%	81.3%
Total (where a sector is declared)	100.0%	100.0%	100.0%
1983 dissimilarity index	34.4% [d]	28.5%	35.9%
Women's share in employment	35.7% [d]	40.7%	40.9%
1989 dissimilarity index	32.3%	28.5%	34.1%
Women's share in employment	31.3%	42.3%	43.1%

continued

	Greece	Ireland	Italy
Men's share by sector, 1989			
Agriculture	21.6%	20.9%	9.2%
Energy and water	1.8%	1.8%	1.4%
Extraction of minerals; chemical industry	3.1%	4.0%	4.2%
Metal manufacture; mechanical, electrical and instrument engineering	4.4%	7.0%	8.7%
Other manufacturing industries	11.1%	10.6%	10.2%
Building and civil engineering	9.9%	10.0%	12.1%
Industry : total	30.3%	33.3%	36.5%
Distributive trades, hotels and catering	19.0%	16.5%	20.6%
Transport and communication	9.0%	6.5%	7.2%
Banking, finance and insurance	4.3%	6.8%	3.9%
Public administration	7.1%	6.0%	8.7%
Other services	8.7%	10.0%	13.9%
Services : total	48.1%	45.8%	54.3%
Total (where a sector is declared)	100.0%	100.0%	100.0%
Women's share by sector, 1989			
Agriculture	32.3%	4.5%	9.2%
Energy and water [a]	0.5%	0.0%	0.3%
Extraction of minerals; chemical industry [b]	1.2%	1.7%	2.0%
Metal manufacture; mechanical, electrical and instrument engineering	0.9%	6.2%	3.6%
Other manufacturing industries	14.6%	10.6%	16.1%
Building and civil engineering	0.0%	0.8%	1.3%
Industry : total	17.2%	19.3%	23.2%
Distributive trades, hotels and catering	18.5%	23.5%	22.8%
Transport and communication	2.1%	3.4%	2.3%
Banking, finance and insurance	5.1%	10.9%	4.6%
Public administration	5.9%	4.8%	7.0%
Other services [c]	18.8%	33.6%	31.0%
Services : total	50.5%	76.2%	67.5%
Total (where a sector is declared)	100.0%	100.0%	100.0%
1983 dissimilarity index	27.5%	34.0%	27.4%
Women's share in employment	32.7%	30.6%	32.0%
1989 dissimilarity index	25.2%	34.8%	25.9%
Women's share in employment	35.0%	32.8%	34.1%

continued

	Luxembourg	Netherlands	Portugal
Men's share by sector, 1989			
Agriculture	4.0%	5.7%	16.9%
Energy and water	2.0%	1.5%	1.4%
Extraction of minerals; chemical industry	13.0%	4.1%	4.8%
Metal manufacture; mechanical, electrical and instrument engineering	5.0%	9.4%	6.8%
Other manufacturing industries	9.0%	10.6%	14.1%
Building and civil engineering	12.0%	10.3%	14.1%
Industry : total	41.0%	35.8%	41.3%
Distributive trades, hotels and catering	16.0%	16.8%	18.4%
Transport and communication	8.0%	7.8%	5.9%
Banking, finance and insurance	10.0%	10.9%	3.9%
Public administration	9.0%	7.4%	7.7%
Other services	12.0%	15.6%	5.9%
Services : total	55.0%	58.5%	41.8%
Total (where a sector is declared)	100.0%	100.0%	100.0%
Women's share by sector, 1989			
Agriculture	3.6%	3.1%	22.8%
Energy and water [a]	0.0%	0.4%	0.3%
Extraction of minerals; chemical industry [b]	1.8%	1.1%	2.1%
Metal manufacture; mechanical, electrical and instrument engineering	1.8%	2.2%	1.7%
Other manufacturing industries	3.6%	6.1%	20.7%
Building and civil engineering	1.8%	1.5%	0.6%
Industry : total	9.1%	11.3%	25.4%
Distributive trades, hotels and catering	27.3%	21.2%	16.1%
Transport and communication	3.6%	3.2%	2.0%
Banking, finance and insurance	16.4%	10.3%	2.7%
Public administration	7.3%	5.1%	5.7%
Other services [c]	32.7%	45.8%	25.4%
Services : total	87.3%	85.6%	51.8%
Total (where a sector is declared)	100.0%	100.0%	100.0%
1983 dissimilarity index	40.1%	36.9%	33.4% [e]
Women's share in employment	32.9%	33.1%	39.9% [e]
1989 dissimilarity index	38.4%	34.6%	31.9%
Women's share in employment	35.5%	37.1%	41.7%

a. Industry in the ex-German Democratic Republic.
b. Small-scale private manufacturing industry in the ex-German Democratic Republic.
c. Other non-manufacturing sectors in the ex-German Democratic Republic.
d. On the basis of data from Alcobendas Tirado (1991).
e. 1986.
Source : Eurostat (1983c and 1989c), *Labour Force Survey*.

Table A2.1.3
Women's share in employment

	Germany	Ex-GDR	Belgium	Denmark
Women's share in employment 1983				
Agriculture	49.9%	40.0%	28.9%	23.9%
Energy and water [a]	10.5%	42.1%	6.3%	17.6%
Extraction of minerals; chemical industry [b]	23.0%	35.7%	11.3%	34.9%
Metal manufacture; mechanical, electrical and instrument engineering	20.9%	-	15.6%	20.4%
Other manufacturing industries	40.5%	55.5%	35.1%	37.2%
Building and civil engineering	9.6%	-	4.8%	9.0%
Industry : total	23.6%	35.8%	18.7%	24.9%
Distributive trades, hotels and catering	52.9%	73.5%	43.7%	48.8%
Transport and communication	21.8%	-	13.0%	23.9%
Banking, finance and insurance	45.4%	-	36.7%	44.9%
Public administration	35.4%	-	29.1%	43.9%
Other services [c]	66.9%	73.1%	61.5%	73.6%
Services : total	49.1%	-	42.8%	56.1%
Total (where a sector is declared)	38.6%	-	34.3%	45.1%
Women's share in employment 1989				
Agriculture	44.8%	37.4%	26.7%	23.3%
Energy and water [a]	10.7%	40.8%	13.0%	0.0%
Extraction of minerals; chemical industry [b]	23.8%	35.9%	14.1%	32.7%
Metal manufacture; mechanical, electrical and instrument engineering	22.4%	-	14.6%	22.2%
Other manufacturing industries	39.4%	56.5%	34.8%	40.8%
Building and civil engineering	10.5%	-	5.0%	10.2%
Industry : total	24.2%	-	19.0%	26.1%
Distributive trades, hotels and catering	52.3%	72.2%	45.4%	45.2%
Transport and communication	25.1%	35.4%	13.6%	26.7%
Banking, finance and insurance	45.9%	-	38.9%	46.1%
Public administration	34.2%	-	37.0%	50.5%
Other services [c]	64.9%	72.4%	63.3%	73.2%
Services : total	49.3%	-	45.9%	55.1%
Total (where a sector is declared)	39.0%	-	36.8%	45.4%

continued

Table A2.1.3 continued

	Spain	France	United Kingdom
Women's share in employment 1983			
Agriculture	26.3%	36.2%	20.5%
Energy and water [a]	5.3%	18.4%	13.7%
Extraction of minerals; chemical industry [b]	13.2%	22.0%	22.8%
Metal manufacture; mechanical, electrical and instrument engineering	9.1%	22.0%	20.3%
Other manufacturing industries	32.8%	42.3%	38.5%
Building and civil engineering	2.0%	8.2%	7.5%
Industry : total	-	24.5%	22.4%
Distributive trades, hotels and catering	36.0%	44.4%	54.2%
Transport and communication	9.1%	24.9%	19.3%
Banking, finance and insurance	22.5%	48.6%	47.6%
Public administration	-	46.7%	38.6%
Other services [c]	55.1%	66.8%	67.6%
Services : total	-	50.6%	52.5%
Total (where a sector is declared)	-	40.7%	40.9%
Women's share in employment 1989			
Agriculture	26.7%	34.9%	19.4%
Energy and water [a]	6.9%	19.3%	15.2%
Extraction of minerals; chemical industry [b]	13.4%	24.6%	24.3%
Metal manufacture; mechanical, electrical and instrument engineering	10.3%	21.9%	22.2%
Other manufacturing industries	32.5%	40.9%	38.5%
Building and civil engineering	2.4%	8.2%	8.7%
Industry : total	16.3%	24.3%	23.3%
Distributive trades, hotels and catering	37.8%	45.6%	53.0%
Transport and communication	11.5%	26.0%	23.6%
Banking, finance and insurance	29.1%	48.7%	48.9%
Public administration	30.4%	46.2%	40.7%
Other services [c]	65.4%	67.8%	69.7%
Services : total	41.4%	51.9%	53.9%
Total (where a sector is declared)	31.3%	42.3%	43.1%

continued

60

	Greece	Ireland	Italy
Women's share in employment 1983			
Agriculture	43.4%	13.3%	35.5%
Energy and water [a]	11.9%	0.0%	8.7%
Extraction of minerals; chemical industry [b]	15.0%	13.2%	18.1%
Metal manufacture; mechanical, electrical and instrument engineering	10.1%	26.6%	17.8%
Other manufacturing industries	38.8%	29.4%	44.4%
Building and civil engineering	1.5%	4.1%	3.8%
Industry : total	20.8%	18.5%	23.5%
Distributive trades, hotels and catering	31.7%	39.1%	33.8%
Transport and communication	10.0%	21.7%	11.1%
Banking, finance and insurance	35.2%	43.2%	31.6%
Public administration	26.7%	29.9%	31.0%
Other services [c]	51.8%	61.1%	54.5%
Services : total	32.7%	43.4%	37.1%
Total (where a sector is declared)	32.7%	30.6%	32.0%
Women's share in employment 1989			
Agriculture	44.6%	9.5%	34.3%
Energy and water [a]	12.5%	0.0%	9.3%
Extraction of minerals; chemical industry [b]	17.0%	17.1%	19.5%
Metal manufacture; mechanical, electrical and instrument engineering	10.3%	30.1%	17.6%
Other manufacturing industries	41.4%	32.8%	45.0%
Building and civil engineering	0.0%	3.9%	5.2%
Industry : total	23.4%	22.0%	24.7%
Distributive trades, hotels and catering	34.3%	41.0%	36.4%
Transport and communication	11.2%	20.0%	14.0%
Banking, finance and insurance	39.1%	43.8%	37.9%
Public administration	30.9%	27.9%	29.4%
Other services [c]	53.9%	62.2%	53.4%
Services : total	36.1%	44.7%	39.1%
Total (where a sector is declared)	35.0%	32.8%	34.1%

continued

	Luxembourg	Netherlands	Portugal
Women's share in employment 1983			
Agriculture	28.6%	19.7%	-
Energy and water [a]	0.0%	9.4%	-
Extraction of minerals; chemical industry [b]	6.3%	12.0%	-
Metal manufacture; mechanical, electrical and instrument engineering	20.0%	9.9%	-
Other manufacturing industries	27.3%	24.6%	-
Building and civil engineering	7.7%	6.2%	-
Industry : total	12.8%	14.0%	-
Distributive trades, hotels and catering	46.7%	38.6%	-
Transport and communication	11.1%	15.0%	-
Banking, finance and insurance	41.7%	34.1%	-
Public administration	25.0%	22.6%	-
Other services [c]	61.5%	60.9%	-
Services : total	43.8%	42.7%	-
Total (where a sector is declared)	32.9%	33.1%	-
Women's share in employment 1989			
Agriculture	33.3%	24.5%	49.1%
Energy and water [a]	0.0%	12.5%	11.6%
Extraction of minerals; chemical industry [b]	7.1%	13.9%	24.0%
Metal manufacture; mechanical, electrical and instrument engineering	16.7%	11.9%	15.3%
Other manufacturing industries	18.2%	25.6%	51.2%
Building and civil engineering	7.7%	7.8%	3.1%
Industry : total	10.9%	15.6%	30.6%
Distributive trades, hotels and catering	48.4%	42.7%	38.4%
Transport and communication	20.0%	19.5%	19.4%
Banking, finance and insurance	47.4%	35.8%	33.1%
Public administration	30.8%	28.8%	34.6%
Other services [c]	60.0%	63.4%	75.4%
Services : total	46.6%	46.3%	47.0%
Total (where a sector is declared)	35.5%	37.1%	41.7%

a. Industry in the ex-German Democratic Republic.
b. Small-scale private manufacturing industry in the ex-German Democratic Republic.
c. Other non-manufacturing sectors in the ex-German Democratic Republic.
Sources : Eurostat (1983c and 1989c), *Labour Force Survey*.
Figge, Quack and Schäfgen (1991) for the ex-German Democratic Republic.
Alcobendas Tirado (1991) for the 1983 data.
Calculations DULBEA.

Distribution of employment in agriculture by status

		Germany	Ex-GDR	Belgium	Denmark
Distribution by professional status, 1989					
Men	Employers and self-employed	58.5 -	-	81.2 ↑	60.6 ↓
	Employees	31.7 ↑	-	9.7 ↓	39.3 ↑
	Family workers	9.8 ↓	-	9.1 ↑	-
Women	Employers and self-employed	9.6 ↓	-	25.8 ↓	(9.9) ↑
	Employees	16.7 ↑	-	-	36.7 ↑
	Family workers	73.7 ↓	-	67.1 ↑	53.4 ↓
The arrows indicate tendencies since 1983.					
Share in part-time employment, 1983					
1983	Men	9.6	-	-	5.5
	Women	33.8	28.5	16.9	27.9
1989	Men	8.4	-	-	13.1
	Women	31.8	26.8	17.0	39.1
Share in temporary employment, 1983					
1983	Men	-	-	7.1	-
	Women	-	-	7.7	-
1989	Men	16.7	-	7.1	12.2
	Women	19.4	-	4.5	20.5

		Spain	France	United Kingdom
Distribution by professional status, 1989				
Men	Employers and self-employed	52.7	71.0 ↓	55.2 -
	Employees	35.9	20.4 ↑	44.8 ↓
	Family workers	11.4	8.7 ↓	-
Women	Employers and self-employed	39.0	33.2 ↑	36.7 ↑
	Employees	14.9	12.2 ↑	63.3 ↓
	Family workers	46.1	54.7 ↓	-
The arrows indicate tendencies since 1983.				
Share in part-time employment, 1983				
1983	Men	-	5.9	5.6
	Women	-	35.3	51.7
1989	Men	-	6.1	6.4
	Women	-	31.7	51.5
Share in temporary employment, 1983				
1983	Men	-	3.7	7.4
	Women	-	10.7	23.1
1989	Men	45.4	9.3	6.0
	Women	77.7	18.5	10.4

continued

		Greece	Ireland	Italy
Distribution by professional status, 1989				
Men	Employers and self-employed	79.5 ↑	77.5 ↑	56.7 ↓
	Employees	5.1 ↑	13.6 ↑	37.7 ↑
	Family workers	15.4 ↓	8.9 ↓	5.6 ↓
Women	Employers and self-employed	25.2 -	36.2 ↑	33.7 ↑
	Employees	3.1 -	-	41.8 ↑
	Family workers	71.7 -	51.4 ↓	24.6 ↓
The arrows indicate tendencies since 1983.				
Share in part-time employment, 1983				
1983	Men	5.7	3.9	8.4
	Women	13.7	45.0	22.2
1989	Men	3.7	(2.4)	10.3
	Women	8.9	35.1	14.5
Share in temporary employment, 1983				
1983	Men	45.6	7.0	25.5
	Women	63.2	11.1	52.9
1989	Men	49.2	9.7	20.7
	Women	73.4	30.0	40.3

		Luxembourg	Netherlands	Portugal
Distribution by professional status, 1989				
Men	Employers and self-employed	82.0	58.8 ↓	65.0
	Employees	-	38.3 ↑	23.6
	Family workers	-	2.9 ↓	11.4
Women	Employers and self-employed	-	12.1 ↑	75.1
	Employees	-	28.8 ↑	10.6
	Family workers	(68.2)	59.1 ↓	14.3
The arrows indicate tendencies since 1983.				
Share in part-time employment, 1983				
1983	Men	-	6.1	-
	Women	(38.7)	67.4	-
1989	Men	-	12.7	9.8
	Women	-	75.7	14.3
Share in temporary employment, 1983				
1983	Men	-	9.2	-
	Women	-	20.2	-
1989	Men	-	10.8	22.9
	Women	-	20.1	49.4

Source : Eurostat (1983c and 1989c), *Labour Force Survey*.

	1983 ≥ 14 Men	1983 ≥ 14 Women	1988 ≥ 14 Men	1988 ≥ 14 Women	1988 25-54 Men	1988 25-54 Women
Europe 12	-	-	68.1	41.2	94.4	60.2
Belgium	64.7	35.6	60.7	35.9	92.7	59.2
Flanders	66.1	36.0	62.1	36.4	94.0	58.4
Wallonia	62.0	33.9	59.2	35.5	91.7	59.7
Brussels region	65.3	39.7	57.1	34.8	87.7	62.0
Denmark	71.7	57.3	74.3	60.0	95.0	86.5
Metropolitan region	79.0	67.0	82.0	71.0	-	-
Jutland	78.0	64.0	81.0	68.0	-	-
Islands	75.0	61.0	79.0	65.0	-	-
Germany	70.3	40.1	70.2	41.7	93.7	60.9
Schleswig-Holstein	70.4	41.1	71.4	40.7	94.8	61.9
Hamburg	68.2	42.7	68.3	44.4	90.6	68.0
Lower Saxony	69.7	38.4	67.8	40.5	93.9	60.9
Bremen	62.7	35.1	68.8	39.7	94.4	61.3
North Rhine-Westphalia	69.3	35.0	68.2	36.7	93.0	53.4
Hesse	70.8	40.6	70.8	43.1	94.6	62.2
Rhineland Palatinate	71.7	38.3	71.1	39.6	95.6	55.3
Baden-Württemberg	70.9	45.2	72.3	44.3	93.8	62.9
Bavaria	72.7	45.6	73.1	47.3	94.8	68.3
Saar	68.7	29.5	65.0	33.6	91.1	50.2
West Berlin	66.2	42.1	70.1	49.0	89.6	77.3
Ex-GDR	84.8	83.0	82.0	85.0	-	-
East Berlin	87.7	84.7	83.0	84.0	-	-
Cottbus	82.0	84.7	82.0	86.9	-	-
Dresden	84.2	87.1	85.1	88.6	-	-
Erfut	83.6	83.1	84.4	85.6	-	-
Frankfurt/O	69.3	72.6	69.9	75.2	-	-
Gera	80.2	84.9	81.0	86.9	-	-
Halle	83.8	82.5	83.0	85.4	-	-
Karl-Marx-Stadt	82.8	87.4	84.0	88.9	-	-
Leipzig	83.2	84.1	88.5	85.7	-	-
Magdeburg	84.1	82.1	84.0	85.2	-	-
Neubrandenburg	77.1	78.7	77.9	82.0	-	-
Postdam	75.4	77.0	76.8	79.8	-	-
Rostock	82.2	79.2	81.1	81.2	-	-
Schwerin	77.5	80.2	78.5	82.8	-	-
Suhl	85.9	88.3	85.3	90.1	-	-
Greece	70.8	33.1	66.6	35.2	94.5	50.2
Northern Greece	71.2	31.8	68.1	36.6	95.2	53.1
Central Greece	70.4	33.6	68.6	40.3	95.6	57.0
Attica	-	-	63.5	31.1	93.1	45.2
Islands	72.3	34.5	68.9	35.6	95.2	48.4

continued

Table A2.1.5 continued

	1983 ≥ 14 Men	1983 ≥ 14 Women	1988 ≥ 14 Men	1988 ≥ 14 Women	1988 25-54 Men	1988 25-54 Women
Spain	-	-	64.6	31.0	94.0	42.9
North-West	-	-	62.5	37.0	92.6	52.4
North-East	-	-	63.6	30.3	94.7	44.2
Madrid	-	-	65.3	29.0	95.2	41.6
Centre	-	-	63.3	26.1	93.7	36.8
East	-	-	66.0	34.9	95.0	47.6
South	-	-	64.7	27.5	92.8	34.9
Canary Islands	-	-	67.1	30.4	93.2	41.1
France	68.9	45.1	65.7	45.9	95.8	70.9
Ile de France	73.2	52.9	70.7	53.7	96.6	77.6
Greater Paris area	68.8	46.6	66.1	45.5	96.2	70.5
North/-Pas-de-Calais	67.6	39.5	61.8	39.2	93.0	60.3
East	70.9	41.5	67.2	43.8	96.0	65.3
West	67.0	45.6	65.2	45.8	95.8	72.9
South-West	65.9	42.1	62.2	44.0	95.3	72.6
Centre-East	69.8	45.8	66.1	47.2	96.7	72.1
Mediterranean	64.8	36.8	61.4	39.8	94.8	64.8
Ireland	73.7	33.4	70.3	33.5	94.0	42.1
Italy	67.7	32.3	65.7	34.2	94.2	50.7
North-West	64.2	33.6	62.9	35.1	94.3	56.8
Lombardy	69.8	36.3	67.7	37.3	95.1	55.8
North-East	70.3	33.8	67.4	35.2	94.3	50.3
Emilia-Romagna	66.6	38.9	64.6	40.7	94.9	67.1
Centre	66.3	35.0	62.9	35.8	94.8	56.5
Lazio	68.5	29.7	66.7	32.6	95.3	48.0
Campania	69.4	30.9	67.8	31.6	93.7	42.4
Abruzzi-Molise	67.3	33.8	64.5	36.7	93.6	55.0
South	66.2	29.3	64.2	31.5	92.6	44.7
Sicily	67.4	22.0	66.8	26.3	93.9	36.7
Sardinia	66.2	26.3	65.0	30.9	92.0	41.6
Luxembourg	-	32.1	68.1	33.9	96.1	46.6
Netherlands	67.0	33.3	69.1	41.3	93.2	55.1
North	64.0	29.3	65.4	37.0	92.3	50.4
East	66.7	32.0	69.1	40.3	93.4	53.4
West	67.8	35.3	69.7	43.2	93.4	58.3
South Netherlands	67.1	32.1	69.5	40.1	93.1	52.1
Portugal	-	-	70.7	45.9	93.6	64.7
Mainland	-	-	70.5	46.3	93.6	65.3
Azores	-	-	76.5	26.4	94.8	37.6
Madeira	-	-	74.8	50.9	93.0	65.8

continued

Table A2.1.5 continued

	1983		1988		1988	
	≥ 14 Men	≥ 14 Women	≥ 14 Men	≥ 14 Women	25-54 Men	25-54 Women
United Kingdom	72.0	45.1	72.9	49.9	95.0	70.7
North	70.1	43.1	70.9	48.4	93.2	69.0
Yorkshire and Humberside	70.9	45.5	71.2	48.5	94.7	71.1
East Midlands	72.4	46.1	72.8	50.7	95.6	71.7
East Anglia	73.2	46.0	73.6	53.1	97.1	73.3
South-East	74.1	46.8	75.7	51.9	96.5	71.6
South-West	70.7	43.3	71.9	49.8	96.6	72.4
West Midlands	72.3	45.0	73.6	49.8	95.2	71.2
North-West	70.5	45.3	71.5	50.2	93.6	72.8
Wales	67.0	39.4	67.3	43.8	90.2	65.3
Scotland	72.8	45.3	72.0	48.3	93.7	68.3
Northern Ireland	69.8	40.8	69.8	43.7	91.8	60.1

Sources : Eurostat (1985), *Regional Statistics Yearbook.*
Eurostat (1990a), *Rapid Report, Regions.*
Danish regions : Knudsen (1991), activity rates for persons aged
between 15 and 74 in 1984 and 1989 - data not comparable with
Eurostat data.
Ex-German Democratic Republic : Figge, Quack and Schäfgen
(1991), table 1.24, 1983-89.

Table A2.1.6
Sectoral distribution of female employment expressed
as percentages of female employment by region;
the share of part-time working in female employment

1989	Total Agriculture	Industry	Services	Part-time
Belgium	2.4%	16.2%	81.4%	25.0%
Flanders	2.3%	20.2%	77.5%	25.9%
Wallonia	3.4%	9.6%	87.1%	26.5%
Brussels region	0.2%	13.0%	86.9%	14.2%
Denmark	2.9%	15.8%	81.3%	40.1%
Germany	4.4%	24.9%	70.7%	30.7%
Schleswig-Holstein	3.4%	17.4%	79.3%	39.0%
Hamburg	0.2%	14.4%	85.4%	29.7%
Lower Saxony	6.2%	22.0%	71.8%	32.6%
Bremen	0.0%	17.5%	82.5%	39.3%
North Rhine-Westphalia	1.7%	23.9%	74.3%	28.3%
Hesse	3.8%	21.7%	74.5%	33.1%
Rhineland Palatinate	5.5%	25.7%	68.7%	30.7%
Baden-Wurttemberg	3.8%	31.8%	64.4%	31.5%
Bavaria	9.0%	28.1%	62.9%	29.1%
Saar	0.5%	19.6%	79.9%	24.0%
West Berlin	0.5%	17.8%	81.7%	32.0%
Greece	32.3%	17.3%	50.4%	8.1%
Northern Greece	41.1%	20.3%	38.5%	6.3%
Central Greece	58.7%	9.0%	32.3%	9.1%
Attica	1.6%	23.4%	75.0%	8.3%
Islands	44.3%	6.0%	49.7%	10.8%
Spain	11.2%	17.0%	71.8%	11.9%
North-West	42.8%	7.8%	49.4%	9.1%
North-East	3.3%	18.9%	77.8%	15.7%
Madrid	0.1%	15.3%	84.6%	4.7%
Centre	13.6%	15.1%	71.3%	15.9%
East	3.3%	25.8%	70.9%	13.4%
South	9.7%	12.5%	77.8%	12.6%
Canary Islands	9.3%	5.6%	85.1%	11.0%
France	5.7%	17.4%	76.9%	23.7%
Ile de France	0.3%	16.2%	83.5%	15.6%
Greater Paris area	7.1%	20.9%	71.9%	24.5%
North/Pas-de-Calais	3.4%	19.1%	77.5%	26.1%
East	4.0%	21.3%	74.7%	26.5%
West	10.9%	17.6%	71.5%	29.4%
South-West	12.2%	12.7%	75.1%	25.8%
Centre-East	4.9%	20.9%	74.1%	25.4%
Mediterranean	6.3%	9.5%	84.2%	26.0%

continued

1989	Total Agriculture	Industry	Services	Part-time
Ireland	3.2%	19.8%	77.0%	15.3%
Italy	9.2%	23.2%	67.6%	10.9%
North-West	8.2%	24.3%	67.4%	9.9%
Lombardy	1.9%	34.5%	63.6%	10.3%
North-East	5.5%	30.2%	64.3%	13.2%
Emilia-Romagna	8.7%	29.7%	61.5%	10.7%
Centre	6.2%	29.2%	64.6%	11.2%
Lazio	7.1%	7.8%	85.1%	9.6%
Campania	20.7%	12.3%	67.0%	12.5%
Abruzzi-Molise	18.5%	19.4%	62.0%	7.7%
South	25.8%	11.0%	63.2%	12.3%
Sicily	12.5%	4.5%	83.0%	8.9%
Sardinia	6.8%	5.6%	87.7%	12.3%
Luxembourg	3.4%	8.5%	88.1%	16.4%
Netherlands	3.1%	11.2%	85.6%	60.1%
North	4.8%	10.3%	84.9%	62.8%
East	4.4%	12.4%	83.2%	61.7%
West	2.2%	8.6%	89.2%	59.4%
South Netherlands	3.6%	17.0%	79.4%	59.2%
Portugal	22.8%	25.4%	51.9%	10.0%
Mainland	23.2%	24.9%	51.9%	9.5%
Azores	4.7%	18.0%	77.3%	13.7%
Madeira	18.2%	43.9%	37.9%	22.0%
United Kingdom	1.0%	17.7%	81.3%	43.7%
North	0.8%	18.5%	80.7%	48.0%
Yorkshire and Humberside	1.0%	18.8%	80.2%	49.1%
East Midlands	0.7%	23.2%	76.1%	48.0%
East Anglia	2.1%	17.4%	80.5%	48.8%
South-East	0.7%	15.4%	83.9%	40.3%
South-West	1.6%	16.1%	82.3%	45.8%
West Midlands	1.1%	22.9%	75.9%	44.6%
North-West	0.6%	18.4%	81.0%	43.4%
Wales	1.5%	16.0%	82.5%	45.9%
Scotland	1.6%	16.8%	81.6%	40.6%
Northern Ireland	1.5%	15.6%	82.9%	35.6%

Source : Eurostat (1989c), *Labour Force Survey.*

Table A2.1.7
Activity rates and the sectoral composition of employment by region in the United Kingdom

	Manufacturing industry		Private services		Men			Women		
	1980	1990	1980	1990	1983 (%)	1990 (%)	Change	1983 (%)	1990 (%)	Change
South										
South-East	22.7	15.0	39.8	49.9	91.6	93.4	1.8	67.5	81.3	13.8
Greater London	18.9	10.6	43.9	56.3	-	-	-	-	-	-
Rest of the South-East	26.2	18.7	35.8	44.5	-	-	-	-	-	-
East Anglia	25.4	19.4	33.6	41.8	86.9	86.5	-0.5	59.5	70.5	11.1
South-West	24.0	18.9	35.7	42.7	84.2	84.0	-0.2	60.5	71.5	11.0
West Midlands	40.0	28.7	28.4	38.3	88.1	82.8	-5.3	61.6	69.5	7.9
East Midlands	34.7	28.2	29.1	36.0	85.4	81.4	-4.0	60.8	70.6	9.8
Wales	26.2	21.7	29.3	36.0	80.1	81.5	1.4	55.1	63.9	8.7
North										
Yorks and Humberside	31.8	24.0	30.5	39.5	84.3	78.7	-5.6	59.8	68.0	8.2
North-West	32.9	25.2	33.7	40.8	83.4	81.6	-1.9	63.5	71.2	7.6
North	30.5	24.0	30.6	37.8	80.3	76.5	-3.8	58.3	64.2	5.9
Scotland	25.3	19.8	34.2	40.2	85.1	83.3	-1.9	62.5	69.5	7.0
Northern Ireland	22.8	17.8	29.0	34.9	86.2	81.1	-5.0	59.5	62.0	2.5
United Kingdom	28.0	20.6	34.3	42.9	86.6	85.4	-1.3	62.8	72.7	9.9

Source : Humphries and Rubery, 1991.

70

3 Employment types and status: no improvement between 1983 and 1989

Did demands for flexibility and the desire to reduce firms' wage bills in the 1980s lead to the creation of low-grade badly paid jobs with onerous conditions of employment and little in the way of social security coverage ? This is the question which we will be looking at in this chapter, which deals with developments in the types of jobs where women are employed. The first part looks at the status of the self-employed, of those in subordinate direct employment and of family assistants while the second deals with atypical employment such as part-time and temporary jobs and jobs with complex working hours.

The ex-German Democratic Republic has been omitted from this chapter since, firstly, the country's employment policy was based on unlimited full-time activity, secondly no distinction can be made between employees and the self-employed, and thirdly there was no ban on women working nights.

1. The majority are still in subordinate direct employment

Developments in total employment mask some important differences in its circumstances and conditions; a spouse helping on a farm, a civil servant and the owner of a business have all been counted in the same way.

In most of the European countries the various types of employment do not enjoy the same conditions of employment. Thus, maternity leave, a guaranteed minimum wage, and the regulation of working hours, for example, are mainly the appanage of subordinate direct employment. These disparities between conditions of employment and their prospects have made it necessary to undertake a study of employment in terms of professional status.

71

Table 3.1
Employment according to professional status

	Wage earners				Family workers			
	Percentage of female employment in 1989	Changes in this percentage between 1983 and 1989	Indication of these changes in 1983-89 values	Percentage of male employment in 1989	Percentage of female employment in 1989	Changes in this percentage between 1983 and 1989	Indication of these changes in 1983-89 values	Percentage of male employment in 1989
Germany	90	+2.91	+	88	4.6	-3.32	-	0.5
France	87	+2.84	+	83	5.7	-3.24	-	0.9
Italy	75	+1.28	+	69	8.2	-2.02	-	2.4
Netherlands [a]	88	-0.51	+	88	4.8	-2.15	-	0.3
Belgium	82	+1.68	+	80	6.8	-1.88	-	1.0
Luxembourg	89	+3.57	+	89	4.1	-3.54	-	0.4
United Kingdom	93	-1.43	+	82	n.a.	n.a.	n.a.	n.a.
Ireland	89	+3.01	+	68	3.7	-3.10	-	2.1
Denmark	93	+2.96	+	85	4.0	-2.73	-	0.1
Greece	50	+5.53	+	52	31.3	-4.81	-	5.1
Portugal [b]	68	+2.42	+	71	4.9	-2.41	-	2.9
Spain [b]	71	+3.29	+	73	11.8	-2.60	-	3.4
Europe 10	86	+1,65	+	80	5,1	-2,35	-	1,0
Europe 12	84	n.a.	n.a.	79	5,6	n.a.	n.a.	1,3

72

	Employers				Self-employed			
	Percentage of female employment in 1989	Changes in this percentage between 1983 and 1989	Indication of these changes in 1983-89 values	Percentage of male employment in 1989	Percentage of female employment in 1989	Changes in this percentage between 1983 and 1989	Indication of these changes in 1983-89 values	Percentage of male employment in 1989
Germany	2.6	+0.40	+	6.6	3.1	+0.04	+	4.8
France	2.3	+0.40	+	6.1	4.7	0.00	+	10.2
Italy	0.5	-0.04	-	1.3	16.4	+0.77	+	27.3
Netherlands a	1.3	-0.09	+	4.6	6.0	+2.75	+	6.8
Belgium	0.5	-0.03	+	2.1	10.2	+0.23	+	17.1
Luxembourg	1.4	-0.20	-	3.5	5.0	+0.17	+	7.3
United Kingdom	2.1	-0.01	+	5.8	5.2	+1.44	+	12.2
Ireland	2.2	+0.50	+	6.5	5.3	-0.41	-	22.9
Denmark	n.a.	n.a.	n.a.	n.a.	n.a.	n.a.	n.a.	n.a.
Greece	1.7	+0.30	+	7.6	16.8	-1.00	+	35.1
Portugal b	2.0	+0.50	+	5.8	24.6	-0.52	+	20.4
Spain b	1.5	+0.30	+	4.5	15.3	-0.97	+	19.3
Europe 10	1.9	+0,12	+	5,1	6.8	+0.58	+	13,7
Europe 12	1.9	n.a.	n.a.	5,0	8,1	n.a.	n.a.	14,5

a. In the case of the Netherlands, the interpretation is distorted due to changes occurring in the definition during the period.
b. Changes between 1986 and 1989.

Source : Eurostat (1983, 1986 and 1989), *Labour Force Survey.*

1.1 Subordinate direct employment

In 1989, the vast majority of working women were in subordinate direct employment and between 1983 and 1989 the subordinate direct employment of women increased in all the countries, as did its relative proportion in overall female employment in all the countries except the United Kingdom and the Netherlands. Subordinate direct employment accounted for more than 90 per cent of female employment in Denmark, the United Kingdom and Germany. Although on the increase in the countries of southern Europe with their greater share of employment in agriculture, it still remained less extensive there. In 1989, Greece stood out with a proportion of female subordinate direct paid employment of no more than 50 per cent (see table 3.1).

The transition rate to regular paid employment has been greater for women than for men in all the countries except Portugal, Spain and Greece. In none of the European countries were the 1980s marked by an assault on the status of the employed, and only the United Kingdom (Humphries and Rubery, 1991, p. 33) reported a large increase in the number of men and women entering self-employment.

1.2 Self-employment : decrease in family workers

As the United Kingdom report (Humphries and Rubery, 1991, p. 33) points out, there may be some ambiguity in the classification into subgroups of this residual category, which accounts for persons classified in the labour force survey as not being in subordinate direct employment. These include - and in this section we will use the Eurostat categories - the following :

employers with one or more employees;
self-employed persons with no employees;
family workers.

In the United Kingdom family workers are not classified separately, and in Denmark no distinction is made in the labour force survey between employers and the self-employed.

Of these three categories, that of family worker is the least enviable since it sanctions a worker's dependence on the activity of a member of his family. Women are overrepresented in this category, with most of them in the position of wives helping spouses active in agriculture or the distributive trades. Few rights are associated with this category, the relative share of which is diminishing in women's employment in all the countries of the Community. This decline is particularly marked in agriculture, which remains the most important sector in Germany, France, Luxembourg, Ireland, Greece and Portugal. Between 1986 and 1989 there was also a decline in the services sector, though not in Portugal and Spain. In 1989, this form of employment still accounted for 31 per cent of female employment in Greece, while in the other countries of the Community the figure was situated in the vicinity of 5 per cent. The decline can be explained by decrease of family business in agriculture and trade and maybe also by the miserable quality of this status, which is avoided by women in Denmark (Knudsen, 1991, p. 47).

The other two forms of self-employment do not have such negative connotations in terms of quality. This is particularly so in the case of employers who, unfortunately, rarely account for more than a ridiculously small percentage (0.46 per cent) of female employment in Italy and Belgium. In 1989 the figure reached a maximum of 2.56 per cent for Germany, and exceeded 2 per cent only in France, the United Kingdom, Ireland and Portugal while distinctly higher percentages (about three times as high) were recorded for men in all the countries.

The relative share of employers in overall female employment remained fairly stable between 1983 and 1989; however, it often rose slightly in absolute terms, and particularly in the services sector where this type of female employment is concentrated.

So the 1980s were not marked by any significant increase in the number of women at the head of businesses. As far as self-employment without employees is concerned, there were contrasting developments according to country. These developments generally stemmed from the balancing out of a decline in this form of employment in agriculture and its increase in the services, a phenomenon which is reflected in the relative decline in the extent of this form of employment in women's employment in Ireland, Greece, Portugal and Spain and a relative increase in its extent in the other countries, particularly the Netherlands, the United Kingdom and Italy, [1] where the most dynamic element in women's self-employment seems to be located in the services sector and particularly in business and other services. This may parallel an increase in consumer services and the use of subcontracting.

An examination of the data on the status of employers and family workers leaves the impression of an enduring gender-bound occupational segregation in self-employment, which seems to be an expression of quality in the case of men, and very much the opposite in that of women.

The quality of self-employment and the either positive or negative image associated with its promotion have been subjects of discussion in a number of the Community countries. The positive image is supported by arguments based on a search for independence and self-fulfilment in work outside the traditional hierarchies while the negative image evokes the decay of the labour market and the inability of the system to create jobs. Seen from this angle, self-employment is claimed to be the only means of avoiding unemployment in contradistinction to the first hypothesis, which seems to envisage a quality situation associated with advanced qualifications and a first-class financial return that would justify the encouragement and the financial and other assistance provided by governments.

Humphries and Rubery (1991, p. 37) point out that

> ... while self-employment and homeworking may have emerged as an alternative to unemployment for specific labour market groups, there is little to suggest that the general growth of self-employment can be explained as a response to unemployment. The fastest rates of growth in self-employment have been in the areas with the lowest unemployment rates and thus suggest that self-employment opportunities tend to increase in areas of fastest growth.

The following questions can be asked in an attempt to judge the quality of the female self-employment which was generated in the 1980s :

> - Are the sectors involved 'advanced' tertiary ones involving personally enhancing intellectual activity, or are they 'manual' ones, whose development is concomitant with marginalization on the labour market ?

- What are the conditions of remuneration in female self-employment ?
- What are the levels of qualification in female self-employment ?
- What hours are worked in this form of employment ?
- What is the survival rate in the case of independent enterprise ?

As far as the different sectors of activity are concerned, the breakdown of the data by sector is not sufficiently detailed to provide an answer. The German report (Figge, Quack and Schäfgen, 1991, p. 20) quotes Büchtemann and Gout (1988) who state that 'women are quite clearly setting themselves up on their own, and this is particularly so in fields where the number of men has declined in recent years because of poor returns'.

Altieri and Villa (1991, p. 59) also recall that self-employment remains concentrated in agriculture and the distributive trades, where it has already existed. These arguments favouring the 'negative' image are corroborated by self-employed women's poor qualifications and remuneration, which do not fit in with an image of skilled and personally enhancing employment.

In the case of Germany, 'in 1984, 33 per cent of self-employed women - as opposed to 5 per cent of men - had a net monthly income of less than 1,000 DM, with one in five having less than 600 DM (Mayer, 1987)' (Figge, Quack and Schäfgen, 1991, p. 20); in Italy, '50 per cent of self-employed women are school dropouts, while the average for women of this category in subordinate direct employment is 26.7 per cent. Improvements were recorded in 1983 and 1989, however, with 67.3 per cent as the corresponding 1983 percentages for self-employed women, and a mean of 39.7 per cent' (Altieri and Villa, 1991, p. 59). To this must be added the insecurity and the risk inherent in self-employment. In Germany, 'since only 20 per cent of newly established firms survive longer than five years, self-employment does not seem to be a solid long-term economic prospect' (Berg, 1990, quoted by Figge, Quack and Schäfgen, 1991, p. 20).

As far as working hours are concerned two apparently contradictory points have been noted, and these are no doubt linked to the various sectors of activity. On the one hand, the large number of hours worked in Italy may well be due to the size of the agricultural sector while, on the other, there has been the development of part-time self-employment, particularly in Germany and the Netherlands.

These two points strengthen the negative image of self-employment. Rather than giving credit to the thesis of self-employment with a positive face, these observations seem to confirm the negative image that was already emphasized in a study of atypical employment (Meulders and Plasman, 1989a). In the majority of cases, women's choice of self-employment is a matter of second best.

2. Atypical employment : part-time work remains a characteristic of women in northern Europe

Women's activity rates are on the increase, and women are occupying an increasingly more important position on the labour market. An analysis of the sectoral distribution of female employment has already enabled us to demonstrate firstly that there is still a long way to go before women enjoy an equal degree of representation in all sectors of economic life, and secondly that the

76

concentration of women in certain types of activity has certainly not been due to chance. In parallel with the distribution of female employment in the various sectors of the economy, the frequency of temporary and part-time working affects the quality of female employment.

2.1 Part-time working : differentiated evolutions

Part-time working : its extent and the sectors affected. With the exception of Denmark and Greece, the relative share of part-time working in the various countries showed an upward trend between 1983 and 1989 for subordinate direct employment and overall employment alike (see table 3.2). In the United Kingdom, there has been a slight decrease in the relative amount of part-time working since 1987 (Humphries and Rubery, 1991, p. 39).

This development was similar for both men and women except in Belgium, where the relative share of part-time working decreased for men and increased for women, and in Denmark, where the relative share of part-time employment increased for men mainly as the result of the spread of a combination of short-term part-time employment and training for young men, and a decrease in the relative share of part-time working for women. The OECD (1991a, p. 44) expresses the hypothesis that 'in the Nordic countries, where the proportion of part-time working is the highest, the figures may have reached their peak around the beginning of the eighties'. At all events, this point does not seem to have been reached in the Netherlands where, in 1989, a record 60 per cent of female employment was part-time. The corresponding figures were 44 per cent for the United Kingdom, 40 per cent for Denmark, 25 per cent for Belgium and 24 per cent for France, while the percentages for the countries of southern Europe were noticeably lower : 10 per cent for Portugal, 11 per cent for Italy, 12 per cent for Spain and 8 per cent for Greece. Unlike Greece and Portugal, Italy and Spain showed no signs of an upward trend.

In these countries, the share of part-time self-employment is also more considerable and can be explained in part by the relative weight of agriculture on the employment scene in comparison with the other countries.

Part-time working essentially involves women; in the case of men, the relative share of part-time working lies between 15 per cent in the Netherlands and 1.6 per cent in Spain. These percentages are distinctly lower than those for women, whose share of part-time working was as high as 89.6 per cent in Belgium and Germany and as low as 64.4 per cent in Greece. Between 1983 and 1989 this share diminished in Denmark, Germany, France, the United Kingdom, the Netherlands and Luxembourg.

In certain countries (see table 3.3), the rise in female employment between 1983 and 1989 can be largely attributed to the growth of part-time jobs; this was the case for France where, of the net number of jobs established for women between 1983 and 1989, 87 per cent were part-time. The figure for the Netherlands [2] was 88 per cent, for Belgium 66 per cent, for the United Kingdom 51 per cent, for Ireland 41 per cent and for Germany 41 per cent; no such trend was visible either in Denmark, or in the countries of southern Europe. In Greece, there was a decline in the part-time employment of women.

In the case of the major sectors (see table 3.4), the distribution of part-time female employment confirms the traditional picture of an overall decrease in

Table 3.2

Part-time working in the countries of the European Economic Community, developments between 1983 and 1989
(in percentage of the corresponding employment)

	Overall employment			Subordinate direct employment			Overall women's employment			Women's subordinate direct employment			Overall men's employment			Men's subordinate direct employment		
	1983	1989	Developments	1983	1989	Developments	1983	1989	Developments	1983	1989	Developments	1983	1989	Developments	1983	1989	Developments
Belgium	8.1	10.2	↑	8.3	11.7	↑	19.7	25.0	↑	20.7	28.0	↑	2.0	1.7	→	1.9	1.8	→
Denmark	23.8	23.4	→	25.8	24.5	→	44.7	40.1	→	46.3	40.6	→	6.6	9.4	↑	7.1	9.9	↑
Germany	12.6	13.4	↑	12.0	13.0	↑	30.0	30.7	↑	29.6	30.4	↑	1.7	2.3	↑	1.1	1.7	↑
Greece	6.5	4.4	→	4.9	3.7	→	12.1	8.0	→	8.5	6.8	→	3.7	2.4	→	3.3	2.1	→
Spain	n.a.	4.8	n.a.	n.a.	4.1	n.a.	n.a.	11.9	n.a.	n.a.	11.1	n.a.	n.a.	1.6	n.a.	n.a.	1.0	n.a.
France	9.7	12.1	↑	9.0	12.2	↑	20.0	23.8	↑	18.7	23.6	↑	2.5	3.5	↑	2.0	3.3	↑
Ireland	6.7	7.5	↑	5.8	8.0	↑	15.6	16.5	↑	11.9	15.3	↑	2.7	3.1	↑	2.4	3.4	↑
Italy	4.6	5.7	↑	3.5	5.2	↑	9.4	10.9	↑	7.5	10.0	↑	2.4	3.1	↑	1.5	2.5	↑
Luxembourg	6.7	6.9	↑	6.2	6.9	↑	18.0	16.4	→	17.1	16.4	→	(1.2)	1.9	↑	(1.0)	1.8	↑
Netherlands	21.2	31.7	↑	21.0	30.9	↑	50.3	60.1	↑	49.5	58.4	↑	6.9	15.0	↑	6.8	14.8	↑
Portugal	6.0*	5.9	→	3.9*	3.7	→	10.0*	10.0	=	8.1*	7.7	=	3.4*	3.1	→	1.3*	0.9	→
United Kingdom	19.0	21.7	↑	19.5	22.6	↑	42.1	43.6	↑	41.8	43.5	↑	3.3	5.0	↑	3.1	4.6	↑
Europe 10	12,1	14,4	↑	12,2	14,9	↑	27,6	30,2	↑	27,8	30,8	↑	2,8	4,1	↑	2,3	3,8	↑
Europe 12	n.a.	13,2	n.a.	n.a.	13,7	n.a.	n.a.	28,0	n.a.	n.a.	28,9	n.a.	n.a.	3,8	n.a.	n.a.	3,4	n.a.

* 1986.

Source : Eurostat (1983c, 1986c and 1989c), *Labour Force Survey.*

Europe. In Greece, there was a decline in the part-time employment of women.

Table 3.3
Women's employment and part-time employment

	Increase in women's employment between 1983 and 1989			Share of part-time working in the increase in women's employment	Women's share in part-time working		
	Total	Part-time	Full-time		1983	1989	Developments
Belgium	12.6	8.4	4.3	66.2	84.0	89.6	↑
Denmark	10.1	0.5	9.7	4.5	84.7	78.0	↓
Germany	6.8	2.8	4.0	40.8	91.9	89.6	↓
Greece	12.1	-3.1	15.3	-25.9	61.2	64.4	↑
Spain	n.a.	n.a.	n.a.	n.a.	n.a.	77.2	n.a.
France	5.8	5.0	0.8	86.8	84.4	83.3	↓
Ireland	5.0	2.0	2.9	41.2	71.6	73.2	↑
Italy	7.7	2.4	5.3	31.0	64.8	64.7	=
Luxembourg	10.4	2.1	8.3	20.0	88.9	81.8	↓
Netherlands	36.3	32.0	4.3	88.1	77.3	70.2	↓
Portugal	n.a.	n.a.	n.a.	n.a.	65.9 *	69.8	↑
United Kingdom	20.2	10.3	10.0	50.7	89.8	87.0	↓
Europe 10	11,6	6,1	5,5	52,7	85,7	82,8	↓
Europe 12	n.a.	n.a.	n.a.	n.a.	n.a.	82,4	n.a.

* 1986.

Source : Eurostat (1983c, 1986c and 1989c), *Labour Force Survey.*

In the case of the major sectors (see table 3.4), the distribution of part-time female employment confirms the traditional picture of an overall decrease in employment in agriculture and hence a decrease in the relative share of part-time female employment in agriculture accompanied a decrease in the relative share of part-time female employment in industry and an increase in the relative share of part-time female employment in the services.

The increase in women's part-time employment and its greatest concentration has taken place in the services sector, where it accounts for 91 per cent of part-time female employment in Belgium, for 88 per cent in the United Kingdom, for 87 per cent in the Netherlands, for 85 per cent in Germany, and so on.

An analysis of the distribution and development of part-time working by subsector is more difficult due to problems connected with the representativeness of the samples. However, it seems that between 1983 and 1989, the

Table 3.4
Sectoral distribution of part-time employment

| | Share of part-time in female employment by sector | | | | | | | | | Distribution of part-time female employment by sector | | | | | | | | |
| | Agriculture | | | Industry | | | Services | | | Agriculture | | | Industry | | | Services | | |
	1983	1989	Devia-tion	1983	1989	Devia-tion	1983	1989	Devia-tion	1983	1989	Devia-tion	1983	1989	Devia-tion	1983	1989	Devia-tion
Belgium	17.6	16.1	-1.5	8.9	11.2	2.3	22.3	27.9	5.6	2.6	1.5	-1.1	8.2	7.3	-0.9	89.2	91.2	2.0
Denmark	29.0	40.0	11.0	33.1	27.8	-5.3	47.5	42.5	-5.0	1.9	2.9	1.0	11.5	10.9	-0.5	86.6	86.1	-0.5
Germany	33.8	31.9	-1.9	24.0	22.7	-1.3	31.9	33.5	1.6	8.3	4.6	-3.7	20.0	18.3	-1.7	71.6	77.1	5.5
Greece	13.6	8.9	-4.7	8.6	4.1	-4.6	12.2	8.8	-3.4	44.6	35.9	-8.7	12.2	8.7	-3.5	43.2	55.3	12.2
France	35.3	31.7	-3.6	11.3	14.1	2.8	20.9	25.3	4.4	13.2	7.6	-5.5	11.3	10.3	-1.0	75.5	82.0	6.5
Ireland	46.2	35.3	-10.9	7.8	7.1	-0.7	14.7	17.6	3.0	22.2	10.2	-12.1	9.3	8.5	-0.8	68.5	81.4	12.8
Italy	22.3	24.4	2.2	6.0	7.7	1.7	8.0	10.2	2.2	31.6	20.6	-11.0	16.9	16.3	-0.6	51.5	63.1	11.6
Netherlands *	67.3	75.7	8.4	38.9	45.8	6.9	51.3	61.4	10.1	4.3	4.0	-0.3	9.5	8.5	-0.9	86.2	87.5	1.3
United Kingdom	51.7	51.8	0.1	26.2	27.1	0.9	46.0	47.2	1.1	1.6	1.2	-0.4	12.3	11.0	-1.3	86.2	87.8	1.7
Portugal	14.0	14.3	0.3	5.6	4.8	-0.8	10.0	10.6	0.6	36.5	32.8	-3.7	13.8	12.2	-1.6	49.7	55.0	5.3
Spain	n.a.	13.8	n.a.	n.a.	6.8	n.a.	n.a.	12.9	n.a.	36.5	13.0	n.a.	n.a.	9.7	n.a.	n.a.	77.4	n.a.
Europe 12	n.a.	24.1	n.a.	n.a.	17.7	n.a.	n.a.	31.1	n.a.	n.a.	5.5	n.a.	n.a.	12.5	n.a.	n.a.	82.0	n.a.
Europe 10	28.8	27.8	-0.9	18.0	19.2	1.2	30.3	33.2	+2.9	7.8	4.8	-3.0	14.2	12.6	-1.6	78.0	82.6	4.6

* In the case of the Netherlands, the interpretation is distorted due to changes occurring in the definition during the period.

Source : Eurostat (1983c, 1986c and 1989c), *Labour Force Survey.*

greatest increases in part-time female employment were recorded in subsectors where the employment of women was already extremely widespread, i.e. :

- hotels and catering (NACE 66),
- sanitary services (NACE 92),
- medical and other health services (NACE 95),
- domestic services (NACE 9a),
- other services (NACE 96),
- recreational services and other cultural services (NACE 97),
- personal services (NACE 98),

sectors which, in certain countries, account for more than 30 per cent of part-time female employment. Such a concentration is a clear pointer to occupational segregation in part-time female employment.

In Belgium,

> ... part-time employment is particularly high in the sanitary sector (NACE 92), with 60.83 per cent (5.10 per cent) of female (male) employment in 1989 and 59.20 per cent (5.68 per cent) in 1983. As the Women's Employment Council emphasizes, certain jobs are so onerous that they are designed to be carried out only a few hours a day, i.e. on a part-time basis. This is typically the case for cleaning, and the bulk of the part-time work coming under NACE 92 can thus be easily explained. This is extremely unfair on certain female workers whose (full-time) wages are often very low as it is. In a number of other sectors it also happens that the work is often too onerous both physically and mentally to be carried out full-time. This applies in particular to NACE 66 (hotels and catering), to NACE 95 (medical, other health and veterinary services) where most nurses are employed, to NACE 96 (other services to the general public) which includes the welfare organizations, to NACE 97 (recreational and other cultural services) and to NACE 9a (domestic services). The share of part-time working in overall female (and male) employment in these sectors is still very high (respectively 29.9 per cent (7.8 per cent); 33.9 per cent (2.1 per cent); 34.9 per cent (6.7 per cent); 39.6 per cent (5.9 per cent) and 35.9 per cent (7.9 per cent) in 1989). In certain sectors such as retail distribution (NACE 64/65) and hotels and catering (NACE 66), staff must only be available during peak periods. In these sectors, part-time employment accounts for respectively 28.3 per cent (3.4 per cent) and 29.2 per cent (7.8 per cent) of overall female (male) employment. In such circumstances, part-time working does not enable women to offset their family and working lives more effectively since the working hours are often variable and unpredictable (Meulders and Vander Stricht, 1991, p. 48).

The extent and development of part-time employment in the services sector and, more particularly, in certain of its subsectors point to labour demand and so to the various enterprises as being also behind this form of employment.

In this respect, Gauvin and Silvera (1991, pp. 30-1) quote the results of a research project carried out by Maruani and Nicole (1989) for France into the conditions of employment in the distributive trades : 'In the survey, part-time employment emerges as one of the basic axes of new style labour management'. It is a type of employment that is part and parcel of job status (and not of a particular way of organizing labour).

The extent to which part-time employment is made use of may, of course, vary. We can go further than this, however, and say that the nature of a person's professional status can be ascertained through observing his career development. i.e.

- part-time working is linked to a high level of instability;
- a move into full-time employment is often seen as a promotion.

In the firms studied, details of qualifications and conditions of payment differ according to whether employment is full- or part-time. Another striking point is that as part of the process of organizing labour, part-time employment is often substituted in place of other earlier forms of employment such as the use of seasonal workers, 'extras' and auxiliaries. Part-time employment also constitutes an aspect of labour organization to the extent that it is an instrument associated not only with the selection and turnover of the labour force, but also with its instability. Part-time employment thus serves the objective of tighter and more flexible corporate management. The authors note that of all the particular forms of employment, part-timing is surely the one which involves the greatest number of employees and which is developing 'to women's advantage as well as to their cost' (Maruani and Nicole, 1989). Indeed, between 1983 and 1989, the net balance of full-time employment was positive (+67,000), though it is totally out of proportion with the net balance of part-time employment (+430,000). Part-time employment is evolving principally through the creation of new jobs and less through modifications to labour contracts. These observations confirm, for France, the thesis of its non-voluntary nature.

Working hours with respect to part-time employment. An analysis of developments in the working hours associated with part-time employment is possible on the basis of the labour force survey because, unlike many of the national statistics, the survey's definition of part-time employment is not based on the fact of working less than a number of hours fixed *a priori*, but rather on interviewees declaring that they work part-time (except in the Netherlands). [2] The data taken into consideration relate to hours normally worked. The subjective definition of part-time employment used in the surveys naturally reflects national characteristics; a person working a thirty-six hour week in Denmark can look upon himself as working part time, while the same number of hours worked in another country will be described as full-time.

In terms of the definition employed in the labour force surveys, part-time workers appear in a number of extremely different circumstances ranging from a student jobbing for a few hours a week to a person working more than thirty hours a week who will describe his employment as full or part-time according to the definition current in his country.

Knudsen (1991, p. 52) has made the following calculation for Denmark :

> If part-time employment is defined as an up to twenty-four hours week, the percentage of women employed part-time in 1989 is cut from 44 per cent to 22 per cent, i.e. by half, and if listing is limited to persons over twenty, i.e. if schoolchildren's and students' jobbing is discounted, the picture of part-time employment changes since the 15-19 age group accounts for 10 per cent of part-time employment and, in 1989, half of these young people worked less than fifteen hours a week.

Cross-country comparisons and an analysis of the data (see Appendix 3.1) on the distribution of part-time employment by hours normally worked must be carried out while taking cognizance of the national character of the subjective definitions. In fact, it seems difficult to cross-compare the countries and since developments between 1983-89 and the distributions contained in table 3.5 are so very different from country to country, no common trend emerges.

Two countries with fairly similar profiles stand out, however. These two countries are the United Kingdom and Denmark, where short-, part-time employment is extremely widespread (in 1989, 53 per cent of male and 23 per cent of female part-time employees in Denmark worked less than ten hours; in the United Kingdom, the corresponding percentages were 40 per cent and 24 per cent), and increased for both men and women between 1983 and 1989.

In 1989, part-time subordinate direct employment with long working hours (more than twenty-four hours) was very widespread among women in Denmark (43.8 per cent), while for men, part-time employment of less than twenty hours accounted for 85.5 per cent of part-time subordinate direct employment.

In 1989, part-time employment of under eight hours was more widespread in the 14-24 age group in the United Kingdom, and also among the over-sixties.

According to the German experts, short-term part-time employment is underestimated in the statistics. In Germany, women are particularly affected by the expansion of part-time jobs limited to a few hours but involving the irregular sort of attendances that are very common in the distributive trades and cleaning firms; in Germany, employment for under fifteen hours attracts virtually no social security coverage. The insufficiency of social security coverage for short-term part-time employment is emphasized (Meulders and Plasman, 1989a) in our study of atypical employment.

The European Community Council [3] has proposed three directives aiming to improve certain types of employment relations involving conditions of employment and the distortion of competition which have not yet been adopted by Council. These proposals would not be applied to employees who, on average, work less than eight hours a week. This means that they would not be treated in the same way as full-time workers with respect to :

- access to companies' vocational training schemes;
- the setting up of workers' corporate representative bodies;
- payments in cash or kind made under the auspices of welfare or non-contributory social security schemes';
- coverage under compulsory social security schemes and professional welfare funds (such coverage should depend on the same basis and criteria and take account of time worked and wages earned);
- etc.

Persons employed for less than eight hours would thus be debarred from the benefits of these directives, which could come into force at the end of 1992. Even if these proposals are a first step towards a better protection of certain categories of employees, one point that is open to speculation is the impact of this situation on the demands of firms that might wish to make use of a greater amount of less costly part-time employment of less than eight hours with its accompanying lower level of social security coverage.

83

Table 3.5
Part-time employment over thirty hours (employees), under ten hours
(employees) and under eight hours (aggregate)

		Men		Developments	Women		Developments
		1983	1989	ments	1983	1989	ments
France	< 8 hours aggregate	6.9	5.8	↓	5.1	4.0	↓
	> 10 hours employees	9.8	8.7	↓	15.6	12.2	↓
	> 30 hours employees	29.7	17.3	↓	9.8	14.6	↑
	average working hours employees	25.3	23.3	↓	20.4	21.6	↑
Germany	< 8 hours aggregate	-	3.5	-	0.0	5.8	-
	> 10 hours employees	16.1	18.0	↑	11.2	9.5	↓
	> 30 hours employees	15.2	4.5	↓↓	5.5	5.4	=
	average working hours employees	21.8	19.1	↓	20.6	20.8	=
Italy	< 8 hours aggregate	3.4	2.7	↓	4.1	1.4	↓
	> 10 hours employees	10.5	13.4	↑	9.7	12.1	↑
	> 30 hours employees	13.1	47.7	↑↑	5.2	15.3	↑↑
	average working hours employees	24.0	29.8	↑	21.4	22.8	↑
United Kingdom	< 8 hours aggregate	11.4	12.6	↑	18.0	20.3	↑
	> 10 hours employees	32.2	39.6	↑	22.3	24.5	↑
	> 30 hours employees	10.2	6.7	↓	5.8	5.5	↓
	average working hours employees	17.4	15.4	↓	18.1	17.6	↓
Belgium	< 8 hours aggregate	4.7	3.0	↓	4.5	4.6	=
	> 10 hours employees	-	-	-	10.2	9.1	↓
	> 30 hours employees	-	-	-	7.0	6.2	↓
	average working hours employees	23.1	21.4	↓	20.2	20.3	=
Denmark	< 8 hours aggregate	4.3	11.2	↑	21.4	29.2	↑
	> 10 hours employees	35.8	53.1	↑	8.9	20.0	↑
	> 30 hours employees	7.1	2.2	↓	7.9	11.1	↑
	average working hours employees	16.1	12.7	↓	21.9	21.0	↓
Ireland	< 8 hours aggregate	9.4	8.6	↓	8.9	8.4	↓
	> 10 hours employees	-	-	-	21.7	21.0	↓
	> 30 hours employees	-	-	-	10.5	32.0	↑↑
	average working hours employees	25.4	19.2	↓	19.1	17.5	↓
Greece	< 8 hours aggregate	2.4	4.1	↑	1.3	2.0	↑
	> 10 hours employees	-	-	-	8.6	12.6	↑
	> 30 hours employees	-	-	-	17.4	5.4	↓
	average working hours employees	28.1	22.4	↓	23.3	20.9	↓
Spain	< 8 hours aggregate	-	7.1	-	-	4.2	-
	> 10 hours employees	-	-	-	-	17.6	-
	> 30 hours employees	-	-	-	-	0.9	-
	average working hours employees	-	19.6	-	-	17.8	-
Portugal (86-89)	< 8 hours aggregate	6.2 [b]	8.5	↑	2.0 [b]	6.0	↑
	> 10 hours employees	-	-	-	21.0	24.5	↑
	> 30 hours employees	-	-	-	7.0	6.1	↓
	average working hours employees	27.0 [b]	24.5	↓	18.5 [b]	18.1	↓
Netherlands [a]	< 8 hours aggregate	13.5	18.5	↑	11.2	28.0	↑
	average working hours employees	20.9	15.9	↓	17.1	16.8	↓

a. In the case of the Netherlands, the interpretation is distorted due to changes occurring in the definition during the period.
b. 1986.

Source : Eurostat (1983c, 1986c and 1989c), *Labour Force Survey*.

Table 3.5 contains data concerning part-timers working under eight hours a week. These data are not limited to employees and so overestimate the number of persons not affected by the directives. It should be noted, however, that the number is not negligible. In their way, these directives sanction the duality apparent in part-time employment - a duality that would seem to make a distinction between part-time working involving long as opposed to short hours. In France (Lehmann, 1985, quoted by Gauvin and Silvera, 1991, p. 30), it is among part-timers working between twenty and thirty-two hours that employees are most frequently found who have control over the hours that they work, while those who have no control are more numerous in the 'less than twenty hour' bracket. Plantenga (1991, p. 37) shares this opinion : 'in the case of small-scale part-time jobs it may be expected that the percentage of people stating that they did not select this option voluntarily will be higher than in the case of part-time jobs with longer hours'. She concludes that the growth of small-scale part-time jobs is due to demand factors while in the case of part-time employment with longer hours, it is supply that is the determining factor.

Features characterizing part-time workers : age, gender and family status. The distribution of part-time employment by age is very different according to gender (see Appendix 3.2). In the case of men, the distribution takes the form of a U shaped curve with concentrations composed of young people in the 14-24 age group and the over-fifty-fives. In the case of young people, the concentrations correspond to various combinations of studies and part-time work and, in the case of the older generation, to the semi-retired. The women's U is inverted and flattened, with the 35-44 and 25-35 age groups standing out (Portugal, Greece, Belgium and Italy).

This difference between the male and the female distributions may be linked to the reasons given by men and women alike to account for their being in part-time employment. In 1989 in the Netherlands (Plantenga, 1991, p. 36) training was given by 75 per cent of male under twenty-fives (representing 52 per cent of male part-timers), while family reasons were given by 48 per cent of female part-timers with a percentage as high as 59 per cent for women between twenty-five and forty-four.

In Belgium, family reasons were given by 40 per cent of women between twenty-five and twenty-nine and/or 54 per cent of women between thirty and thirty-four.

Taken all round, part-time employment in Italy affects mature women - those with dependent families - less than in the other countries, with 42 per cent of female part-timers not wishing to work full time.

In France, 'three-quarters of all part-time employees between the ages of twenty-five and thirty have children, and part-time working increases with their numbers' (Gauvin and Silvera, 1991, p. 30). According to Lehmann (1985, quoted by Gauvin and Silvera, 1991, p. 30) :

... 33 per cent of all part-time employees - or to be more exact, 37.2 per cent of women and 19.6 per cent of men - are able to be selective over their working hours. So, in two cases out of every three, part-time working is brought in at the employer's instigation. The sectors with the highest proportion of non-selective part-time working are also those where female part-time employment is the most widespread.

The distributive trades are an example of this.

In the United Kingdom, 'married women also have a higher share of part-time work, at 50.7 per cent, but the share of part-time work for non-married women is still significant in international comparative terms' (Humphries and Rubery, 1991, p. 39). In 1990, 79 per cent of married women part-timers said that they did not wish to work full-time; the corresponding figure for non-married women was 40.5 per cent.

The situation in the United Kingdom seems to be particular because the percentage of women stating that they worked part-time through not having obtained full-time employment was particularly low and declining, with 5.1 per cent as the 1990 figure; in the other countries, the 1989 percentage was noticeably higher, i.e. 26 per cent in Belgium, 26 per cent in Spain, 29 per cent in the Netherlands and 31 per cent in Italy.

However, Humphries and Rubery (1991, p. 42) state that

> ... the absence of a large group of women who consider themselves to be in part-time work when they would prefer full-time work does not of course mean that part-time work would be their preferred option if there was different child care provision, or that the choice of part-time work does not represent severe costs to women in terms of pay, status and career opportunities.

The compatibility between a woman's role as a mother and her undertaking part-time employment does not always seem to be obvious.

> For many women, part-time works seems to be the ideal solution to the problem of offsetting family life and employment. They hope to have more time to devote themselves to their children or to a hobby. Hours are often inconvenient, however, and since they allegedly have more free time, they are burdened with housework and their partners in full-time employment do not feel the urge to help out. Much more than full-timers, part-timers can be employed any time of the day - mornings, afternoons, nights or days alternating with one day off and two of eight hours on (Meulders and Vander Stricht, 1991, pp. 52-3).

In the United Kingdom, 'a significant share of the part-time workforce has to provide flexible hours to meet employers' requirements and are involved in unsocial hours, working with no compensation in terms of premia' (Horrell and Rubery, 1991, quoted by Humphries and Rubery, 1991, p. 43).

In France too,

> ... in terms of constraints and work tempo, part-time employment in whatever form should not be classified as a sort of better class sequence of working and free time, to the advantage of the latter. An inquiry into employment conditions (Bue and Cristofari, 1986, quoted by Gauvin and Silvera, 1991, p. 29) shows that :
> - part-time working does not seem to exclude very long working days and, consequently, staggered hours;
> - part-time working does not seem to exclude longer weeks;
> - part-time working is characterized not only by working hours varying with greater frequency from day to day at the employer's behest, but also by the number of days worked varying from week to week. For part-time employees, autonomy with respect to working hours is less frequent.

86

Part-time employees are obliged to work weekends more frequently than full-time employees (women particularly on Saturdays, and a greater number of both men and women regularly on both Saturdays and Sundays).

Another negative aspect brought out in the French survey of Bue and Cristofari (1986) is that the work is less frequently multivalent and more frequently repetitive :

Amongst the jobs mainly done by part-timers are :
- caretaking, cleaning and maintenance, both indoors and out;
- accounting, data processing and secretarial and other types of administrative work;
- welfare, sanitary, educational and cultural duties;
- working as a cashier, a counter clerk or in sales or other types of duties in commerce (Bue and Cristofari, 1986, quoted by Gauvin and Silvera, 1991, p. 29).

In Italy (Altieri and Villa, 1991, p. 66) too, part-time employment has spread to jobs requiring few or no qualifications such as cashier, shop assistant, seasonal worker in agriculture and domestic help.

The percentage of temporary workers among part-time employees (see table 3.6) is often greater than the same percentage calculated for full-timers, and this higher percentage reinforces the image of insecurity that can be linked to part-time employment. In the United Kingdom (Humphries and Rubery, 1991, p. 40), however, a number of studies support the conclusion that most women part-timers do not look upon their jobs as insecure and say that they are in stable employment. In that country, part-time employment cannot be classified together with temporary employment, and this also seems to be the case in some of the other countries where, even if the percentage of those in temporary employment is higher for part-timers, it is nevertheless relatively low (Denmark, Germany, Belgium and the Netherlands); in others, (Greece, Ireland, Italy, Spain and Portugal), the correlation between part-time and temporary employment is more visible.

Table 3.6
Share of temporary employees in part-time and full-time employment, 1989

| | Women | | Men | |
	Part-time	Full-time	Part-time	Full-time
Luxembourg	20.5 % >	1.0 %	86.7 % >	0.6 %
United Kingdom	12.5 % >	3.4 %	35.4 % >	2.2 %
Ireland	40.1 % >	6.9 %	62.2 % >	4.5 %
Denmark	6.9 % <	12.4 %	17.1 % >	9.0 %
Greece	51.9 % >	13.0 %	83.9 % >	16.6 %
Spain	52.8 % >	28.6 %	55.4 % >	24.2 %
Portugal	34.6 % >	17.9 %	49.7 % >	15.0 %
Germany	7.8 % <	14.3 %	31.2 % >	9.8 %
France	13.1 % >	8.3 %	31.8 % >	7.0 %
Italy	44.8 % >	4.7 %	68.6 % >	3.3 %
Netherlands	13.2 % >	9.1 %	17.8 % >	4.8 %
Belgium	12.8 % >	6.7 %	37.0 % >	2.5 %

Source : Eurostat (1989c), *Labour Force Survey.*

The role of the public authorities. In our study of atypical forms of employment (Meulders and Plasman, 1989) we drew attention to the policies implemented during the 1980s with respect to part-time employment. In that study, we identified legislative action that we classified as passive (the adaptation of labour and social security legislation so as to extend to part-timers the legislation applicable to full-timers in Germany, Belgium, France, Spain and Italy) as well as legislation that we classified as active (for the purpose of promoting part-time employment by introducing it into the public service, as in Belgium, Italy, Ireland, Luxembourg, Portugal and France), by introducing financial aid for job sharing (Belgium and France), by granting tax exemptions (Ireland), and by increasing opportunities for semi-retirement (France).

In Chapter 2 we dealt with the development of employment in the public sector. As far as the passive type of policy is concerned, Altieri and Villa (1991, p. 64) state that, in Italy, the regulations liberalizing and regulating part-time employment in the private sector (law no. 863/1984) and in the civil service (law no. 554/1988) have not noticeably influenced labour supply and demand in the direction of this form of employment. As far as the active policies are concerned, attention must be drawn to a provision in the unemployment legislation which, since 1982, [4] has authorized the 100 per cent unemployed in Belgium to undertake part-time employment while continuing to draw unemployment benefit. The number of unemployed undertaking part-time work to escape unemployment has been on the increase since 1983; in June 1991, 195,000 persons including 165,000 women were involved. In 1989, 162,000 women and 37,000 men were affected by this provision while, according to the labour force survey, the part-time employment figures were 277,000 for women and 38,000 for men. Even though the sources are not comparable in terms of definitions, there is no doubt that most part-time employees are in fact registered as unemployed and draw unemployment benefit in addition to their wages for their part-time work.

This type of arrangement gives rise to the question of the part-time employment trap where, under the combined effect of the tax and transfer system, a person would no longer see any purpose in switching from part-time to full-time employment because an increase in taxation and social security contributions in conjunction with a decrease in benefits would only lead to a small increase in their disposal income, or even to a fall in some cases.

A recent study (Demazy, 1991) shows that in Belgium, there are lowly paid workers who would be affected by marginal rates in excess of 80 per cent if they switched from the status of unemployed persons in part-time employment to that of fully employed persons; in the case of lone persons, the rates exceed 100 per cent.

In 1992, as part of a programme of budget cuts, the Belgian government took two measures that indicate a shift in policy on part-time work. Employers will be obliged to pay a levy for each part-time worker they employ who has taken the job to avoid unemployment, and limits in benefits were introduced to encourage the individuals concerned to look for full-time jobs.

2.2 Temporary employment : development in the countries of southern Europe

Temporary employment accounts for very different types of employment ranging from temporary contracts to seasonal employment to interim and occasional activity. The data given in the labour force survey relate to the subjective definition of permanency of employment and concern employees only. According to the explanatory notes accompanying the Community questionnaire, employment can be considered as temporary if it is understood by the employer and the employee that the termination of a period of employment is determined by objective conditions such as reaching a certain date, the completion of an assignment or the return of an employee who has been temporarily replaced. In the case of a fixed term contract, the contract generally specifies the conditions for its termination.

Included in this category are :

- workers employed on a seasonal basis;
- workers employed by an employment agency and hired out to a third party for the carrying out of an assignment (unless there is a written labour contract of unlimited duration with the employment agency);
- workers with specific training contracts.

As Knudsen (1991, p. 55) points out, the question asked of employees in the labour force survey concerning the permanency of their employment relates to the reference week only. Seasonal and occasional employment is only recorded if carried out during that particular week. It is thus probable that relatively long-term temporary contracts have not been declared as temporary. The number of temporary jobs counted in the surveys would thus seem to be an underestimate.

Table 3.7
The temporary element in overall employment, 1989

Country	Women				Men			
	1983		1989	1983		1989	
Luxembourg	4.3 %	=	4.2 %	1.8 %	↑	2.0 %
United Kingdom	7.3 %	=	7.4 %	4.1 %	↓	3.7 %
Ireland	8.8 %	↑	11.9 %	4.7 %	↑	6.5 %
Denmark	n.a.		10.2 %	n.a.		9.8 %
Greece	15.5 %	=	15.6 %	16.5 %	↑	18.0 %
Spain	n.a.		31.2 %	n.a.		24.5 %
Portugal	n.a.		19.2 %	n.a.		15.3 %
Germany	n.a.		12.3 %	n.a.		10.2 %
France	3.4 %	↑	9.4 %	3.3 %	↑	7.8 %
Italy	9.4 %	↓	8.7 %	5.3 %		4.9 %
Netherlands	9.2 %	↑	11.5 %	4.1 %	↑	6.8 %
Belgium	8.5 %	=	8.4 %	3.8 %	↓	3.1 %

Source : Eurostat (1983c and 1989c), *Labour Force Survey.*

An examination of the labour force survey data (see table 3.7) indicates that generally speaking, more women than men hold temporary jobs and that, in the 1980s, not every country experienced an increase in the percentage of temporary employees. Significant increases were recorded in France, where the percentage of women in temporary employment tripled between 1983 and 1989, and in Spain and Ireland; in Germany, there was an increase until 1986, and since then the number of fixed term contracts has diminished. In Portugal temporary, and particularly occasional, employment is seasonal; while it remains stable in agriculture, it is on the increase in the distributive trades and is declining in the services.

While the tertiary sector is the main user of temporary labour in France, industry does tend to abuse it, particularly in the form of interim jobs. In Luxembourg and Belgium this form of employment is concentrated in the services.

In the various countries temporary employment often marks entry into the labour market with the share of temporary employment greater in the 14-24 age group, where it reflects the manner in which young people slot themselves into the working world. However, while temporary employment is decreasing for men over twenty-four, for women it remains a form of employment that they run up against throughout their working lives (Plasman and Plasman, 1991, p. 36). Silvera and Gauvin (1991, p. 36) [5] submit data on labour mobility in France, where

> ... fixed term contracts were involved in 75 per cent of all recruitment in 1987 (60 per cent in 1983). The proportion of fixed term contracts is continuing to grow, while the number of male employees already in post on fixed term contracts is estimated at about 3 per cent. Fixed term contracts are more a phenomenon affecting women as such, women under twenty-five and women with no qualifications.

In Italy too, 'an inquiry carried out in Turin city shows that recruitment to insecure jobs mainly involves young people with low levels of academic achievement' (Altieri and Villa, 1991, p. 73). On the other hand, Alcobendas Tirado (1991) points out that, in Spain, temporary contracts are more a matter for women with middle level schooling or vocational training.

In most of the countries, temporary employment is an unwanted form of employment both for men and for women; the percentage of women stating that they are in temporary employment through having failed to find a job of unlimited duration is generally very high. An exception is the United Kingdom, where the proportion has dropped since 1983 and was as low as 19 per cent in 1989. However, as the United Kingdom experts point out,

> ... this conclusion must be interpreted in the context of the United Kingdom labour market and United Kingdom labour law where firms have relative freedom to dismiss workers even when employed on so called permanent contracts. Employees cannot claim unfair dismissal unless they have been employed for two years continuously at sixteen hours a week (or five years if working between eight and sixteen hours). Firms in fact have little incentive to employ staff on explicit temporary contracts (Humphries and Rubery, 1991, p. 40).

The percentage of part-timers amongst women in temporary employment (see table 3.8) is high, and in this connection there seems to be a link between temporary and part-time female employment, particularly in the United Kingdom, Luxembourg, Italy, the Netherlands and Ireland, where more than 50 per cent of women in temporary employment work on a part-time basis. These percentages are distinctly higher than those for women in permanent employment.

More than part-time employment, temporary employment is a phenomenon linked to labour demand.

Whereas in periods of crisis the quest by business and industry to adjust output to track fluctuations in demand and to reduce wage costs is intensified, it is not closely linked to economic recession. Facing up to uncertainty in a context where their status is subject to regulation is a challenge with which firms claim to be confronted whatever the state of the economy. One of the methods of adjusting the amount of 'actual' employment to the amount of 'desired' employment lies in the use of flexible outside

Table 3.8

Share of part-time workers in temporary and permanent employment, 1989

Country	Women			Men		
	Temporary		Permanent	Temporary		Permanent
Luxembourg	80.0 %	>	13.7 %	72.2 %	>	0.2 %
United Kingdom	73.9 %	>	41.1 %	43.4 %	>	3.1 %
Ireland	51.3 %	>	10.4 %	32.8 %	>	1.4 %
Denmark	27.4 %	<	42.1 %	17.3 %	>	9.1 %
Greece	22.6 %	>	3.9 %	10.0 %	>	0.4 %
Spain	18.7 %	>	7.6 %	2.3 %	>	0.6 %
Portugal	14.1 %	>	6.3 %	3.0 %	>	0.6 %
Germany	19.1 %	<	31.8 %	5.1 %	>	1.3 %
France	32.9 %	>	22.7 %	13.7 %	>	2.5 %
Italy	51.5 %	>	6.1 %	34.8 %	>	0.8 %
Netherlands	66.9 %	>	57.3 %	38.9 %	>	13.0 %
Belgium	42.5 %	>	26.7 %	21.3 %	>	1.2 %

Source : Eurostat (1983c and 1989c), *Labour Force Survey.*

labour, which leads to differences in workers' status which, in its turn, brings in fixed term and temporary (or interim) contracts (Gauvin and Silvera, 1991, p. 32).

This idea also features in the Netherlands report (Plantenga, 1991, p. 40) :

From the point of view of business and industry, fixed term employment can be justified in different ways. What may be involved are periods of probation for future permanent staff or a need for seasonal workers or for replacements for temporarily absent staff.

However, as Plantenga points out :

A fixed term contract does not necessarily mean an uncertain job. A study shows, for example, that more than 56 per cent of those with fixed term or flexible contracts in May 1985 had obtained permanent jobs by October 1986. Some 7 per cent had been unemployed in the interim period, and 37 per cent were still in fixed term employment. The researchers also conclude that the hard core of those on fixed term or flexible contracts is probably relatively small and that the number of transitions is considerable (Plantenga, 1991, p. 40).

In France too (Gauvin and Silvera, 1991, p. 37), numbers of jobs recruited for on fixed term contracts are converted into permanencies, with the fixed term contract serving as a means of probation. According to an estimate, [6] this involves between a quarter and a fifth of all such contracts. The employment survey offers a more optimistic estimate of about two out of every three. A study carried out in Italy (Altieri and Villa, 1991, p. 73) on a sample of firms in the province of Turin shows that 73 per cent of the firms considered that they would have to face up to a need for flexibility in the near future, and this would mean recruitment for periods of not more than twelve months. Flexible labour management by means of fixed term contracts is not the prerogative of the private sector; in several of the countries, the government has made large-scale use of this type of contract.

2.3 Rotating, unsocial and split working hours

This section looks at various regimes such as night working, shift working and weekend working. We have no fully correlated data on these regimes, which are determined by very different conditions according to country. Since this is so, we cannot go into them in any great detail.

In a number of the countries of the Community there has been a ban on women working nights and in the cases of Belgium and Germany, [7] the ban has not been lifted. In France, the law of 19 June 1987 increased women's chances of working nights, and in the Netherlands the ban was lifted in 1986, though monitoring continued until 1989 via a system of authorization. Since then, women's night work has been permitted and only pregnant women are subject to restrictions. Authorizing women to work nights should open jobs to them which are associated with this type of working while the fact of being unable to work nights deprives them of promotion and extra earnings. In sectors where work is organized on a shift basis, the ban could serve as an excuse to get rid of them.

A survey carried out in the Netherlands (Ministerie van Sociale Zaken en Werkgelegenheid, 1988b, quoted by Plantenga, 1991, p. 41) amongst women night workers in industry shows that 72 per cent wished to continue working nights since this type of programme enabled them to organize their time better and have access to bonuses. The report also reveals that

> ... the possibility of working nights in no way improves women's position on the labour market. Rather than leading to the recruitment of more women, the opening up of night work to them has brought about the modification of their working hours, with most women night workers having previously worked one or two day shifts. In addition, many women are not firmly ensconced on the labour market, and in the firms investigated about a third of the female workforce were either temporary or had fixed term contracts. It also emerged that the women had less well paid jobs than their male colleagues.

> As Wentholt rightly remarks, these results reflect the well-known 'part-timer's dilemma' : (part-time) night work offers women individually a solution to the problems arising from the need to combine paid employment with household duties. This said, their position in relation to their male colleagues and their employers remains marginal and diverges from the norm. So, from a structural point of view, there can be no thought of a change for the good (Wentholt, 1990, p. 466, quoted by Plantenga, 1991, p. 41).

Night work has never been banned in Denmark (Platz, 1988, quoted by Knudsen, 1991, p. 60), and there are no differences between men and women as far as this type of regime is concerned. Employment of this type involves 7 per cent of employees and 8 per cent of the self-employed, and in 1987, 31 per cent of the self-employed and 15 per cent of employees often worked evenings. This type of regime is less widespread in the private sector than in the public one, where public transport and the sanitary and welfare services are to be found. In France, the first results of the employment survey show that in 1990

> ... women accounted for slightly less than a quarter of regular night workers and fewer than 20 per cent of those only occasionally involved, i.e. 2 per cent of the active female population in the former case, and 4 per cent in the latter. For men, the percentages were 6 per cent and 4 per cent respectively. Whereas men are more involved in night work than women, the increase in the frequency of nights worked also affects the latter, and this was so even before the 1987 law. In 1984, 65 per cent of the women who worked nights were employees or intermediate level staff in medical establishments, hotels and care taking firms. However, there was an enormous increase in frequent night working among both male and female manual workers upon the signing of a series of collective agreements (Gauvin and Silvera, 1991, p. 39).

But a lack of enthusiasm about women working nights is sometimes expressed by men, particularly when it is to their advantage to do so. Thus, the management of the Angers (Maine-et-Loire) Bull plant had to stop recruiting women to their electronic card production line. The unions were against it. Henceforth, these jobs will go to men (*Le Monde*, 22 May 1991, quoted by Gauvin and Silvera, 1991, p. 39).

A ban on night work is an obstacle to women's undertaking shift work because shiftwork forms an integral part of continuous and semi-continuous production. This partly explains why shift work is more frequent in the case of men than of women in the countries where the ban is maintained. At the same time, however, an explanation for this disparity between men and women is also to be found in the fact that this type of employment is concentrated in the industrial sector. In the United Kingdom (Humphries and Rubery, 1991, p. 46), a quarter of male manual workers as opposed to 12 per cent of female full-timers and 5 per cent of female part-timers is involved in shift work. In Belgium (Meulders and Vander Stricht, 1991, p. 62), 21.7 per cent of men and 14.7 per cent of women employed in industry work shifts as opposed to 8.8 per cent and 8.4 per cent respectively in the services. Between 1985 and 1989 there was an increase in the proportion of shift working in overall employment, with a greater increase in the case of women than of men. In 1983, the proportion of women on shift work was very low in the ex-German Democratic Republic (Figge, Quack and Schäfgen, 1991, p. 25), a factor which goes a long way towards accounting for the disparity in men's and women's incomes.

Two forms of weekend working must be distinguished, namely :

> - a traditional form in the distributive trades, in certain services and in the weekend schedules of shift workers engaged in round-the-clock working.
> - a more innovatory form associated with weekend working only which, in a wider context, forms part of an experiment into the organization of working time. These forms are often, but not always, associated with a reduction in working hours. For firms extending their activities to six or seven days what is involved is the rotation of four shifts over six days, shifts on short hours and the setting up of substitute shifts

for Friday/Saturday, Saturday/Sunday or Friday/Saturday/Sunday (FS, SS, or FSS) (Gauvin and Silvera, 1991, p. 39).

At our disposal we have data on for four countries. In the case of France,

... regular Saturday working affects women (25.8 per cent) more than men (15 per cent). A similar percentage of men and women (46 per cent) occasionally work on Saturdays. Regular Saturday working affects 84 per cent of women employed in the distributive trades (61 per cent of men) and 65 per cent of men in services dealing directly with the public (46 per cent of women). Among the categories that frequently work on Saturdays there are also senior civil servants, artists and members of the intelligentsia (men : 21 per cent; women : 31 per cent), middle grade civil servants and professionals in education and health (men : 31 per cent; women : 34 per cent). Thus, it is essentially teachers, doctors, artists, nurses and journalists who are involved. Sunday working is less widespread. It affects more or less the same categories, but in different proportions. Between 1978 and 1984 the percentage of employees stating that they worked at least one Sunday per annum rose from 18.8 per cent to 19.9 per cent. But regular Sunday working is low and static (2.9 per cent for men and 3.2 per cent for women), and those involved are mainly in the distributive trades and services dealing directly with the public. It has also been ascertained that there are 486,000 employees working both Saturdays and Sundays without falling within the compass of weekend shifts, which are still in their infancy. On the other hand, part-time working is quite widespread in jobs requiring Saturday and Sunday presences. And last of all, inquiries [8] among users reveal that very few firms in fact make use of weekend shifts on an exclusive and permanent basis. In 1984, such shifts only accounted for 0.01 per cent of employees (Gauvin and Silvera, 1991, p. 40).

In 1990, according to an Equal Opportunities Commission inquiry (quoted by Humphries and Rubery, 1991, p. 46), 46 per cent of the total United Kingdom sample had worked at least one Saturday during the four weeks preceding the inquiry (57 per cent of men; 36 per cent of female full-timers; 32 per cent of female part-timers). Sunday working affected almost 30 per cent of the workforce (37 per cent of men; 24 per cent of female full-timers; and 18 per cent of female part-timers). For full-timers, weekend working often meant more than five days open while for part-timers, weekend working rarely corresponded to more than five days of work. Even though the percentage of women among Sunday workers in Germany (Figge, Quack and Schäfgen, 1991, p. 25) is still far from high, it has been increasing steadily. In Denmark (Knudsen, 1991, p. 62), a fifth of all employees work regularly on Sundays and a quarter do so occasionally. More than two-thirds of employees are not involved in Sunday working and it is mostly in the public sector that weekend working is to be found.

Whereas the particular forms of employment reviewed in the section form important categories, the list is not exhaustive. As Plantenga (1991, p. 42) says, on-call working, mini/maxi contracts and homeworking are other examples whose extent is often difficult to ascertain and which mainly involve women.

3 . Conclusions

As a first point, this chapter on the the less traditional forms of employment evidences strong national disparities. Developments and the proportion of women involved vary from country to country, and it often happens that no Community-wide trend is visible at all. The only constant in employment outside the wage system takes the form of a decrease in family workers, who are overrepresented amongst women. In contrast, the number of women employers - weakly represented in female employment - remains stable. There are contrasting developments in self-employment, and we have echoed the discussion concerning the quality of this type of employment which, in the case of women, is often a matter of second best.

Whereas part-time working remains the exponent *par excellence* of the flexibility of female employment, its relative growth seems to have come to a standstill in both Denmark and the United Kingdom as far as women are concerned and, for men, it is now becoming more a matter of young people offsetting studies and work. In the cases of France, the Netherlands, Belgium, the United Kingdom, Ireland and Germany the increase in female employment between 1983 and 1989 is largely attributable to the growth of part-time employment. In this connection, the difference with respect to the countries of the South of Europe is striking since the proportion of part-time working there is low, and has not increased significantly since 1983. Its concentration in already very close sectors, its non-optional nature, its insecurity and its awkward working hours make part-time employment into a form of employment that is of very little personal value for women even if in the United Kingdom, a majority of women part-timers declare that they do not want to work full-time. In Belgium, unemployment benefits combined with part-time employment prevented a switch from part-time to full-time employment in the case of low wage earners.

Women in temporary employment remain overrepresented, but developments differ from one country to another. Thus, some considerable increases have been recorded in France and in Spain, where temporary employment often disguises entry into the labour market and serves as a vehicle for probation. However, once entry has been gained, the percentage of temporary employment remains higher for women than for men, and this type of employment includes a high proportion of part-time working.

Generally speaking, as far as these different forms of employment are concerned, it seems that while the situation did not degenerate between 1983 and 1989, it did not improve, either. Women remain overrepresented in these forms of employment and are fair game as far as policies aiming for flexibility are concerned.

Notes

1. In Italy, the increase can also be explained by 'legal and fiscal provisions leading to certain illegal activities emerging into broad daylight' (Altieri and Villa, 1991, p. 57).
2. In the Netherlands, the definitions were changed during the period under study. These changes distort the interpretation of the developments observed.
3. EEC, COM (90) 228 final (90/C224/04) and COM 228 final (90/C224/05).

4. Royal decree of 22 March 1982.
5. According to the survey of labour force employment conditions (ACEMO).
6. According to the *'Déclarations de mouvements de main-d'oeuvre'* (DMMO).
7. In Germany this ban only concerns female manual workers, not employees.
8. According to the survey of labour force employment conditions (ACEMO).

Appendix 3.1 : Distribution of the part-time work according to the number of hours working by week

Germany

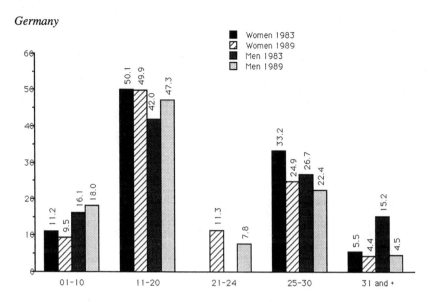

France

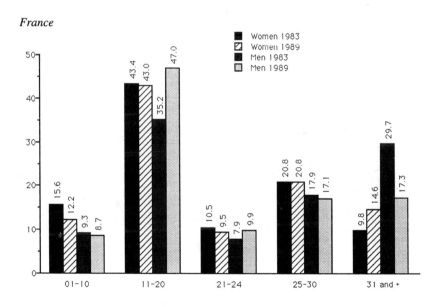

Italy

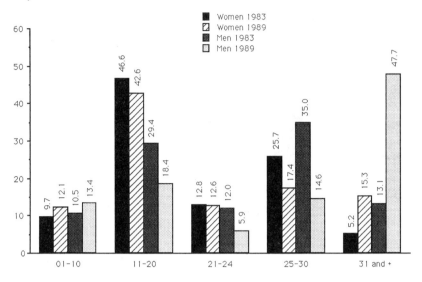

Netherlands

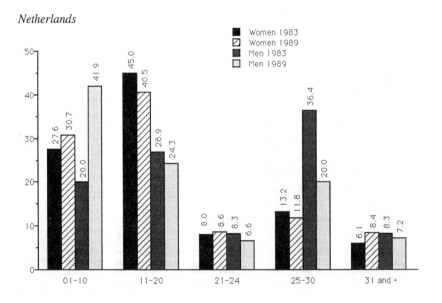

Belgium

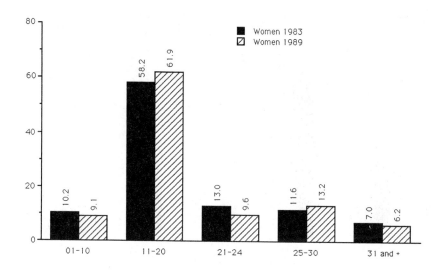

United Kingdom

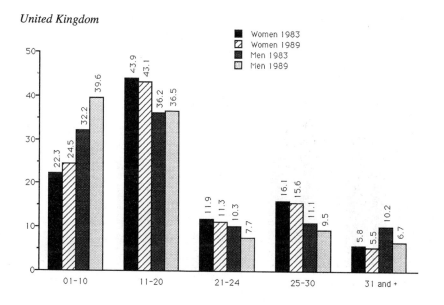

Ireland

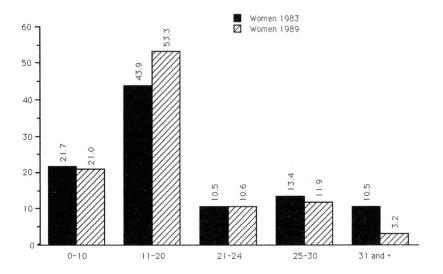

Denmark

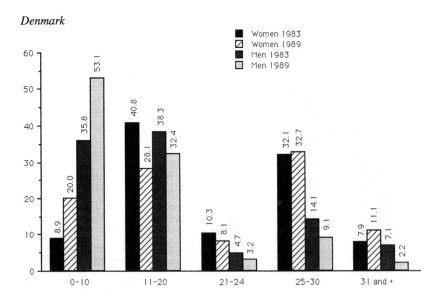

100

Greece

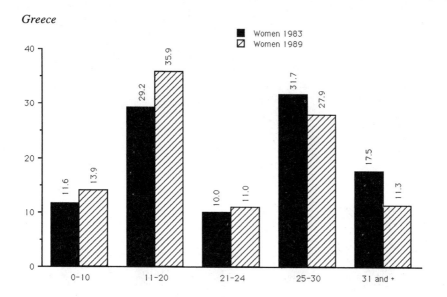

Portugal

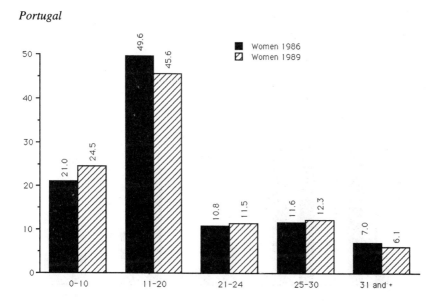

101

Spain

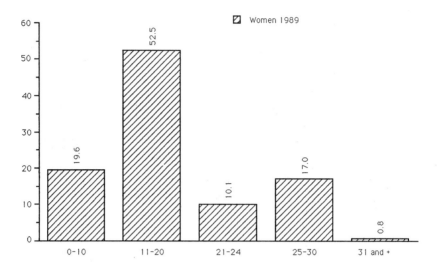

Appendix 3.2 : Distribution of part-time employment by age groups

Germany

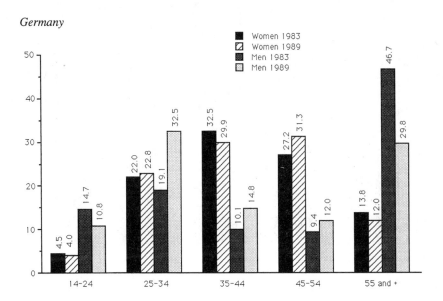

France

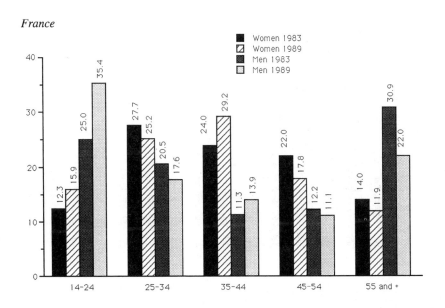

Italy

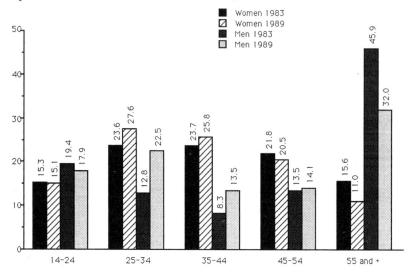

Netherlands

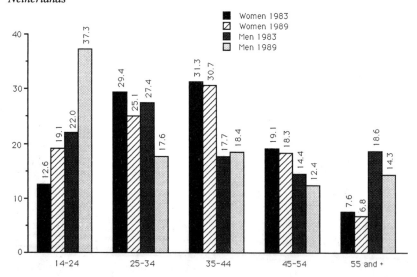

104

Belgium

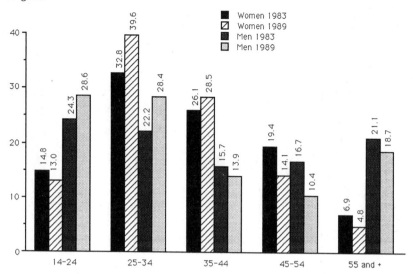

Legend:
- ■ Women 1983
- ◨ Women 1989
- ▨ Men 1983
- ▦ Men 1989

United Kingdom

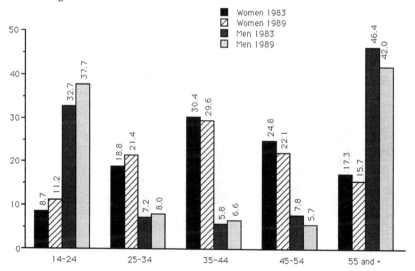

Legend:
- ■ Women 1983
- ◨ Women 1989
- ▨ Men 1983
- ▦ Men 1989

Ireland

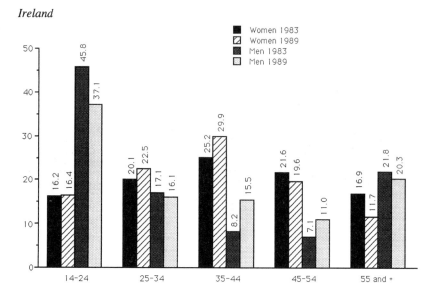

Denmark

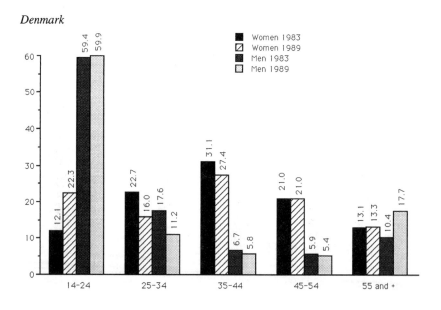

106

Greece

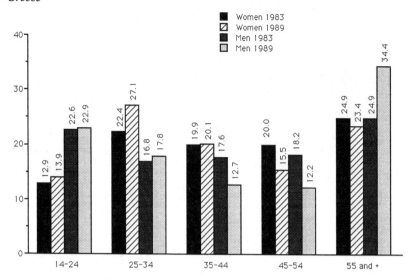

Portugal

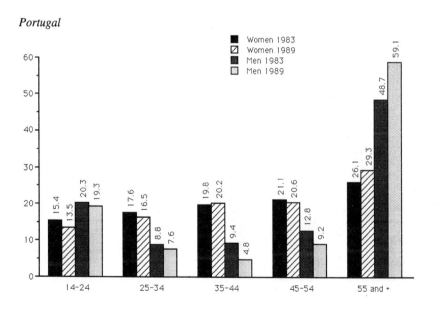

Spain

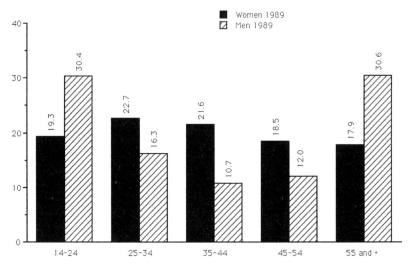

- Women 1989
- Men 1989

	14-24	25-34	35-44	45-54	55 and +
Women	19.3	22.7	21.6	18.5	17.9
Men	30.4	16.3	10.7	12.0	30.6

4 Conditions of remuneration: persistence and increase of the disparities

Equal pay is now legally guaranteed in all the countries of the Community. This is the result of a long work of the European Community Commission and Council to oblige member states to apply the article 119 of the Treaty of Rome which imposes the unambiguous principle of equal pay for equal work regardless of gender (Vogel-Polsky and Vogel, 1991, p. 104). Table 4.1 shows the evolution of the national legislations. Since 1975, directive no. 75/117 (of 10 February 1975) has been complemented by article 119, which includes equality of pay not only for the same work, but also for work of the same value.

> It obliges member states to use the same criteria for either sex in determining pay within the system of job classification, establishes the principle of jurisdictional guarantees, eliminates discrimination whatever its source, and provides protection against dismissal resulting from the application of the principle (Vogel-Polsky and Vogel, 1991, p. 116).

In this chapter we will endeavour to ascertain the extent to which gender wage differentials improved during the 1980s.

1. Harmonized income statistics : an imperfect tool for the analysis of discrimination

On a European level, the only regular harmonized statistics on gender related earnings refer to the gross average hourly earnings of manual workers in industry and the gross average monthly earnings of employees in industry and certain services (see Appendix 4.1). This gives rise to a number of

109

Table 4.1
Equal pay policy in the member countries of the
European Economic Community

Countries	Year	Designation	Sanctioning bodies
Belgium	1975	National employment council's collective labour agreement no. 25, rendered mandatory by royal decree	Collective bargaining parties; Ministry of labour
Denmark	1973	Collective agreement at national level on wage parity	
France	1972	Act no. 72/1143 on equal remuneration for men and women	Ministry of labour; Delegation of the status of women
Germany	1980	Code of civil procedure (paragraph 612)	Ministry of labour and social affairs; Labour courts
Greece	1984	Law no. 1414/84 on the applications of the principle of equality between the sexes in employment	Ministry of labour
Ireland	1974	Anti-discrimination (pay) act (amended by employment equality act)	Employment equality agency; Labour courts
Italy	1960	Equal pay agreement for the industrial sector	Collective bargaining parties
	1964	Equal pay law for the agricultural sector	Ministry of labour
Netherlands	1975	Equal pay act	Civil courts
	1984	(Revised) equal treatment act (integrating the equal pay act of 1975 and the equal treatment act of 1980)	Civil courts
Portugal	1979	Act on equality in work and employment	Equality commission; Labour inspectorate
Spain	1980	Worker's statute Basic employment law	Labour tribunals; Labour inspectorate
United Kingdom	1970	Equal pay act	-
	1975	(in force)	Industrial tribunals
	1984	(amended)	-

Source : OECD (1988), pp. 167-8.

problems. On the one hand, hourly and monthly earnings are determined on the basis of the total corporate wage bill divided by the number of male and female workers respectively.

> The wage is thus an average which is of little interest from the point of view of an analysis of labour market discrimination since in the case of static and intersectoral comparisons it obscures any interenterprise and interindustry difference in qualifications, seniority and types of employment across the various gender groups. Given a similar pay structure, the average wage in a sector will increase in proportion to the number of skilled workers that it employs. Similarly, as far as both sectors and individual enterprises are concerned, the average male wage will be above the average female one even if there are proportionately more women in posts where qualifications, seniority and the type of employment are less well remunerated, and even if there is no direct or indirect discrimination as such. Hourly and monthly earnings are thus a sign of direct and indirect discrimination as well as of the different structure of the workforce according to sector or labour force group (Plasman and Plasman, 1991, p. 41).

On the other hand, hourly earnings include items (such as piece rate payments, productivity bonuses, overtime payments, etc.) which are the cause of gender related wage disparity because of differences in the quantity and quality of the work (Eurostat, 1983b, p. XLV).

As a final point, the Eurostat data cover little more that industry. Those covering the services are incomplete and cannot be compared to those covering industry. In addition, no information is given on part-time workers' earnings. What is needed for these data to serve as a means of comparing wage discrimination from country to country is that :

a) they should cover a reasonably large segment of total employment and relatively equivalent percentages of malc and female employment;
b) within total employment, the amount of employment in the sectors covered by the survey should maintain the same proportion over time;
c) the relative levels of male/female earnings in these sectors should serve as a good indicator of relative pay levels in sectors not included in the survey;
d) the extent and stability of the sectors covered should be similar in all the member states (Rubery, 1991, p. 11).

Now, an analysis of sectoral distribution (Chapter 2) shows that men's share in industry is much higher than women's, that the share of employment in industry is on the decline, and that the size of the industrial sector varies from one country to another. The relative levels of male/female earnings in industry do not seem to be a good indicator of what is happening in the remaining sectors. Altieri and Villa (1991, p. 87) emphasize that, according to data from the Italian Treasury, the gender wage differential is relatively lower in industry than in agriculture and the services, whereas it is relatively higher in Spain (Alcobendas Tirado, 1991).

Furthermore, the harmonized data on earnings only cover full-time employment, so excluding a considerable number of women from the survey (see Chapter 3). This is not without consequence. If part-time and full-time earnings had followed the same line of development, the statistics on full-time earnings would suffice but, as Humphries and Rubery (1991, pp. 51-2) show for the United Kingdom, the differential between full and part-timers' pay widened over the 1980s, with the ratio of female part-time hourly pay to female full-time hourly pay falling from 79 per cent to 75 per cent between 1983 and 1990. As a final point, Spain does not provide data by gender and Italy has not done so since 1985.

> There is always the extra problem of changes occurring in the structures of the aggregates under study whenever developments in disparities relating to pay, sector and/or gender are examined. Employment is not stable and when fluctuations occur, the bulk of the categories under study are not affected in an identical manner. The last-in-first-out principle is often applied when a sector goes in for large-scale dismissals. If seniority is an important factor in determining pay, the average wage level will be affected positively without there being any thought of pay adjustments or reductions in pay discrimination (Plasman and Plasman, 1991, p. 41).

A European comparison. All these points must be taken into consideration when the ratio of male to female earnings (see table 4.2) is employed as a discrimination index. In 1989, the ratio of the gross average hourly earnings of female manual workers to those of male manual workers in manufacturing varied from 84.5 per cent in Denmark to 58.5 per cent in Luxembourg. In Germany, Belgium, France, Greece and Ireland there was a trend towards an improvement in this ratio in comparison with 1983, but it deteriorated in Denmark, the United Kingdom, Luxembourg and the Netherlands. As far as monthly earnings are concerned, the ratio of women's earnings to men's was less marked, ranging from 71.5 per cent in Portugal to 55 per cent in Luxembourg and the United Kingdom. This stemmed in part from differences in working hours. There was a tendency for the ratio to improve in all the countries except Germany and the United Kingdom where it remained fairly stable.

An analysis by sector shows that, in all the countries, the ratio of women's pay to men's is declining in a number of sectors (see Appendix 4.1).

Even if caution is *de rigueur* in interpreting these data, they do show that gender pay differentials persist and are even on the increase in certain cases; there is thus nothing to justify our stating that they are on the decline.

2. The development and position of women's relative earnings : persistence and worsening of the differences

Gender pay differentials are widening in Italy, Denmark and Portugal. In Italy, according to data from the Ministero delle Finanze (quoted by Altieri and Villa, 1991, p. 81), relative female earnings in Italy passed from 79.42 per cent in 1982 to 76.80 per cent in 1986; this trend has been confirmed by other surveys.

> An examination by sector points to an increase in this differential over the period 1982-86 in all sectors excepting agriculture, wholesaling and transport, where the degree of compression between average income levels remained very low. More problematic is the fact that this differential increased in the public administration, with a ratio passing from 86.91 per cent to 84.40 per cent. Moreover, it emerged that whereas the gender pay differential diminished noticeably over the 1982-83 period, it increased again between 1983 and 1986. This phenomenon, already emphasized in other

Table 4.2
Relative gross earnings of women (1983-89) (in percentage of male gross earnings)

	Germany	Belgium	Denmark	Spain	France	United Kingdom	Greece	Ireland	Italy	Luxembourg	Netherlands	Portugal
Manual worker's gross average hourly earnings												
Industry as a whole												
Women's earnings / men's earnings 1989	73.4	75.1	n.a.	n.a.	80.8	68.8	n.a.	68.6	n.a.	63.2	75.9	69.4
Difference 1989-83	1.2	1.2	n.a.	n.a.	+0.7	0.0	n.a.	n.a.	n.a.	-2.0	+1.9	n.a.
Manufacturing												
1989	72.8	74.0	84.5	n.a.	79.5	68.3	79.7	69.3	n.a.	58.5	75.4	68.0
Difference 1989-83	0.2	0.6	-1.0	n.a.	+1.1	-0.2	+5.1	+0.8	n.a.	-2.9	-0.4	n.a.
Employees' gross monthly earnings												
Industry as a whole												
Women's earnings / men's earnings 1989	66.5	64.5	n.a.	n.a.	64.9	55.2	n.a.	n.a.	n.a.	55.6	64.5	73.4
Difference 1989-83	0.0	1.9	n.a.	n.a.	2.6	0.4	n.a.	n.a.	n.a.	1.6	3.4	n.a.
Manufacturing												
Women's earnings / men's earnings 1989	66.5	64.1	n.a.	n.a.	65.0	55.1	66.2	n.a.	n.a.	55.0	63.7	71.5
Difference 1989-83	-0.2	1.4	n.a.	n.a.	2.6	0.1	6.2	n.a.	n.a.	1.1	2.8	n.a.

Source : Eurostat (1990c), *Earnings, Industry and Services.*

surveys (Bettio, 1985, quoted by Altieri and Villa, 1991, p. 82), can be linked to very precise causes. Thus, whereas before 1983 the effects of a trade union policy were felt which led to the flattening out of wage distributions and a compression of gender wage levels, after 1983 a new wage slide was observed with a reversed trend brought about by important agreements between the representative bodies and the government in order to curb labour costs through the setting of maximum ceilings for pay increases. In addition, after 1983 the reabsorption of inflation led to a loss of importance for wage indexing which, up to that time, had contributed to the flattening-out process. The effects of this wage policy were not slow in manifesting themselves in terms of women's pay levels and, after 1983, there was a resurgence of wage differentials and so of serious discrimination against women workers (Altieri and Villa, 1991, pp. 82-3).

Before the implementation of wage parity, women's hourly earnings in Denmark were less than 80 per cent of men's. For a number of years, women's average earnings were closer to men's - in 1977 by as much as 91.7 per cent. After 1978 the percentage slowly declined, before nosediving in 1985. There was another improvement in parity after 1987, and at the beginning of 1990 the hourly wage differential stood at 10 per cent, i.e. the same as in 1975. An increase in women's pay in percentage points of men's took place at the same time as the principle of equal pay was introduced. There have been many attempts to explain why this development did not continue and why there are still vast differences in remuneration for work of equal value (Knudsen, 1991, pp. 63-5).

'The pay differential, exacerbated over a number of years, could be explained by the adverse economic conditions which have been the cause of structural changes in Danish economic life since the end of the seventies'. The hypothesis that the exacerbation of gender pay differentials can be explained by the higher level of female unemployment has also been put forward.

Knudsen (1991, p. 69) also emphasizes that

...post-1975 incomes policy has influenced wage determination in various ways and has thus acted as a brake on wage parity. The regulation of cost of living allowances imposed by the post-May 1977 austerity programme has played a very large part, as has the fact that the unions have had to shelve the priority accorded to the elimination of wage differentials in favour of a less supportive wages policy.

In the United Kingdom there is a growing lack of equality within the female workforce : much of the improvement in women's average pay has resulted from steep increases in pay for higher paid women workers (Humphries and Rubery, 1991, p. 50). Moreover, the differential is increasing between full-time and part-time wages. This may stem from the acceleration of the trend towards the decentralization of pay determination. Firms largely set their pay through direct negotiations with the unions or independently, without any guidelines from national agreements (Ingram and Cahill, 1989, quoted by Humphries and Rubery, 1991, p. 64). Generally speaking, there has been no decrease in gender pay differentials, and the explanations put forward by the Italian and Danish experts seem to show that the austerity policies of recent years have had something to do with this.

The United Kingdom experts emphasize the role played by the economic policy of the eighties in the widening of pay differentials.

The eighties has seen a continuation and acceleration of the trend towards decentralization of pay determination; industry wide agreements have continued to lose their influence and in many cases have disappeared (including, for example, the largest of them all, covering the engineering industry). Firms largely set their pay through direct negotiations with unions or independently, without any guidelines from national agreements (Ingram and Cahill, 1989, quoted by Humphries and Rubery, 1991, p. 64). The breakdown of the national bargaining system is likely to have most effect in small firms and on the weakest labour force groups. One explanation of the increasing polarization of earnings among women may be this fragmentation of the pay determination system. In addition, the powers of the wage councils which set legal minimum wages in certain industries, mainly female dominated service sectors, have been weakened and the incidence of avoidance of the legislation has increased. Many woman workers have also been taken outside the protection of the public sector pay bargaining system by the privatization of ancilliary services such as catering and cleaning. There is also a general trend away from centralized pay determination in the public sector, a development which is likely to increase the gender gap as the pay hierarchy lengthens, and to widen pay differentials between women as both occupational and regional pay differentials increase. Greater differentiation with and between industries in pay levels can thus be expected, with significant negative consequences on the lowest paid female workers (Humphries and Rubery, 1991, pp. 64-5).

2.1 Differentials by age

In the Netherlands,

> ...gender pay differentials increase according to age until the 45-49 age group is reached. They then remain relatively stable until they increase again among the over-sixties. This profile no doubt reflects women's fragmented careers. Based on 1982 data, a study of the effects of career breaks on the basic wage shows that the loss of earnings capacity can be set at 2 per cent per year of non-activity. This means, for example, that after a ten year period of non-activity the basic wage is about 20 per cent below the level that would have been earned but for the break (Groot et al., 1988, quoted by Plantenga, 1991, p. 45). Data provided by the Netherlands expert show that there is already a considerable pay differential in the youngest age groups. Thus, in 1989, an eighteen year old girl earned on average 8 per cent less than a youth of the same age. A survey carried out in 1984 among young people of school age provided some striking further detail on the subject. This survey showed that with the exception of seventeen year-old final year high school students, boys benefited from a higher hourly wage than girls whatever the combination of age and school type. This difference amounted to a minimum of 0.25 gulden for seventeen year-old youths on senior secondary vocational education and a maximum of 1.80 gulden for eighteen year-old youths studying for the senior general secondary eduction (Groot et al., 1988, quoted by Plantenga, 1991, p. 45).

In Italy (Altieri and Villa, 1991, p. 86), there is a greater compression of the gender pay differential among young people on the one hand, and a gap which increases according to age on the other.

> Blackwell (1989) records an interesting model connected with the relative incomes of young male and female manual workers in Ireland. His data show that adolescents are on particularly low wages immediately after leaving school - so much so that 55 per cent of the female school leavers in a 1987 Ministry of Labour inquiry were earning

115

less than seventy Irish punts a week. Basing himself on a list of special tables in the Ministry of Labour's 1987 report on 1986 school leavers, he established that female adolescents earned an average of 71.68 punts a week while male adolescents at the same stage were on an average of 69.3 punts in the years after entering the labour market (Blackwell, 1989, table 6.6, quoted by Barry, 1991). He attributes this situation to the following facts : there is a certain number of reasons why, in certain occupations, girls' incomes approach and even exceed boys'. The first is that a much higher number of boys are in apprenticeships, and this means low earnings during the period of transition. The second is that a considerable number of girls are in sectors where adult wages are paid relatively early on (Blackwell, 1989, p. 49, quoted by Barry, 1991).

2.2 Differentials by levels of educational attainment

A study carried out in Italy (Biagioli, 1987, quoted by Altieri and Villa, 1991, p. 87) emphasizes that gender pay differentials are relatively higher at either end of the educational scale, i.e. the primary school leaving certificate on the one hand, and a university degree on the other. Hence the interpretation according to which poorly educated and qualified women are probably employed in less well paid jobs in the ancilliary segment of the labour market. On the other hand, where educated of a higher standard the huge gap between male and female workers' average earnings is probably due to women's tendency to be less career oriented than men and to take less advantage of the wage formulae available (Altieri and Villa, 1991, p. 88).

3. Vertical and horizontal segregation, the underevaluation of women's work and premia systems : points explaining gender pay differentials

Two types of explanation can be distinguished :

1) The different gender distributions across the various sectors and occupations and in the different hierarchical grades. This is in fact a return to the old question of vertical and horizontal segregation in female employment.
2) The underevaluation of women's work and the payment of premia to men more frequently than to women.

3.1 Differences in the distribution of employment by gender

The concentration of women's employment in some sectors where the pay level is low is one of the explanatory factors related to male/female earnings differentials. The high share of textile-clothing industry in women's industrial employment illustrate the correlation between the percentage of women in a sector and the pay level. 'The national summary tables suggest the same conclusions for all countries : the average salary in textile-clothing is below the average salary in manufacturing industry...' (Meulders and Plasman, 1991, p. 52). The share of women's employment in the public sector also plays an important role : Rubery (1991, p. 102) mentions that

116

...in Britain, women public sector workers have suffered overall relative declines in pay but the experience has been slightly variable with for example nurses improving their pay but health services ancilliaries suffering a significant decline in relative pay. In Germany, all public sector workers appear to have suffered some relative fall in pay but the position of groups within the sector has remained relatively stable : moreover women occupy a not significant share of higher pay jobs in the public sector.

In Italy, a recent survey shows that intra-occupational gender ratios are often 90 per cent or more, so that most of the overall wage disparity between men and women is caused by the distribution and concentration of women in certain areas of employment rather than to differences within occupations (Rubery, 1991, quoted by Altieri and Villa, 1991, p. 87).

The German experts (Gottschall, 1987 and Fiedler and Regenhard, 1987, quoted by Figge, Quack and Schäfgen, 1991, pp. 27-8) emphasize that at the time of their recruitment women are generally allocated to lower grade posts and more frequently remain in new entrants' jobs.

3.2 Underevaluation of women's work

The German experts emphasize that, even though the qualification levels for male and female employees are the same for both sexes in Germany, the disparities between men and women are greater in this category. They emphasize the part played by the

...consistent failure to award bonuses for merit and to pay the employer's share of social security contributions - typical features of the everyday working lives of women employed in the services as cashiers, secretaries and nurses, for instance (Kurz-Sherf, 1986, quoted by Figge, Quack and Schäfgen, 1991, p. 28). As the result of the 1955 ban on restricted pay clauses for women low wage groups were introduced, with the criterion distinguishing them from the better paid groups in industry depending on job facility or the amount of physical effort involved. Regardless of the approach used wage scale-based job evaluation criteria incorporate women's activities in an unsatisfactory manner only. The establishment of the scale of effort in industry is based on the notion of a very narrow ergonomic load depending on no more than actual muscular effort and the concomitant energy production (Judisch et al., 1990, quoted by Figge, Quack and Schäfgen, 1991, p. 28). In conjunction with an occupational training certificate, dynamic muscular strength is the factor determining wage group differentials. Despite the associated nervous and psychological strain, the monotony, and the lack of movement etc., typical women's work such as static overhaul and maintenance and tasks requiring a high degree of sensitivity and precision of movement is classified as being easy and is covered by the bottom pay group (Drohsel, 1986 and Kurz-Scherf, 1986, quoted by Figge, Quack and Schäfgen, 1991, p. 28).

As far as the ex-German Democratic Republic is concerned, the under 600/700 DM wage group is represented to a much greater extent in spheres normally considered to be the preserve of women (trade, science, education, culture, health, housing, local affairs and finance), than in spheres with higher levels of male employment (industry and the building trades) (Figge, Quack and Schäfgen, 1991, p. 30).

It would seem that in connection with tedious jobs and spheres of activity less well protected by the unions there is a mechanism in Italy that tends to reward the thankless aspects of men's work and to undervalue women's (Altieri and Villa, 1991, p. 87).

In the Netherlands, about a quarter of the firms with upwards of twenty employees make use of job evaluation (Plantenga, 1991, pp. 48-9). Pay is no longer based on an individual's training and experience (the theory of human capital), but on an evaluation of his job. Job evaluation systems may adopt various roles in the explanation of pay differentials :

- an incorrect description of women's (and men's) jobs;
- the structure of job evaluation systems has an (indirectly) discriminatory effect for women;
- the implementation of job evaluation systems is not without its discri minatory aspects.

If a job is to be evaluated, an accurate description is required : what has not been described cannot be evaluated. Even though empirical observations on the subject are rare, there is a certain tendency to describe women's jobs as being less difficult. Thus, a 1988 study of some eight jobs held by women showed that the existing job descriptions were incomplete : the main duties were not fully listed and the degree of autonomy and responsibility were underestimated. But the principal weakness in the job descriptions was connected with the management aspect. Management was an important part of the duties of seven of the eight job holders investigated, yet management was only mentioned in three of the descriptions, and then only in general terms (De Bruijn, 1988, p. 79, quoted by Plantenga, 1991, p. 49).

The structure of job evaluation systems may be discriminatory to the extent that the aspects upon which jobs are evaluated do not wholly fit the types of jobs generally held by women. It thus appears from a recent case study on job evaluation in a large multinational that the 'employment conditions' aspect attracts more points when a job is based in a workshop or a laboratory. This means that a mechanic moving around the premises obtains more points because of this than a telephone operator who works in a concentrated state in one spot surrounded by various other people (who talk all the time). The situation is the same with respect to the 'physical stress' aspect, which seems to have little to do with the kinds of jobs generally done by women. Mental stress is not included under this heading any more than simple and repetitive tasks like typing (Veldman, 1989, pp. 26-7, quoted by Plantenga, 1991, p. 49). On a more general level it can be safely said that job evaluation systems afford little or nothing in the way of opportunities to express human qualities such as human contact and the various degrees of responsibility that such contact includes. In other words, while such systems are relatively generous in the credit that they allocate to responsibilities with a bearing on tangible assets and money, they are avaricious when it comes to people, particularly children (De Bruijn, 1991, p. 28, quoted by Plantenga, 1991, p. 49).

Hitherto, most research has been into the possible discriminatory uses of existing job evaluation systems. In a piece of research carried out in 1988 and 1989 the Loontechnische Dienst looked at the application of job evaluation systems in the private and public sectors. They came to the conclusion that there could be no thought of discrimination in the application of such systems (Loontechnische Dienst, 1988b and 1989, quoted by Plantenga, 1991, p. 49).

3.3 The influence of premia systems

It seems that, in most European countries, the more frequent payment of premia to men than to women explains certain aspects of pay differentials. In Germany,

> ...among manual workers and employees, men's uninterrupted working life serves as criterion for payments rewarding long service and experience. Time devoted to the up-bringing of children despite a lack of child care facilities is not taken into considera-tion in the granting of premia for seniority (Kurz-Scherf, 1986, quoted by Figge, Quack and Schäfgen, 1991, p. 29). The 'family premia' paid to male employees up to the end of the seventies have been replaced by neutral premia which are more usually granted to men. This is why certain critics plead for the inclusion of the whole reward package in the analysis of wage differentials; in addition to the wage/flat rate aspect, this analysis should also include payments in kind, fringe benefits, attendance allow-ances, corporate pension schemes and other special payments (Pfarr and Bertelsmann, 1981, quoted by Figge, Quack and Schäfgen, 1991, p. 29).

Knudsen (1991, pp. 69-70) states that men are more skilled than women at obtaining premia and that, amongst these, there are some which are disguised as head of family allowances.

The United Kingdom experts provide a clear demonstration of how premia systems lead to gender discrimination even if they appear to be 'legitimate' as, for example, overtime pay.

> If overtime pay is included in gross weekly earnings for manual workers, the gender differential only showed a slight improvement from 61 per cent in 1983 to 62 per cent in 1990, but if overtime is taken out, there is clearer evidence of a narrowing of the gap in gross weekly earnings from 67 per cent in 1983 to 70 per cent in 1990. Thus, overtime working has served to offset in part the gains made in equalizing basic pay over the eighties. The effect of overtime working is much lower for non-manual workers, but nevertheless the effect on the gender gap for all workers of including or not including overtime pay, remains significant; with overtime, women's earnings are only 68 per cent of men's, but without overtime they rise to 73 per cent (Humphries and Rubery, 1991, pp. 57-8).

> Differences in pay which can be accounted for by differences in hours worked are large-ly regarded as 'legitimate', that is not evidence of direct discrimination, provided of course that women have access to the same overtime opportunities and the same over-time premia. In practice, these latter conditions are not always met as even if overtime premia are available in principle to female full-timers, many firms in the service sector use part-timers to cover extra hours, thereby avoiding the payment of premia (Horrel and Rubery, 1991, quoted by Humphries and Rubery , 1991, p. 58).

Overtime is not the only factor leading to differences in make up of pay : other factors include payment by results, bonuses, merit pay and shift and other allowances for unsocial or special conditions. A recent survey in Britain (Industrial Relations Services / Equal Opportunities Commission, 1991, quoted by Humphries and Rubery, 1991, p. 58) into payment structures has concluded that although men and women tend to be eligible in principle for these additional pay elements, women are less likely in practice to be in receipt of these pay supplements. This disparity arises for several reasons : firstly, firms tend to use different pay structures for different groups of workers, and these pay structures tend to be either male dominated or female dominated; female dominated pay structures are less likely to have provision for additional payments. The share of both these premia in total pay is decreasing although there is still a strong bias in favour of male workers, particularly manual workers. Moreover, the survey revealed considerable evidence that these differences in eligibility for bonus could lead to major distortions in the relative earnings structure of occupations.

The United Kingdom experts show that, in local government in Britain, jobs where performance premia are available are held mainly by men.

> The same study found that male manual workers' maximum pay in local authorities often exceeded maximum pay for female non-manual workers graded considerably higher and with higher basic pay levels.
>
> Other methods than bonus are increasingly being used to reward individuals for either performance or merit; these are various forms of merit or performance pay systems. Again, these payment systems are found most often in managerial grades so that more men are eligible to receive these payments, although merit pay is also common in clerical grades dominated by women. Where these payments are made, they are done on an individualized and essentially secretive basis which reopens the opportunity for sex bias in pay.
>
> These types of payment systems are undoubtedly leading to a widening of differentials as they apply mainly to higher grade or managerial staff. While the overall effect may be to widen the gender differential, these payment systems are also likely to be implicated in the increasing polarization of earnings among women workers as in certain areas such as the health service some female dominated grades are for the first time to be included in the performance pay system. Another important element in the reward package where there is unequal access for female employees is that of fringe benefits. Various surveys suggest that the main divergence in eligibility for fringe benefits is not between male and female full-time workers, but between full and part-time workers. Indeed, it is in the provision of fringe benefits that there is most evidence of 'direct discrimination' in the rewards for part-timers : there is relatively little evidence of part-timers being a paid lower hourly wage rate for the same job as full-timers, but they are often not eligible for the same benefits including sick pay, pensions, maternity leave and even holiday with pay as full-timers. The United Kingdom employers' opposition to the part-time directive would require equalization of benefits reflects the low provision currently made for part-timers in the United Kingdom (Humphries and Rubery, 1991, pp. 58-60).

4. Conclusions

Women's average pay is lower than men's in all the countries - even in those where women's activity rates are very close to men's (Denmark and the ex-German Democratic Republic).

One explanation is the different gender employment distribution. Women are concentrated in the worst paid sectors and in jobs at the lower end of the hierarchy.

In addition, women's work is often undervalued. Characterized though it is by nervous and psychological strain, monotony and a lack of movement etc., typical women's work such as static overhaul and maintenance and tasks requiring a high degree of sensitivity and precision of movement remains badly paid.

The 'conditions of employment' aspect is better remunerated when a job is based on a workshop or a laboratory rather than on an office. Generally speaking, human qualities attract little in the way of financial reward. Responsibilities with a bearing on tangible assets and money are generally better remunerated than responsibilities relating to people, particularly children.

In addition, premia are more frequently paid to men than to women. This may seem legitimate in the case of overtime, but as Humphries and Rubery (1991) remark, in the services with their predominantly female workforce employers prefer to use part-timers, so avoiding the payment of premia. In addition, premia are paid on an individualized and essentially secretive basis, so reopening the opportunity for sex bias in pay.

The development of women's relative pay in the1980s shows that gender differentials are not on the decline. Measures aiming at reducing pay discrimination seem to have been relegated to a secondary role by measures taken in the interest of wage moderation. In the United Kingdom, the decentralization of wage determination plays a major part in the widening of pay differentials.

Appendix 4.1 : Relative earnings of women by NACE sectors (woman's earnings / man's earnings, in percentage)

See NACE codes p. 127.

	Belgium		Denmark		Germany		Greece		France	
	1989	1989-83	1989	1989-83	1989	1989-83	1989	1989-83	1989	1989-83
Gross hourly earnings of manual workers										
10. Energy and water										
	69.9	-	-	-	77.9	3.1	-	-	-	-
11.	-	-	-	-	-	-	-	-	-	-
12.	-	-	-	-	-	-	-	-	-	-
13.	-	-	-	-	-	-	-	-	-	-
14.	-	-	97.9	2.2	71.7	0.9	60.6	-16.5	-	-
15.	-	-	-	-	76.5	-5.2	-	-	-	-
16.	-	-	-	-	74.7	1.3	-	-	-	-
17.	-	-	-	-	83.7	6.7	-	-	-	-
20. Mineral extraction, chemicals										
21.	-	-	-	-	-	-	-	-	-	-
22.	72.7	-5.5	87.6	-0.4	75.5	-1.4	60.3	-5.9	-	-
23.	-	-	90.5	-1.6	72.0	-0.6	-	-	-	-
24.	72.8	-5.0	94.7	-1.7	74.3	0.3	79.2	2.3	79.5	1.8
25.	71.2	2.2	86.8	-9.6	73.8	-0.1	77.7	7.3	77.4	-1.2
26.[a]	70.6	-1.5	-	-	79.4	-0.4	69.8	6.0	76.8	-
30. Metal manufacture, engineering										
	86.7	3.8	85.7	-1.7	75.7	-	-	-	83.9	1.2
31.	83.0	-0.8	87.6	-0.4	75.7	0.9	84.4	2.2	82.9	1.5
32.	81.4	-2.7	85.2	-2.7	76.6	-0.3	84.7	-12.5	81.6	0.4
33.	82.6	-	85.2	-2.7	82.5	1.7	-	-	91.6	-3.3
34.	87.4	4.2	85.2	-2.7	77.2	0.1	94.4	7.3	86.1	1.3
35.	87.8	4.0	78.5	8.8	81.0	-0.5	89.0	0.3	86.4	1.4
36.	81.5	2.6	78.6	3.9	75.6	0.8	62.4	-3.8	78.5	3.0
37.	86.4	10.2	90.5	-1.6	79.2	-0.6	86.5	-1.7	81.1	-2.3
40. Other manufacturing industries										
41/42.	85.2	2.1	87.3	0.7	70.5	0.8	88.1	8.3	80.9	1.1
43.	77.9	-0.1	85.1	-1.6	80.7	0.2	85.3	4.1	86.3	-0.9
44.[b]	86.0	-3.2	92.9	1.4	74.7	1.4	85.9	8.8	89.3	2.0
45.	81.5	0.6	94.1	-0.9	80.0	1.6	81.2	0.3	86.7	1.0
46.	88.9	-1.2	84.1	-6.8	79.7	1.1	-	15.4	87.1	0.4
47.	74.0	1.8	77.0	-1.9	71.2	2.3	80.2	2.6	75.5	2.3
48.	78.3	-2.3	97.1	1.4	74.8	-0.3	75.4	0.9	83.6	1.7
49.	91.9	7.4	90.5	-1.6	77.6	2.3	95.3	6.7	88.6	2.1
50. Building and civil engineering [c]										
	-	-	-	-	-	-	-	-	-	-
A. All industries [d]										
	75.1	1.2	-	-	73.4	1.2	-	-	80.8	0.7

a. Belgium 1989-82; b. Greece 1989-82; c. Germany 1989-82; d. NACE 1-5.

	Belgium		Denmark		Germany		Greece		France	
	1989	1989-83	1989	1989-83	1989	1989-83	1989	1989-83	1989	1989-83

B. All industries [a]

	Belgium		Denmark		Germany		Greece		France	
	75.1	1.2	84.5	-1.0	73.6	1.1	-	-	80.8	0.7

C. Mining and quarrying [b]

	Belgium		Denmark		Germany		Greece		France	
	72.9	72.9	90.5	-1.6	65.2	1.4	-	-	-	-

D. Manufacturing industries [c]

	Belgium		Denmark		Germany		Greece		France	
	74.0	0.6	84.5	-1.0	72.8	0.2	79.7	5.1	79.5	1.1

Gross monthly earnings of non-manual workers

	Belgium		Denmark		Germany		Greece		France	
10. Energy and water										
	76.6	-0.1	-	-	69.4	-0.2	-	-	-	-
11.	89.3	25.9	-	-	67.2	2.1	69.0	-2.5	-	-
12.	67.7	6.8	-	-	-	-	-	-	-	-
13.	-	-	-	-	65.9	2.8	-	-	-	-
14.	59.7	-1.3	-	-	69.6	-0.7	64.0	4.3	-	-
15.	-	-	-	-	67.8	-0.7	-	-	-	-
16.	80.1	-2.5	-	-	71.1	-0.3	-	-	-	-
17.	69.2	-0.5	-	-	71.8	-1.5	-	-	-	-
20. Mineral extraction, chemicals										
21.	-	-	-	-	72.4	5.7	-	-	65.9	-0.4
22.	65.6	1.0	-	-	66.2	-1.3	60.2	-0.7	71.8	4.8
23.	68.8	3.8	-	-	67.8	2.5	-	-	60.3	2.8
24.	64.8	-1.3	-	-	67.1	-	70.0	3.0	62.8	2.4
25.	65.3	0.8	-	-	72.3	0.4	63.8	5.6	65.6	2.8
26.	69.7	10.7	-	-	70.5	-1.5	69.2	6.9	-	-
30. Metal manufacture, engineering										
	66.4	2.2	-	-	65.3	-0.4	-	-	65.7	2.5
31.	67.7	3.4	-	-	64.3	-0.6	63.9	4.4	63.1	2.6
32.	63.5	0.8	-	-	63.7	-1.3	64.6	0.2	63.1	1.4
33.	-	-	-	-	68.9	2.5	-	-	67.9	-0.2
34.	69.5	3.6	-	-	66.7	-0.5	66.2	-2.9	64.9	0.9
35.	65.7	-0.1	-	-	67.3	1.3	69.4	6.8	70.5	3.3
36.	69.0	5.9	-	-	66.0	-0.5	63.4	4.6	71.2	3.2
37.	62.8		-	-	68.6	0.4	71.3	-3.4	62.0	3.0
40. Other manufacturing industries										
41/42	66.6	2.4	-	-	69.7	0.5	72.6	6.9	59.8	1.4
43.	62.4	0.5	-	-	69.5	0.8	70.8	6.8	61.2	1.0
44.	69.1	1.1	-	-	63.4	-0.9	64.4	9.7	62.9	2.8
45.	-	-	-	-	70.3	0.2	69.7	-0.6	64.9	3.1
46.	69.4	1.1	-	-	63.2	0.5	66.8	5.5	64.2	3.3
47.	63.9	1.3	-	-	65.6	0.4	69.8	4.8	63.0	2.4
48.	66.0	1.3	-	-	66.0	-0.8	67.8	4.5	66.3	2.5
49.	61.8	6.2	-	-	67.7	-0.4	62.1	-13.5	65.4	4.3
50. Building and civil engineering										
	64.6	3.2	-	-	61.4	-0.1	-	-	63.0	1.6

a. NACE 1-5 excepted for 16 and 17; b. NACE 11, 13, 21, 23; c. NACE 12, 14, 15, 22, 24, 26, 3, 4.

	Belgium		Denmark		Germany		Greece		France	
	1989	1989-83	1989	1989-83	1989	1989-83	1989	1989-83	1989	1989-83
A. All industries [a]										
	64.5	1.9	-	-	66.5	0.0	-	-	64.9	2.6
B. All industries [b]										
	64.5	2.0	-	-	66.3	0.0	-	-	64.9	2.6
C. Mining and quarrying [c]										
	84.3	18.8	-	-	66.5	2.1	-	-	-	-
D. Manufacturing industries [d]										
	64.1	1.4	-	-	66.5	-0.2	66.2	6.2	65.0	2.6
E. Wholesale and retail distribution										
	62.6	-1.4	-	-	65.8	2.1	-	-	-	-
F. Wholesale distribution										
	65.4	0.0	-	-	69.0	1.0	-	-	65.2	4.3
G. Retail distribution										
	71.9	-0.1	-	-	68.0	2.2	75.5	6.0	68.5	4.7
H. Credit institutions										
	78.4	1.6	-	-	76.7	-0.7	80.1	-	75.2	2.1
I. Insurance (except social institutions)										
	75.4	2.0	-	-	78.4	1.3	76.5	-	70.0	1.6

a. NACE 1-5; b. NACE 1-5 excepted for 16 and 17; c. NACE 11, 13, 21, 23; d. NACE 12, 14, 15, 22, 24, 26, 3, 4.

	Ireland		Italy	Luxembourg		Netherlands		Portugal	United Kingdom	
	1989	1989-83	1983	1989	1989-83	1989	1989-83	1989	1989	1989-83
Gross hourly earnings of manual workers										
10. Energy and water										
	-	-	-	99.2	42.7	-	-	-	-	-
11.	-	-	-	-	-	-	-	-	-	-
12.	-	-	-	-	-	-	-	-	-	-
13.	-	-	81.9	-	-	-	-	-	-	-
14.	-	-	80.6	-	-	-	-	88.2	-	-
15.	-	-	-	-	-	-	-	-	-	-
16.	-	-	93.2	99.5	43.1	-	-	74.3	68.2	-6.0
17.	-	-	90.9	-	-	-	-	91.4	-	-
20. Mineral extraction, chemicals										
21.	-	-	-	-	-	-	-	-	-	-
22.	-	-	84.0	73.0	2.7	-	-	64.5	61.3	-3.3
23.	-	-	90.1	-	-	-	-	81.4	-	-
24.	73.3	-2.1	93.0	80.5	-4.9	-	-	78.6	69.8	0.8
25.	63.0	-2.3	89.1	63.7	-9.8	-	-	76.6	70.1	0.3
26.	-	-	90.7	-	-	-	-	49.7	68.8	1.6
30. Metal manufacture, engineering										
	77.6	-	-	63.6	-3.7	82.4	-0.4	86.8	73.5	-2.1
31.	76.3	4.4	90.3	74.6	-0.6	-	-	83.2	71.2	-1.4
32.	80.9	8.2	90.7	69.9	-2.4	-	-	86.9	77.8	0.1

continued

	Ireland		Italy	Luxembourg		Netherlands		Portugal	United Kingdom	
	1989	1989-83	1983	1989	1989-83	1989	1989-83	1989	1989	1989-83
33.	84.3	6.0	92.6	-	-	-	-	-	73.7	-6.4
34.	77.7	2.4	91.9	-	-	83.3	-2.1	84.9	75.6	-1.8
35.	-	-	92.1	-	-	-	-	69.7	83.7	4.1
36.	-	-	90.7	-	-	-	-	51.1	79.1	2.0
37.	69.7	-3.3	90.4	69.7	-	-	-	76.9	80.7	2.5
40. Other manufacturing industries										
41/42.[a]	74.7	-4.6	92.0	71.2	2.0	74.8	-3.0	66.8	76.5	-1.0
43.	57.6	-7.5	91.5	-	-	-	-	78.3	74.3	0.4
44.	76.4	16.8	92.2	-	-	-	-	81.3	72.7	-1.7
45.[a]	73.8	1.5	95.9	36.8	-8.5	-	-	80.4	75.6	2.8
46.	83.3	2.6	93.7	74.8	4.5	-	-	79.1	84.0	2.3
47.	64.9	0.9	82.7	65.0	2.8	-	-	66.4	67.9	2.3
48.[a]	70.8	5.7	88.5	67.7	-3.5	-	-	75.7	67.0	-2.1
49.	72.5	-9.9	90.4	-	-	-	-	71.1	71.5	-2.1
50. Building and civil engineering										
	-	-	90.2	73.9	5.0	-	-	82.6	63.9	2.7
A. All industries [b]										
	68.6	-	85.9	63.2	-2.0	75.9	1.9	69.4	68.8	0.0
B. All industries [c]										
	69.2	0.9	87.2	63.4	-1.8	75.9	1.9	72.1	69.5	0.0
C. Mining and quarrying [d]										
	-	-	88.5	-	-	-	-	81.4	-	-
D. Manufacturing industries [e]										
	69.3	0.8	87.6	58.5	-2.9	75.4	-0.4	68.0	68.3	-0.2
Gross monthly earnings of non-manual workers										
10. Energy and water										
	-	-	-	-	-	-	-	-	55.6	-
11.	-	-	-	-	-	-	-	-	-	-
12.	-	-	81.7	-	-	-	-	-	-	-
13.	-	-	71.2	-	-	-	-	-	-	-
14.	-	-	79.9	-	-	-	-	73.8	-	-
15.	-	-	-	-	-	-	-	-	-	-
16.	-	-	84.2	74.3	-1.2	-	-	7.7	56.5	-1.4
17.	-	-	86.5	66.4	-1.8	-	-	91.4	-	-
20. Mineral extraction, chemicals										
21.	-	-	71.3	-	-	-	-	-	-	-
22.	-	-	73.8	62.5	0.4	-	-	70.0	56.8	1.9
23.	-	-	72.7	63.6	11.0	-	-	72.9	-	-
24.	-	-	71.2	58.4	3.7	-	-	78.1	-	-
25.	-	-	72.2	55.0	1.1	-	-	73.6	57.2	1.8
26.	-	-	76.8	-	-	-	-	66.8	-	-

a. Ireland 1989-82; b. NACE 1-5; c. NACE 1-5 excepted for 16 and 17; d. NACE 11, 13, 21, 23; e. NACE 12, 14, 15, 22, 24, 26, 3, 4.

	Ireland		Italy	Luxembourg		Netherlands		Portugal	United Kingdom	
	1989	1989-83	1983	1989	1989-83	1989	1989-83	1989	1989	1989-83
30. Metal manufacture, engineering										
	-	-	-	56.6	2.4	64.2	3.6	72.8	54.9	1.5
31.	-	-	70.1	54.5	0.1	-	-	75.2	-	-
32.	-	-	68.9	58.6	3.9	-	-	72.1	52.0	0.9
33.	-	-	70.8	-	-	-	-	-	-	-
34.	-	-	72.6	-	-	-	-	71.1	54.7	0.5
35.	-	-	71.4	-	-	-	-	82.5	55.3	1.1
36.	-	-	77.2	-	-	-	-	72.1	-	-
37.	-	-	69.2	-	-	-	-	59.1	-	-
40. Other manufacturing industries										
41/42	-	-	70.7	53.1	2.4	61.5	1.6	71.7	52.9	-2.8
43.	-	-	70.5	-	-	-	-	72.6	-	-
44.	-	-	70.3	-	-	-	-	82.0	-	-
45. [a]	-	-	71.1	49.4	13.9	-	-	71.7	-	-
46. [a]	-	-	72.9	54.8	-6.0	-	-	92.7	-	-
47.	-	-	69.3	60.5	1.1	69.3	5.6	71.6	58.0	-1.4
48.	-	-	68.1	54.4	2.4	-	-	68.6	52.0	-0.4
49.	-	-	64.8	-	-	-	-	51.5	-	-
50. Building and civil engineering										
	-	-	71.3	62.5	6.7	-	-	80.5	53.7	3.2
A. All industries [b]										
	-	-	71.6	55.6	1.6	64.5	3.4	73.4	55.2	0.4
B. All industries [c]										
	-	-	71.1	54.9	1.9	63.8	3.3	73.7	54.9	0.6
C. Mining and quarrying [d]										
	-	-	74.3	63.6	11.0	-	-	72.9	-	-
D. Manufacturing industries [e]										
	-	-	71.1	55.0	1.1	63.7	2.8	71.5	55.1	0.1
E. Wholesale and retail distribution										
	-	-	-	57.1	1.7	59.7	1.8	-	55.2	0.3
F. Wholesale distribution										
	-	-	-	63.1	1.6	64.0	1.9	-	54.5	-0.3
G. Retail distribution										
	-	-	-	60.5	4.1	65.7	1.6	-	59.3	0.4
H. Credit institutions										
	-	-	-	68.6	3.1	60.6	0.9	86.0	52.6	-2.7
I. Insurance (except social institutions)										
	-	-	-	65.6	-0.3	67.2	1.0	-	52.6	1.2

a. United Kingdom 1989-82; b. NACE 1-5; c. NACE 1-5 excepted for 16 and 17; d. NACE 11, 13, 21, 23; e. NACE 12, 14, 15, 22, 24, 26, 3, 4.

Source : Eurostat (1990c), *Earnings, Industry and Services.*
Calculations DULBEA.

00	Agriculture, hunting, forestry and fishing

01	Agriculture and hunting
02	Forestry
03	Fishing

10	Energy and water

11	Extraction and briquetting of solid fuels
12	Coke ovens
13	Extraction of petroleum and natural gas
14	Mineral oil refining
15	Nuclear fuels industry
16	Production and distribution of electricity, gas, steam and hot water
17	Water supply : collection, purification and distribution of water

20	Extraction and processing of non-energy producing minerals and derived products; chemical industry

21	Extraction and preparation of metalliferous ores
22	Production and preliminary processing of metals
23	Extraction of minerals other than metalliferous and energy producing minerals; peat extraction
24	Manufacture of non-metallic mineral products
25	Chemical industry
26	Manmade fibres industry

30	Metal manufacture; mechanical, electrical and instrument engineering

31	Manufacture of metal articles (except for mechanical, electrical and instrument engineering and vehicles)
32	Mechanical engineering
33	Manufacture of office machinery and data processing machinery
34	Electrical engineering
35	Manufacture of motor vehicles and of motor vehicle parts and accessories
36	Manufacture of other means of transport
37	Instrument engineering

40	Other manufacturing industries

41/42	Food, drink and tobacco industry
43	Textile industry
44	Leather and leather goods industry (except footwear and clothing)
45	Footwear and clothing industry
46	Timber and wooden furniture industries
47	Manufacture of paper and paper products; printing and publishing
48	Processing of rubber and plastics
49	Other manufacturing industries

50	Building and civil engineering
60	Distributive trades, hotels, catering, repairs

61	Wholesale distribution (except dealing in scrap and waste materials)
62	Dealing in scrap and waste materials
63	Agents
64/65	Retail distribution
66	Hotels and catering
67	Repair of consumer goods and vehicles

70	Transport and communication

71	Railways
72	Other land transport (urban transport, road transport, etc.)
73	Inland water transport
74	Sea transport and coastal shipping
75	Air transport
76	Supporting services to transport
77	Travel agents, freight brokers and other agents facilitating the transport of passengers or goods; storage and warehousing
79	Communication

80	Banking and finance, insurance, business services, renting

81	Banking and finance
82	Insurance except for compulsory social insurance
83	Activities auxiliary to banking, finance and insurance; real estate transactions (except letting of real estate by the owner), business services
84	Renting, leasing and hiring of movables
85	Letting of real estate by the owner

90	Other services

91	Public administration, national defence and compulsory social security
92	Sanitary services and administration of cemeteries
93	Education
94	Research and development
95	Medical and other health services, veterinary services
96	Other services provided to the general public
97	Recreational services and other cultural services
98	Personal services
9A	Domestic services
9B	Diplomatic representation, international organizations and allied armed forces

5 The unemployment of women

With a very few exceptions, such as the United Kingdom, the relatively high growth in employment in the Community at the end of the 1980s did not lead to comparable decreases in unemployment rates. The increase in the population of working age and the rise in participation rates contributed to the growth of employment more than the decrease in the number of unemployed. The growing proportion of long-term unemployment and the relative decrease in young people's unemployment tend to show that employers preferred to make use of young persons entering the labour market rather than the unemployed. These developments are different for men and for women.

In this chapter we will highlight trends according to age, region and levels of educational attainment. Having done this, we will then examine the reasons for unemployment, its length and its compensation. In the last section we will consider unemployment in the five new German *Länder*.

1. Inequalities as to the extent and development of unemployment [1]

With the exception of the United Kingdom, women's unemployment rates are consistently higher than men's, and the relationship between the two brings out differences that are sometimes considerable. In 1983, the rate of female unemployment for the whole of the European Community was 11.8 per cent, or 1.38 times the rate for men, while in 1990 it was 11.2 per cent, or 1.7 times that for men. In the majority of cases, the lack of parity at the beginning of the period was worse in 1990.

In Portugal, women's and men's unemployment rates decreased considerably between 1983 and 1989.

As Figge, Quack and Schäfgen (1991, p. 32) point out :

> Unlike men's, women's unemployment does not rise and fall according to the state of the economic crisis, but undergoes a more than proportional increase in the phase following cyclical depression. These anticyclical variations can be explained by the fact that few women are employed in sectors very sensitive to cyclical recession, but congregate in the services sector, which is only affected by cyclical developments after the event.

In fact, an examination of the 1983-89 European Community unemployment rates for men and women confirms a certain phase displacement in their development (see figure 5.1 and table 5.1). Whereas the men's rate began to decline with effect from 1986, the women's remained at 13 per cent from 1985 to 1987 and showed no signs of dipping before 1988, i.e. two years after the men's. Moreover, not only do movements in women's unemployment rates lag behind men's, but they are smaller. These two reasons explain the increase observed in unemployment rate differentials.

A classification of the countries into three groups according to the sizes of their 1989 unemployment rate differentials gives Greece, Belgium, Italy, Portugal and Luxembourg as the five countries with the biggest disparities and women's unemployment rates more than double the men's. The second group includes Spain, the Netherlands, France and Germany and is made up of those countries whose unemployment differentials are slightly above the European average. Lastly, in Denmark, Ireland and, of course, the United Kingdom, the disparity in unemployment rates is significantly lower than in the Community as a whole.

It will be seen that this classification does not correspond to a grouping of the countries according to the extent of their aggregate unemployment rates. Ireland and Spain, for example, have very high unemployment rates, but whereas in Ireland men and women experience an equal degree of difficulty, in Spain male unemployment is high, but women's is practically double. A horizontal comparison across various of the countries does not seem to indicate that the higher a country's unemployment rate, the worse women's position is in relation to their male counterparts'.

These women's unemployment rates can also be considered in the light of their demographic weight taken in conjunction with the greater or lesser extent of their participation in the active population. Whereas in 1983 the ratio of men to women in the active population in the European Community was 0.61, in 1989 it was 0.67. The weight of women in the active population is increasing. Around the European average there are contrasting situations like Denmark, where the ratio has stabilized itself at 0.85, and Ireland, with a ratio slightly over half of the Danish one.

Table 5.2 situates each of the countries in terms of the three variables mentioned above (aggregate unemployment rates, the differential between the unemployment rates for the two sexes, and the weight of the active female population). The table should be read as follows : vertically, the countries are arranged according to the degree of disparity between the male and female unemployment rates : the higher a country is on the list, the worse the female unemployment rate is in relation to the male. Horizontally, there is a twofold

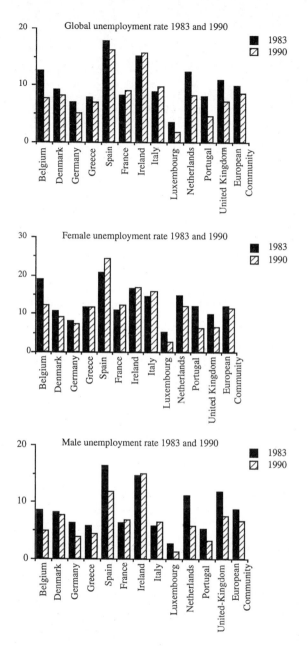

Figure 5.1   Evolution of unemployment rates between 1983 and 1990

Source : Eurostat (1991b), *Unemployment*.

Table 5.1

Unemployment rates, yearly averages (in per cent)

	Europe 12	Belgium	Denmark	Germany	Greece *	Spain	France	Ireland	Italy	Luxembourg	Netherlands	Portugal	United Kingdom
Total men/women													
1983	9.9	12.5	9.3	6.9	7.8	17.8	8.2	15.2	8.8	3.5	12.4	8.0	11.1
1984	10.7	12.5	8.7	7.1	8.1	20.6	9.8	16.8	9.3	3.1	12.3	8.7	11.3
1985	10.8	11.6	7.2	7.1	7.8	21.8	10.2	18.2	9.6	2.9	10.5	8.8	11.4
1986	10.7	11.6	5.6	6.3	7.4	21.0	10.3	18.2	10.5	2.6	10.2	8.2	11.4
1987	10.3	11.4	5.7	6.2	7.4	20.4	10.4	18.1	10.2	2.6	10.0	6.8	10.4
1988	9.7	10.0	6.5	6.1	7.7	19.3	9.9	17.6	10.8	2.1	9.3	5.6	8.5
1989	8.9	8.5	7.7	5.5	7.5	17.1	9.4	17.0	10.7	1.8	8.7	5.0	7.0
1990	8.5	7.7	8.2	5.1	7.0	16.1	9.1	15.6	9.8	1.7	8.1	4.6	7.1
Men													
1983	8.7	8.6	8.2	6.2	5.8	16.5	6.3	14.6	5.8	2.6	11.1	5.3	11.9
1984	9.4	8.4	7.4	6.1	6.0	19.4	7.9	16.3	6.2	2.4	11.0	6.5	11.9
1985	9.4	7.5	5.6	6.1	5.6	20.3	8.4	17.5	6.3	2.1	9.2	6.7	11.7
1986	9.2	7.4	4.0	5.2	5.1	19.2	8.5	17.5	7.1	1.8	8.4	6.4	11.8
1987	8.6	7.5	4.5	5.1	5.1	16.8	8.3	17.4	7.0	1.8	7.5	5.1	10.8
1988	7.8	6.7	5.5	4.9	4.9	15.0	7.7	17.0	7.2	1.5	7.2	3.9	8.7
1989	7.0	5.4	6.8	4.3	4.6	12.9	7.0	16.1	7.2	1.3	6.5	3.4	7.2
1990	6.6	4.9	7.7	3.9	4.3	11.9	6.9	15.0	6.5	1.2	5.8	3.2	7.4
Women													
1983	11.8	19.0	10.5	8.0	11.7	20.8	10.8	16.5	14.4	5.3	14.7	11.8	9.9
1984	12.7	19.3	10.2	8.6	12.1	23.3	12.3	18.0	15.2	4.4	14.9	11.9	10.6
1985	13.0	18.4	9.1	8.7	11.7	25.2	12.6	19.7	15.7	4.3	12.8	11.7	11.0
1986	13.0	18.5	7.4	8.1	11.6	25.2	12.8	19.9	16.7	4.0	13.4	10.9	11.0
1987	13.0	17.6	7.0	7.9	11.4	27.7	13.3	19.3	16.1	3.9	14.0	9.2	9.9
1988	12.6	15.2	7.6	7.9	12.5	27.5	12.8	18.9	17.0	3.1	12.8	7.9	8.3
1989	11.7	13.3	8.6	7.4	12.4	25.2	12.4	18.8	16.9	2.7	12.1	7.1	6.7
1990	11.2	12.1	8.9	7.0	11.7	24.1	12.0	16.8	15.7	2.5	11.9	6.4	6.6

* Spring.

Source : Eurostat (1990b and 1991b), *Unemployment.*

132

subdivision. Firstly, the left-hand column shows the countries whose aggregate unemployment rates are below the European level (8.9 per cent), while the right-hand column indicates those where they are higher; secondly, the first and third columns list the countries where women's weight in the active population is less than the European average, while the second and fourth columns show countries where it is more.

Table 5.2
Basic typology of unemployment rates (1990)

	Unemployment rates below 8.5 per cent		Unemployment rates above 8.5 per cent	
	Women's low weight in the active population	Women's significant weight in the active population	Women's low weight in the active population	Women's significant weight in the active population
Extremely high unemployment rate differential (women/men)	Greece Belgium Luxembourg	Portugal	Italy	
High unemployment rate differential (women/men)	Netherlands Germany		Spain	France
Low unemployment rate differential (women/men)		Denmark United Kingdom	Ireland	

No significant grouping of the countries can be ascertained using the three variables considered. If Luxembourg is discounted (as, indeed, it will be in the rest of this chapter), there are no more than two countries in any group sharing the same characteristics.

So, no link can be established between a high rate of unemployment and the extensive participation of women as part of the active population (this only occurs in France). Similarly - as we have already pointed out - there is an extreme lack of parity between male and female unemployment in a country where unemployment is serious (Italy), and one where it is less so (Greece).

2. Marked differences in terms of age, region and levels of educational attainment

2.1 Women's unemployment by age

Which are the worst affected age groups ? (see table 5.3). The under twenty-fives are affected by a consistently higher rate of unemployment than the active population taken as a whole. Young people - men as well as women - are victims of unemployment rates which, in certain cases, may be three or

133

Table 5.3
Unemployment rates by age groups

	Europe	Belgium	Denmark	Germany	Greece	Spain	France	Ireland	Italy	Netherlands	Portugal	United Kingdom
1983												
Total	9.9	11.7	9.7	6.4	7.8	17.8	7.9	14.8	8.7	11.9	8.0	11.1
Women												
14-24	24.5	28.9	19.8	11.1	29.8	44.4	23.9	19.0	35.3	19.1	24.4	17.5
25-49	-	15.5	8.7	7.1	9.3	-	7.5	15.6	8.6	12.4	-	8.3
50-64	-	9.1	6.6	4.8	(2.8)	-	6.4	9.4	3.3	6.4	-	4.6
Men												
14-24	21.4	19.3	18.1	10.2	17.0	41.4	16.0	23.4	24.1	23.0	13.8	22.4
25-49	-	6.3	7.7	5.1	5.1	-	4.2	13.2	2.7	9.3	-	9.5
50-64	-	6.0	6.4	4.3	3.2	-	5.1	8.8	1.7	6.5	-	9.2
1989												
Total	9.1	8.3	8.1	5.7	7.5	17.3	9.6	16.1	11.1	8.8	5.2	7.4
Women												
14-24	20.2	20.2	12.4	5.9	33.9	42.6	23.1	19.6	38.7	14.1	15.7	9.3
25-49	10.6	12.3	8.0	7.6	10.0	22.1	11.3	15.6	13.1	11.7	6.3	6.8
50-64	6.8	7.0	8.2	9.3	2.6	8.4	8.2	12.1	3.3	7.7	1.9	5.7
Men												
14-24	15.2	11.4	10.7	5.2	16.9	27.5	16.2	23.7	26.0	12.7	8.5	11.2
25-49	5.9	4.7	7.2	4.2	3.6	10.7	5.9	15.5	5.0	5.9	2.7	6.2
50-64	5.6	4.0	5.9	5.2	1.9	9.2	6.4	11.6	2.3	4.9	2.0	7.9

Sources : Eurostat (1983c), *Labour Force Survey*, and Eurostat (1990b), *Unemployment*.

134

even four times as high as the national rate (as is the case of young women in Italy and Greece, for example). Young men in Germany constitute the only exception, but in this case the classification of apprentices as part of the active population may have produced an artificially low unemployment figure for the young (Figge, Quack and Schäfgen, 1991, p. 33, note 19).

This point applies to 1983 as well as to 1989. However, it should be noted that between these two reference years there was a tendency towards a narrowing of the gap separating the relative situation of the younger generation with respect to the population as a whole.

If the ratio of the young persons' unemployment rate to the national unemployment rate is worked out for both men and women, what emerges in all the countries except Greece is a decrease in this ratio between 1983 and 1989.

As far as women under twenty-five are concerned, the relative unemployment situation is particularly bad in Greece (unemployment rate of 29.8 in 1989), Italy (unemployment rate of 35.3 in 1989) and Spain (unemployment rate of 44.4 in 1989), three countries that we have already quoted as having enormous male/female unemployment rate differentials. The countries where the differences are less pronounced are Germany, the United Kingdom and, particularly, Ireland.

If a comparison is made in terms of unemployment rates between position of women under twenty-five and the active female population as a whole, what emerges is that, relatively speaking, it is mainly young women in Greece, Italy, France, Spain and Portugal who are in a much more difficult position than women taken as a whole. The differentials are lower in the Netherlands, Germany and Ireland (the unemployment rate for young women recorded in 1989 in Germany was below the rate for women in general but, here again, the German figures must be viewed with caution). What is noteworthy is that, between 1983 and 1989, women's unemployment rate differentials across the various age groups tended downwards.

The same development emerges from an examination of the unemployment rates for men under twenty-five in relation to the national rates. In addition, whereas young women are the victims of extremely high unemployment rates due to their age, young men have unemployment rates that are consistently more divergent from the active male population than women do.

In summary, it can be concluded that, on the whole, women have higher unemployment rates than men. Apart from a few exceptions, the same result is obtained by major age group, namely that in each category, women are harder hit than men. For young women, the position is twice as difficult since age and sex militate against them on the labour market. However, age affects them less than it affects young men, and the positions of young men and women are in fact closer than those of men and women taken across all the age groups.

The proportionally greater drop in unemployment rates for the young (men as well as women) may have a number of causes. To begin with, there is demography. The arrival on the labour market of smaller numbers of individuals to replace the swarms of children born in the 1960s (i.e. the baby-boom years) has served to reduce the tension on this part of the market (Figge, Quack and Schäfgen, 1991, p. 33). Then, more extensive education has contributed to keeping off the market increasing numbers of under twenty-fives. As Altieri and Villa (1991, p. 94) note in speaking of central-northern

Italy, 'the reduced weight (in unemployment) of 14-19 year olds must inevitably be associated with the intensive academic training obtaining in that part of the country'.

Age distribution of the unemployed (see table 5.4). As the development of unemployment rates by age suggests, the overall trend is towards an ageing of the population of active, though unemployed, women. Whereas the absolute number of young unemployed women is not necessarily declining, [2] their relative weight decreased over the period 1983-89. This phenomenon has been observed in the case of both men and women.

No generalizable shift can be ascertained at the other end of the scale. In certain of the countries, steps taken to remove the older unemployed [3] from the active population have led to a reduction in the relative numbers of unemployed aged over fifty. This development is far from general, however, and in certain countries the opposite is taking place (Germany and Spain, for example). There is thus no 'recentring' of the unemployed into the 25-49 age group.

A comparison of the structures of male and female unemployment shows that, more often than not, the number of young unemployed women is greater than that of young unemployed men. Inversely, almost everywhere the weight of the unemployed over fifty is greater in the case of men than of women. This seems to be logical to the extent that women's activity rates are on the increase and older women do not have such high activity rates as younger women. Lastly, it should not be overlooked that the legal retirement age for men and women is different in a number of countries (Belgium and Germany, for example).

2.2   Women's unemployment by region [4]

Belgium (see table 5.5) (Meulders and Vander Stricht, 1991, p. 75). From this it can be seen that, in Belgium, the regional differences were greater for men than for women. Whereas the male unemployment rate was distinctly lower in Flanders, the rates for women were much closer to the rates of the other regions. It seems that the glowing health of the Flemish economy was of no benefit to the women in the region (in 1989, the women's unemployment rate was four times as high as the men's, while it was only twice as high in Wallonia and more or less equal in the Brussels region).

Whereas unemployment diminished in the three regions between 1983 and 1989, the situation deteriorated in Brussels for men and women alike.

Denmark (Knudsen, 1991, p. 71). In Denmark, the highest rates of unemployment were recorded in North Jutland and, more recently, in urban Copenhagen. The unemployment rates for women in these regions were well above the average for the whole country.

Germany (see table 5.6) (Figge, Quack and Schäfgen, 1991, p. 34). An analysis of female unemployment by *Länd* shows a differentiated North-South structure in which the northern regions had the higher unemployment rates (in the South, the Saar was the only exception, with a rate of 14.6 per cent).

It should be noted that men's and women's unemployment figures are not

136

Table 5.4

Unemployment by age groups (in per cent)

	Europe	Belgium	Denmark	Germany	Greece	Spain	France	Ireland	Italy	Netherlands	Portugal	United Kingdom
1983							a	a				a
Women	100.0	100.0	100.0	100.0	100.0	100.0	100.0	100.0	100.0	100.0	100.0	100.0
14-24	50.4	34.6	42.0	32.2	44.6	67.1	50.2	44.2	58.6	42.5	51.5	39.2
25-49	-	56.7	(39.0)	52.4	-	29.2	(38.0)	(45.2)	(31.0)	(52.2)	43.9	48.0
50-64	-	8.7	(19.0)	15.4	-	3.7	(11.8)	(10.6)	(10.4)	(5.3)	4.6	12.8
Men	100.0	100.0	100.0	100.0	100.0	100.0	100.0	100.0	100.0	100.0	100.0	100.0
14-24	42.6	27.5	34.0	26.6	35.1	44.7	40.1	25.9	64.2	33.6	61.6	37.0
25-49	-	49.4	(40.0)	53.7	-	41.4	(43.4)	(55.9)	(26.8)	(55.3)	26.7	44.4
50-64	-	23.1	(26.0)	19.7	-	13.9	(16.5)	(18.2)	(9.0)	(11.1)	11.7	18.6
1989	b				b		b	b				c
Women	100.0	100.0	100.0	100.0	100.0	100.0	100.0	100.0	100.0	100.0	100.0	100.0
14-24	39.1	21.5	30.0	18.1	32.3	45.5	34.6	34.9	48.0	31.6	43.3	30.4
25-49	-	71.5	(44.5)	56.7	-	49.2	(54.6)	(53.8)	(41.2)	(60.9)	50.2	56.3
50-64	-	7.0	(25.5)	25.2	-	5.3	(10.7)	(11.2)	(10.8)	(7.5)	6.5	13.3
Men	100.0	100.0	100.0	100.0	100.0	100.0	100.0	100.0	100.0	100.0	100.0	100.0
14-24	35.9	17.6	24.0	16.4	28.6	36.3	28.6	22.2	51.5	31.4	43.3	31.0
25-49	-	62.9	(52.0)	55.9	-	46.8	(55.5)	(58.7)	(38.1)	(57.8)	41.8	46.4
50-64	-	19.5	(24.0)	27.7	-	16.9	(15.9)	(19.0)	(10.4)	(10.8)	14.9	22.6

a. 1984; b. 1988; c. 1990.

Sources : Eurostat (1986a and 1989a), *Employment and Unemployment*, and Eurostat (1990b), *Unemployment*.

Remark : The figures in brackets have been estimated by ourselves.

137

Table 5.5
Unemployment rates by region in Belgium

	1983	1989
Women	19.0	13.3
Brussels region	13.3	14.0
Flanders	17.6	11.2
Wallonia	20.8	16.1
Men	8.6	5.4
Brussels region	12.0	13.2
Flanders	7.0	2.8
Wallonia	9.6	8.0

Source : Meulders and Vander Stricht (1991), p. 75.

Table 5.6
Unemployment rates by region in Germany

	1983	1989
Women		
Schleswig-Holstein	10.8	10.3
Hamburg	8.9	11.1
Lower Saxony	12.3	12.1
Bremen	12.9	15.6
North Rhine-Westphalia	12.2	12.2
Hesse	8.8	7.7
Rhineland Palatinate	9.9	9.1
Baden-Württemberg	7.1	5.6
Bavaria	9.0	7.2
Saar	14.6	12.6
(West) Berlin	9.7	9.7
Men		
Schleswig-Holstein	10.2	9.1
Hamburg	11.1	12.2
Lower Saxony	10.6	8.7
Bremen	13.2	13.8
North Rhine-Westphalia	9.6	8.6
Hesse	6.8	5.0
Rhineland Palatinate	7.7	5.6
Baden-Württemberg	5.1	3.7
Bavaria	7.5	4.7
Saar	10.4	10.2
(West) Berlin	11.0	9.8

Source : Figge, Quack and Schäfgen (1991), appendix, table V.9.

wholly identical from region to region; while over the two years the order of presentation by region remained largely the same for either sex, a greater difference emerges if all the years are compared. It seems that this can be explained by the differences in the structure of industry and the services in each *Länd*; by the resulting labour supply for women, by the demand for different jobs and by different demographic developments in each region.

Spain (see table 5.7) (Alcobendas Tirado, 1991, item 5.1.2). The unemployment rate for women was particularly high in regions such as Andalusia (36.7 per cent), Extramadura (38.2 per cent) and the Canary Islands (31.3 per cent), which feature among the bottom ten Community regions according to the European Community's 1987 synthetic index of regional disparities.

Italy (see table 5.8) (Altieri and Villa, 1991, p. 96). Generally speaking, what emerges are increased regional disparities in men's and women's unemployment. Whereas unemployment rates fell consistently in the centre and the North, the shift was in the opposite direction in the South.

However, there has been a tendency towards a *rapprochement* between men's and women's circumstances in the South; the situation there is dramatic, but the female unemployment rate is rising proportionately less than the male. In the North and centre, however, the decline is less pronounced for men than for women and, in 1989, the rate of female unemployment was almost three times as high as the male. Most unemployed Italian women live in the South, but the proportion of women is greater in the overall number of unemployed in the centre-North (64 per cent) than in the South (53 per cent). This is only one aspect of the more serious male unemployment in the South and, on a more general level, it serves as an exponent of the lack of demand for labour in the region (Altieri and Villa, 1991, p. 90).

If developments in the activity and unemployment rates in both the various age groups and the two regions are taken into consideration, what emerges is that in northern and central Italy women enter the labour market in greater numbers once they have passed the age of twenty and, even if their proportion is smaller than that of their male counterparts of the same age, they succeed for the most part in finding employment after the age of twenty-five. In the South of the country they enter the market in smaller numbers, but with every likelihood of remaining unemployed into their mature years (Altieri and Villa, 1991, pp. 95-6).

Greece (see table 5.9) (Cavouriaris, 1991a, p. 29). Between 1983 and 1989, unemployment in urban regions remained practically stationary. However its gender-based distribution changed significantly. In 1983, women represented 52.0 per cent of the unemployed and in 1989, they represented 62.5 per cent.

Between 1983 and 1989, in semi-urban regions, unemployment decreased by 3 per cent. But in 1983, women represented 51.1 per cent of the unemployed and in 1989, 59.8 per cent.

In rural regions, the fall in unemployment between the two dates was over 9 per cent, but in 1983 women's unemployment rose from 43.7 per cent of overall unemployment to 54.3 per cent.

The Netherlands (Plantenga, 1991, p. 57). Table 5.10 shows the highest unemployment rates to be in the North for men and women alike.

Inversely, the West is the least affected region. The three largest cities - Amsterdam, Rotterdam and The Hague - and the surrounding areas show higher unemployment rates, however. Unemployment is concentrated in the inner city areas, and particularly in certain districts and amongst certain ethnic minorities.

The United Kingdom (Humphries and Rubery, 1991, p. 67). Men's unemployment rates are always greater than women's rates (see table 5.11), (this

Table 5.7
Unemployment rates by region in Spain

	1983	1989
Women		
Galicia	12.58	14.14
Asturias	24.50	25.20
Cantabria	21.24	22.84
Basque country	31.95	30.54
Navarre	26.97	18.13
Rioja	25.23	12.13
Aragon	25.53	19.12
Madrid	24.31	17.59
Castille-Leon	25.52	26.73
Castille-La Mancha	20.21	23.52
Extremadura	28.21	38.21
Catalonia	26.97	20.68
Valencia	25.17	21.60
Balearic Islands	18.82	15.54
Andalusia	31.23	36.69
Murcia	23.89	26.13
Canary Islands	35.43	31.34
Men		
Galicia	14.96	10.34
Asturias	15.99	12.45
Cantabria	15.51	13.11
Basque country	21.42	13.33
Navarre	14.06	7.02
Rioja	13.36	5.14
Aragon	13.17	4.20
Madrid	18.62	9.58
Castille-Leon	15.29	9.85
Castille-La Mancha	14.28	8.92
Extremadura	28.69	19.69
Catalonia	18.98	7.79
Valencia	17.48	9.74
Balearic Islands	11.07	6.85
Andalusia	29.90	20.64
Murcia	16.03	9.98
Canary Islands	23.66	21.98

Source : Alcobendas Tirado (1991), item V-1-2.

Table 5.8
Unemployment rates by region in Italy

	1983	1989
Women		
Centre-North	13.18	12.26
South	23.39	33.16
Men		
Centre-North	5.21	4.34
South	9.41	14.99

Source : Altieri and Villa (1991), appendix, table 5.4.

Table 5.9
Unemployment rates by region in Greece

	1983	1989
Women		
Urban regions	17.6	16.9
Semi-urban regions	10.3	10.4
Rural regions	3.4	4.1
Men		
Urban regions	7.7	5.8
Semi-urban regions	4.5	3.6
Rural regions	2.7	2.3

Source : Cavouriaris (1991), p. 29.

Table 5.10
Unemployment rates by region in the Netherlands

	1989	1991
Women	6%	5%
North	8%	7%
East	6%	5%
West	5%	5%
South	6%	5%
Men	6%	5%
North	8%	6%
East	8%	6%
West	6%	5%
South	5%	5%

Source : Plantenga (1991), p. 57.

Table 5.11
Unemployment rates by region in the United Kingdom

	1983	1989
Women	7.4	4.2
South-East	5.3	2.7
Greater London	5.5	3.4
East Anglia	6.0	2.7
South-West	6.9	3.3
West Midlands	9.1	4.7
East Midlands	6.9	3.9
Yorks and Humberside	8.0	4.8
North-West	8.9	5.4
North	9.9	6.1
Wales	9.2	4.8
Scotland	9.1	6.1
Northern Ireland	10.6	9.5
Men	12.5	7.9
South-East	9.0	4.9
Greater London	9.4	6.4
East Anglia	9.2	4.2
South-West	9.9	5.3
West Midlands	15.2	7.9
East Midlands	11.1	6.9
Yorks and Humberside	13.6	9.5
North-West	16.3	10.8
North	17.7	12.8
Wales	15.2	9.2
Scotland	14.4	11.8
Northern Ireland	18.6	18.2

Source : Humphries and Rubery (1991), appendix, table 5.2.

difference is probably accentuated by the methods used to record the un-employed even if the European Community's harmonized rates show lower women's rates too).

Apart from the problems inherent in the recruitment of the unemployed, women were less affected by the decline, at the beginning of the 1980s, of manufacturing industry with its heavy regional basis and, in comparison with men, their chances of finding employment improved in all the regions. However, the female labour supply did not increase as much in the regions in a state of decline as in the South; this might stem from women's feeling of discouragement at the idea of offering their labour in an unfavourable economic environment and might be a case of disguised unemployment and so enhance the statistics with reference to them. It should be noted that, firstly, if the employment rates are taken in absolute terms, the regional disparities are more pronounced for men than for women, and that, secondly, during the 1980s, there was a considerable contraction in the scatter of regional un-employment rates for men and women alike.

2.3 Women's unemployment by levels of qualification

The OECD's analysis in the *Employment Outlook* outline the correlation between unemployment and level of qualification :

> There would appear to be no theoretical basis for expecting any particular relationship between educational attainment and unemployment, because the ways in which educational attainment interacts with the factors determining employment prospects are often ambiguous. On the one hand, educational attainment is likely to enhance an individual's general position in the employment queue, making him or her more attractive to employers. Higher levels of educational attainment also may be associated with better labour market information and more effective job search techniques, thereby reducing the likelihood, or the duration, of unemployment. Furthermore, the segmented and dual labour market perspectives predict that those with less schooling will be caught in jobs characterized by frequent turnover, low wages, and high unemployment.
>
> On the other hand, consider an individual who has received advanced education for an occupation with specialized skills. Downturns in demand or excess supply, due to growth in training facilities and sluggishness in downward wage adjustments, can for such an occupation result in long periods of unemployment because the skills are sufficiently advanced and specialized that they do not transfer to other well paid occupations. In addition, the higher the level of education, the wider the range of salaries for which the individual might qualify. But a wider range of salaries suggests that job seekers may have a higher reservation wage, expecting larger potential pay-off to longer periods spent searching for jobs; these longer search periods may imply longer periods of 'search unemployment'.
>
> The balance of such factors will determine the actual relationship of educational attainment and unemployment in each economy (OECD, 1989, p. 58).

According to the OECD, this goes to prove the hypothesis that qualifications reduce the risk of unemployment (OECD, 1989, p. 58).

The OECD also remarks that 'the pay-off of higher levels of educational attainment in the form of reduced unemployment appears to differ by sex, being somewhat lower for women than for men'. Their analysis rests on a comparison across men and women of the relationship between unemployment rates in the case of economically active persons with a lower secondary education and those for persons with at least a university degree. This relationship [5] is greater for men (except in Belgium), and is particularly so in Germany, the Netherlands and Spain, where it is double what it is for women.

Let us now see how far the experts' analysis confirms the OECD survey.

In the Netherlands (Plantenga, 1991, p. 57; analysis based on 1990 data), the rate of unemployment amongst women with a primary education only is below that of men with the same educational level. However, unemployment is higher amongst women than amongst men for all other educational levels.

In the United Kingdom, for the two sexes there is a generally decreasing likelihood of unemployment with higher qualifications; the only exception seems to be that women with no qualifications are slightly less likely to be unemployed than women with lowest level qualifications (Humphries and Rubery, 1991, p. 68). Furthermore, in 1984, having high-level qualifications appeared to confer less of an advantage on women in the labour market;

unemployment rates were certainly lower than for those with low-level qualifications, but were approximately twice those for men with higher qualifications. By 1989, unemployment rates for those with a degree or other higher education had fallen to around 2 per cent for men and around 3 per cent for women (Humphries and Rubery, 1991, p. 69).

In Greece, we can compare the training rates of the unemployed with the training rates of the employed. Women without any training are less likely to be unemployed than men with the same level of training. But women with a lower secondary or an upper secondary education are more vulnerable than men in this category. The risk of unemployment is smaller for women with a higher education whatever the level, except in the case of post graduates (Cavouriaris, 1991a, annexes).

In Spain, the unemployment rate for women with vocational training is 31.64 per cent. Next come women with middle grade schooling, who have an unemployment rate of 30.53 per cent, and they are followed by women with a primary education, whose rate is 20.8 per cent; last of all there are women with a higher education, who have an unemployment rate of 19.78 per cent. For each of these levels the women's unemployment rate is twice the men's (Alcobendas Tirado, 1991 - 1990 data).

In Italy, 'the two extremes - unqualified women on the one hand, and university graduates on the other - always seem to have enjoyed a relative advantage in the context of unemployment rates' (Altieri and Villa, 1991, p. 99).

In the countries where the analysis was carried out by comparing the qualification levels of the male and female unemployed, what emerged was that, unlike female unemployment, male unemployment was more concentrated at the bottom end of the qualifications scale - in Luxembourg (Plasman and Plasman, 1991, p. 48) and Belgium (Meulders and Vander Stricht, 1991, pp. 78-9).

In Denmark, the surveys carried out by the Institute of Social Research (Maerkedahl, 1989, quoted by Knudsen, 1991, p. 74) show that in all age groups and at all levels of educational attainment the female unemployment rate is above the male apart from the 50-59 age group with short-term vocational training, where male unemployment is greater than female.

Figure 5.2 shows the result of a comparison by highest qualification obtained of the unemployment rates for sixty-six classes of training. For sixty-three of these classes, women's unemployment is greater than men's; the three exceptions are short-term health service training and courses in the humanities (translator/secretary, for example). The excessive degree of female unemployment shows huge variations. For certain levels of training the women's unemployment rate is more than 200 per cent higher than the men's. It is only for very few levels of training that the female unemployment rates are less than 50 per cent above the male, and among the unqualified female overunemployment is below that for many levels of training (Knudsen, 1991, p. 74).

In Ireland :

There are no complete data on the link between educational levels and unemployment in the Irish economy. A survey of school leavers carried out in 1990 for the Ministry of Labour looked at the economic status of 1989 school leavers with different qualification levels. The results showed that the higher a young person's qualifications

144

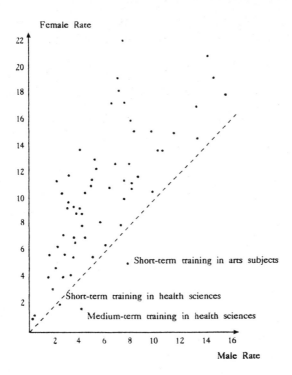

Figure 5.2   Unemployment rates for men and women with the same levels of
training - Sixty-six categories of training - 1986 in Denmark

Source : Reproduced from Maerkedahl, 1989, quoted by Knudsen, 1991, p.
75.

are, the more chance he/she has of finding a job. This model showed itself to be reli-
able for both boys and girls, although it was more pronounced in the case of the girls.
It also emphasized that job quality varied as a direct function of the level of educational attainment (Barry, 1991).

However, this same study showed that young women find it more difficult to
slot themselves into the labour market. Their rates of unemployment and
emigration - particularly in the case of the unqualified - are higher than those
of young men.

The experts' analysis seems to confirm the OECD's conclusions (except for
Ireland, for which the study is incomplete), which state that the advantage
conferred by qualifications is not so great in the case of women.

It must be remembered, however, that women's activity rates increase in
step with their levels of qualification (see chapter 1) and depend much more
on these than in the case of men. Poorly qualified women enter the labour

145

market much less frequently than women with degrees or diplomas. For men, employment is not an option and they enter the labour market willy-nilly.

An analysis of the employment rate (the proportion of the population in employment divided by the aggregate population) brings out a very marked relation with levels of training (Meulders and Vander Stricht, 1991, p. 19).

It must also be borne in mind that, firstly, 'the chances of finding a job or being unemployed depend not only on the levels of qualifications obtained, but also on the route followed (options and/or department) in order to obtain them, and that secondly, there are still some serious differences between men and women in this respect' (Plantenga, 1991, p. 57).

In Germany :

> It is principally those qualified in arts subjects - a field often chosen by women - who cannot find openings corresponding to their qualifications. On the other hand, women graduates from university level business and technical colleges often come from departments slanted towards jobs in the public service - the social services, for instance - and are thus particularly affected by cuts in staffing costs in this area (Krais and Trommer, 1988, quoted by Figge, Quack and Schäfgen, 1991, p. 35).

The Netherlands expert shows that, generally speaking, the likelihood of mobility in employment diverges sharply from the mean in the case of persons whose training is in fields often selected by girls :

> The likelihood of mobility in employment is defined in terms of the percentage of persons in any given category who come off the interim unemployment register after a year. Thus, the likelihood in the case of those with a primary education only or who have studied at the academy of fine arts is about 30 per cent below average. In the case of university drop-outs and graduates in sociocultural subjects, it is 10-15 per cent below. On the other hand, people with qualifications in agriculture, technology, economics/administration and (para)medical subjects have an above average likelihood of mobility of between 20 per cent and 40 per cent (Ministerie van Sociale Zaken en Werkgelegenheid, 1989, p. 21, quoted by Plantenga, 1991, p. 58).

3. Circumstances giving rise to unemployment; returns to the labour market and an end to temporary contracts

3.1 Women seeking a first job or looking for employment after a period of economic inactivity

In all the countries of the Community the number of unemployed women seeking a first job is greater than the number of unemployed men (except in Belgium in 1989; for the other years, the relation remains the same) (Meulders and Vander Stricht, 1991, p. 81). Generally speaking, however, the difference is not significant except in Spain, Greece and, to a lesser extent, Ireland, where the divergences are slightly larger. It seems that there is a significant number of older women in these countries who have never worked and who are looking for a first job.

In Spain, the situation is very significant for women in the 35-49 age group. In this group, 37,000 women were recorded as looking for a first job as opposed to 2,000 men (Alcobendas Tirado, 1991). According to the national data, 52,000 women are looking for a first job in Portugal (Chagas

Lopes, Ferreira and Perista, 1991, p. 33). In Ireland, 'a large percentage of women looking for a first job have been housewives, and this proportion increased between 1983 and 1989. This means that a larger number of women are trying to make the move from the domestic to the official economy' (Barry, 1991). In Italy, the number of men and women in search of a first job is particularly high. But the pre-search situation is different.

> In the case of men, 75 per cent of the job seekers have been involved in training, while the corresponding percentage of women is 45 per cent. Of the women, more than 50 per cent have been housewives. The most interesting point is that the percentage of women over twenty-five with a housewife's background is 73 per cent. It would thus seem that men follow a more linear course which has them academically engaged, then in the forces, and finally looking for a job. Women's initial entry into the world of work follows a more varied course with the fact of being a housewife preceding the rest (Altieri and Villa, 1991, pp. 102-3).

Another category of female job seeker with similar problems covers women looking for work after having interrupted their careers to remain at home. The M shaped age based activity rate configuration in Germany, the United Kingdom and the Netherlands suggests that such women are relatively numerous in these countries. Table 5.12 shows an increase in the numbers of unemployed women looking for work after periods of economic inactivity in Germany, France, Ireland and the Netherlands. They account for a particularly large proportion of the unemployed female population in the United Kingdom and the Netherlands. This point is confirmed in the German report through an analysis of the numbers of newly unemployed on the basis of statistics supplied by the federal employment agency. Thus, whereas two-thirds of the women registering as unemployed in May/June 1983 had previously been in paid employment, in May/June 1990 they accounted for no more than half of the women registered as unemployed. At the same time, the percentage of those registering after a career break or a period of economic inactivity rose from 23 per cent to 43 per cent. The growth of the latter two groups was mainly evident with respect to women in the 35-40 age group (Figge, Quack and Schäfgen, 1991, p. 37). Whereas surveys in Belgium have failed to identify an M shaped group configuration (Meulders and Vander Stricht, 1991, p. 5), they do show that many housewives want to reenter the labour market, and remain at home longer than they would like. A survey (Van Regenmortel and Vandeloo, 1990) shows that the women in question are relatively highly qualified (more than women unemployed on a long-term basis and women wishing to remain at home) and that their vocational background is on the positive side. These women are a boon for the labour market. It is only very recently that governments have understood this and that steps have been taken in the various countries of the Community to facilitate these women's return to the labour market (see Chapter 6).

In the United Kingdom there has been an increase in the number of women entering unemployment from economic inactivity, accounting for 38 per cent of the unemployed in 1984, 46 per cent in 1989 and 60 per cent of unemployed married women (Humphries and Rubery, 1991, p. 69).

Table 5.12
Distribution of unemployed

	Europe 12	Europe 10		Belgium		Denmark		Germany		Greece		Spain	
	1989	1983	1989	1983	1989	1983	1989	1983	1989	1983	1989	1983	1989
Males													
Seeking after loss/leaving job	59.0	22.1	56.2	65.1	68.3	-	80.2	65.1	72.7	62.0	47.7	-	71.6
Seeking first job	21.3	21.6	20.8	17.3	19.9	-	(2.5)	17.3	6.2	25.9	43.0	-	23.3
Seeking work after inactivity	19.0	9.2	22.1	17.1	11.7	-	17.3	17.1	20.1	12.2	9.3	-	5.1
Not stated on group	0.7	47.2	0.9	-	-	-	-	-	(0.9)	-	-	-	-
Males from 14 to 24 years													
Seeking after loss/leaving job	34.8	13.7	32.3	39.9	33.7	-	65.2	-	53.8	30.4	18.9	-	44.6
Seeking first job	47.3	44.8	46.7	43.0	59.5	-	(8.4)	31.4	23.2	54.3	73.2	-	49.5
Seeking work after inactivity	16.9	8.1	19.7	16.2	-	-	26.3	-	20.3	(15.2)	(7.9)	-	6.0
Not stated on group	1.0	33.4	1.3	-	-	-	-	68.6	(2.7)	-	-	-	-
Females													
Seeking after loss/leaving job	38.9	18.3	36.9	53.6	67.0	-	77.1	53.6	57.3	29.8	23.0	-	49.0
Seeking first job	30.0	32.2	27.5	19.1	15.7	-	(3.4)	19.1	7.7	45.2	58.5	-	40.9
Seeking work after inactivity	30.5	17.0	35.0	26.8	17.2	-	18.5	26.8	34.7	25.0	18.5	-	10.1
Not stated on group	0.6	32.6	0.7	-	-	-	-	-	-	-	-	-	-
Females from 14 to 24 years													
Seeking after loss/leaving job	27.8	15.4	25.5	39.0	40.0	-	55.2	-	50.4	23.4	14.8	-	35.9
Seeking first job	54.7	52.1	53.4	42.3	51.0	-	(12.1)	42.9	29.1	63.3	79.9	-	60.0
Seeking work after inactivity	16.8	9.4	20.2	17.8	(8.5)	-	30.2	-	20.0	13.3	5.4	-	4.2
Not stated on group	0.7	23.1	0.9	-	-	-	-	57.1	-	-	-	-	-

148

	France		Ireland		Italy		Luxembourg		Netherlands		Portugal		United Kingdom	
	1983	1989	1983	1989	1983	1989	1983	1989	1983	1989	1983	1989	1983	1989
Males														
Seeking after loss/leaving job	64.5	69.1	72.7	77.5	9.3	15.0	68.3	(61.5)	73.6	56.7	-	38.0	-	66.3
Seeking first job	13.9	7.4	14.9	13.4	61.0	59.6	(22.2)	-	17.1	16.6	-	22.5	13.8	8.1
Seeking work after inactivity	19.4	21.3	12.1	8.6	29.2	24.6	-	-	8.1	26.4	-	39.5	-	25.1
Not stated on group	2.2	2.1	-	-	(0.4)	0.8	-	-	1.2	-	-	-	86.2	(0.4)
Males from 14 to 24 years														
Seeking after loss/leaving job	46.1	51.3	53.4	49.1	4.1	5.9	-	-	-	29.3	-	26.0	-	47.7
Seeking first job	32.7	22.3	37.9	43.1	79.3	80.6	-	-	-	38.0	-	45.3	33.3	23.6
Seeking work after inactivity	18.3	23.4	(7.9)	-	16.2	12.8	-	-	-	32.2	-	28.7	-	27.6
Not stated on group	2.8	3.1	-	-	-	(0.6)	-	-	-	-	-	-	66.7	(1.0)
Females														
Seeking after loss/leaving job	52.8	56.0	34.4	37.5	4.8	6.6	(32.8)	(39.4)	34.4	23.9	-	25.7	-	34.2
Seeking first job	19.4	12.5	23.7	19.1	65.7	65.4	(39.2)	-	27.1	17.7	-	29.1	17.8	8.8
Seeking work after inactivity	26.1	29.5	41.6	42.9	29.0	27.6	(27.8)	-	37.8	58.2	-	44.7	-	57.0
Not stated on group	1.7	2.0	-	-	(0.4)	(0.4)	-	-	-	-	-	-	82.2	-
Females from 14 to 24 years														
Seeking after loss/leaving job	46.1	50.3	37.6	41.3	4.1	4.1	(54.0)	-	-	24.1	-	20.5	-	31.2
Seeking first job	37.9	27.5	44.9	43.8	80.2	83.0	-	-	-	42.7	-	44.5	36.6	24.4
Seeking work after inactivity	13.9	19.3	16.8	(13.8)	15.3	12.6	-	-	-	33.2	-	34.6	-	44.5
Not stated on group	2.1	2.9	-	-	-	-	-	-	-	-	-	-	63.4	-

Source : Eurostat (1983c and 1989c), *Labour Force Survey.*

3.2 Women who have lost their jobs

Altieri and Villa (1991, p. 106) recall that

> ... unemployment may be an incident in the life of someone with a penchant for more or less regular and stable employment (and consequently a passing phase), a state in which a worker finds himself because of the precarious nature of his activity (agricultural day workers, for example) or a more or less permanent condition for young people who have not yet succeeded in finding their way into the structures of employment.

In Italy (Altieri and Villa, 1991, p. 106), women are much more subject than men to recurrent periods of unemployment due to the temporary nature of their jobs (the proportion of women registered as unemployed due to the ending of temporary jobs is 62 per cent, as opposed to 48 per cent for men). In Belgium (Meulders and Vander Stricht, 1991, p. 91) and Luxembourg (Plasman and Plasman, 1991, p. 49), the proportion of women unemployed due to the ending of temporary jobs is also greater for women than for men. In the United Kingdom and Ireland, the proportion of women who have given up work for personal reasons is considerable and is rising.

In the countries for which information is available (Belgium, the United Kingdom, Italy, Luxembourg and Portugal) there is an increase in the numbers of unemployed - particularly women - due to the ending of temporary jobs and a decline in the numbers of unemployed as the result of dismissal or redundancy. In Portugal, the percentage of women unemployed due to the ending of temporary jobs reached 34 per cent for the final year considered (1989).

4 . Length of unemployment

4.1 Situation

Women are affected more than men by long-term unemployment (in excess of two years) in the majority of the countries of the Community.

Not only is the unemployment rate higher for women than for men, but women remain unemployed for longer periods except in Germany, Ireland and the Netherlands (table 5.13). However, Figge, Quack and Schäfgen (1991, p. 38) point out that 'discouragement seems to drive many women unemployed for over a year to give up signing on at their local employment offices or to withdraw altogether from the labour market'.

Barry (1991) explains the smaller proportion of women among the long-term unemployed in terms of women's low level of participation in the Irish labour force potential and also as due to the fact that there is little to encourage them to register as unemployed.

Of all the countries, the United Kingdom stands out thanks to a lower unemployment rate and the smaller number of women, as opposed to men, among the long-term unemployed.

Generally speaking, older rather than younger workers are affected by long-term unemployment.

Table 5.13
Percentage of long-term unemployed and unemployment rates by gender

	Percentage of long-term unemployed among the unemployed	
Unemployment rate	Higher for women	Higher for men
Higher for women	France, Italy, Belgium, Netherlands, Portugal, Denmark, Greece, Spain	Germany, Ireland, Netherlands
Higher for men		United Kingdom

Source : Based on the data given in Appendix 5.1; where no details are given, the position was the same in 1983 and 1989.

In most of the cotries, young people are more likely to find themselves unemployed but to remain so for a shorter period. On the one hand, this may be due to the fact that since they are young, they are less likely to have been economically active for long and on the other, to a possible employers' preference for a younger workforce (see table 5.14).

Table 5.14
Age groups containing the greatest percentage of long-term unemployed

14-24	Italy (men and women, 1989 *)
25-49	Denmark (women, 1983), Greece (men and women, 1983, women, 1989), Spain (women, 1989), Italy (men and women, 1983, women, 1989 *)
50 and over	Belgium, Netherlands, Denmark (men and women, 1989), Germany, France, Ireland, Greece (men, 1989), Portugal, United Kingdom

* Parity.

Source : Based on the data given in Appendix 5.1; where no data are given, the position was the same in 1983 and 1989.

None of this is valid for Italy, where young people's (14-24 age group) share in long-term unemployment (more than one year) is greater than the older generation's.

Altieri and Villa (1991, p. 107) emphasize that 'generally speaking, unemployment in Italy is of a highly exclusive nature (Altieri and Meghnagi, 1986, quoted by Altieri and Villa, 1991, p. 107) to the extent that people who have not had much opportunity to enter employment in the past are more likely to remain out in the cold'.

4.2 Developments

The predominant trend is towards an increase in long-term unemployment in parallel with a fall in the unemployment rate; exceptions are France, Ireland and Italy, where the unemployment rate is increasing, and, in the case of women, Denmark and the United Kingdom, where the unemployment rate and the numbers of long-term unemployed are declining (see table 5.15).

Table 5.15
Percentage of long-term unemployed and unemployment rates

	Percentage of long-term unemployed (in excess of two years)	
Unemployment rate	Rise	Fall
Rise	France, Ireland, Italy	
Fall	Belgium, Germany, Greece, Netherlands, United Kingdom (men)	Denmark, United Kingdom (women)

Source : Based on data given in Appendix 5.1.

The increase in the proportion of long-term unemployed can be explained by the fact that the market sorts out and selects job seekers according to the 'last come, first served' principle. Thus, the cyclical improvement has favoured the most recent job seekers, with the long-term unemployed remaining at the end of the queue. This means that they sag even deeper into unemployment : the more they wait, the more they will be obliged to (Meulders and Vander Stricht, 1991, p. 92).

5. Unemployment compensation : lower for women than for men

In 1989, the overall percentage of unemployed in the European Community drawing benefits was 30 per cent (see table 5.16). The differences between the countries are significant, for both women and men. In the Mediterranean countries (Greece, Italy, Spain and Portugal), very few of the unemployed draw benefits. France and the Netherlands fall between these two extremes.

Roughly speaking, unemployment benefits fall into two major categories. The first is insurance related and generally associated with the payment of contributions over a certain period which, when unemployment occurs, entitle a worker to draw benefits. The second is aid related; it is not paid out on the basis of past contributions, but is usually subject to a means test involving the claimant and his household and is more often lower. The two systems exist in most of the countries (OECD, 1991a, pp. 199-200).

As table 5.16 shows, the numbers of women entitled to one or another of these forms of assistance is consistently lower than the numbers of men (26 per cent of women as opposed to 34 per cent of men for the European Community). In fact, the conditions associated with benefit payments are often a source of indirect discrimination between unemployed men and women.

In the case of unemployment benefits (the insurance principle), women, who have had more career breaks than their male counterparts and who occupy a larger proportion of part-time jobs, find it difficult to fulfil the conditions relating to the period over which contributions are due (Figge, Quack and Schäfgen, 1991, p. 39) (however, in certain countries such as the Netherlands (Plantenga, 1991, p. 62), the period of employment necessary

Table 5.16
Percentage of unemployed people receiving unemployment benefits or allowances

	Europe*	Belgium	Denmark	Germany	Greece	Spain	France	Ireland	Italy	Nether-lands	Portugal	United Kingdom
1983												
Total	50.6	81.4	68.1	59.0	6.5	-	43.5	62.4	-	65.3	-	78.1
Women	37.3	80.3	66.7	47.4	(3.3)	-	39.6	35.0	-	40.7	-	57.4
Men	62.2	82.6	69.4	68.8	9.7	-	48.4	76.1	-	81.2	-	89.5
1989												
Total	30.1	88.2	84.1	61.9	4.8	22.8	42.6	70.2	17.0	43.3	9.8	-
Women	26.5	88.9	84.1	53.6	3.6	14.6	38.8	42.4	16.7	27.5	8.8	-
Men	34.0	87.1	84.0	70.9	6.6	31.2	47.7	84.5	17.3	60.5	11.3	-

* Europe 10.

Source : Eurostat (1983c and 1989c), *Labour Force Survey.*

for the granting of benefits includes child-rearing years). In addition we have already seen that, to a much greater extent than in the case of men, unemployed women are young women under twenty-five, many of whom have had no work experience.

As far as unemployment related national assistance is concerned (the aid principle), the means test often has negative repercussions for married women dependent on their husband's income. So women, who already have higher unemployment rates than men, are doubly penalized because they are less frequently entitled to benefits than their male counterparts. This is particularly so in Germany, the Netherlands, Spain and France. On the other hand, Belgium and Denmark are characterized by greater numbers of unemployed drawing benefits which are virtually the same for men and women.

6. Women's unemployment in the five new *Länder* (Figge, Quack and Schäfgen, 1991, pp. 40-3)

So far, we have not looked at unemployment in the former ex-German Democratic Republic, which has been united with Germany since October 1990. The lack of comparable data and the particular nature of the East German case justify a special section covering female unemployment in the five new *Länder*.

Whereas under the planned command economy the ex-German Democratic Republic was characterized by a shortage of labour and a zero or virtually zero unemployment rate (between 1 per cent and 2 per cent in the final years due to the effects of rationalization) (Stiftung, 1985, quoted by Figge, Quack and Shäfgen, 1991, pp. 40-3), note that since reunification,

> ... with the introduction of the DM (...) and the collapse of economic relations with eastern Europe, enterprises in the ex-German Democratic Republic immediately found themselves plunged into the world market and, because of their underdeveloped productivity, have not been able to sell their products while covering their costs. The result has been a gigantic economic collapse which, since the beginning of 1990, has gradually led to part-time work and total unemployment.

The extent of this unemployment, the novelty of the phenomenon and the lack of experience on the part of the labour organizations explain the lack of statistics on the structure of the unemployment. However, it is possible to present the principal features of the phenomenon.

It is thus justifiable to assume that this

> ... unemployment goes back almost exclusively to dismissals due to rationalization and closures, and that there are no long-term unemployed because unemployment only appeared in 1990 (...). As far as women are concerned, trends are already discernible that show that, all things considered, women are worse hit by unemployment (their percentage among the unemployed has been rising steadily) and their return to working life is not being made easy (Figge, Quack and Schäfgen, 1991, p. 41).

It seems that in enterprises undergoing rationalization, redundancies mainly affect departments with a high proportion of female staff (administration, social services and research and development).

In addition, women are included much less frequently than men in long-term training and retraining programmes, and this may well make it more difficult for them to pick up the reins again and so lead to long-term unemployment.

The steps taken by the communist authorities to allow women access to work are no longer valid. Whether they took the form of obligations placed upon personnel managers or the financing of child care infrastructure, these dispositions no longer exist in the ex-German Democratic Republic. The mass unemployment which is developing and affecting women proportionally more than men may well be greatly resented by the latter, who have internalized this aspect of socialist society and therefore believe employment to be indispensable (Figge, Quack and Schäfgen, 1991, p. 42).

As far as unemployment benefits are concerned, whereas federal law has been applied in the five new *Länder* since reunification, the granting and payment of benefits is proceeding with a great deal of difficulty because of congestion in local employment offices and the enormous number of claims submitted.

7. Conclusions

Except for the United Kingdom, women's unemployment rates are consistently higher than men's, and in most of the countries these differences increased between 1983 and 1989, where they generally affect all age groups.

It seems that no link can be established between the disparities between women's and men's unemployment, general unemployment levels and women's activity rates.

Whereas, on the one hand, there is a tendency for these differences to diminish, on the other, the situation remains particularly critical for the under twenty-fives in certain countries where the age of unemployed women is on the increase.

Regional disparities reveal a duality within the female labour market itself; it seems that there are differences between the various regions of one and the same country.

The advantage conferred by education in relation to the risk of unemployment is smaller for women than for men.

It is becoming increasingly more frequent for women to quote the ending of a period of fixed term employment as a reason for the unemployment. Another expanding group is that made up of women returning to the labour market after bringing up their families.

In most countries of the Community, long-term unemployment affects women more than men and the proportion of long-term unemployment in total unemployment is increasing.

Finally, even if women are overrepresented on the unemployment scene, they nevertheless benefit from much less in the way of substitute incomes; this inequality is explained on the one hand by the irregularity of their careers and their large representation in atypical forms of employment, and on the other by married women's dependence on their husbands' incomes.

As far as the five new German *Länder* are concerned these seems to be a real danger that the liberalization of the labour market will be parally to the emergence of the same inequalities on the unemployment front.

Notes

1. The data used for this section are taken from Eurostat (1990b and 1991b, *Unemployment*, no. 12, topic 3 series B). The International Labour Office's definition of unemployment has been adopted, and the results given here derive from an evaluation on the basis of labour force survey data. It must be emphasized that the methods used to record the unemployed and the presentation of the statistics include subjective elements which are not neutral in the analysis of discrimination.
2. In Spain, for example, there has been practically no change. See Alcobendas Tirado, 1991, item 5.1.1.
3. In Belgium, for example, precise measures have been adopted leading to greater possibilities of early retirement. In addition, certain changes in the definition of unemployed persons over fifty have made it possible to exclude them artificially from the statistics (see Meulders and Vander Stricht, 1991, p. 74).
4. In this section we simply repeat the information contained in the national reports. Problems of country-to-country comparability do arise (i.e. definitions of the unemployed, sources, etc.), but the major interest of this section lies in the analysis of interregional discrepancies in the same country. Few comparability problems arise here.
5. Calculated for Belgium, Germany, Greece, Italy, the Netherlands, Spain and the United Kingdom.

Appendix 5.1 : Distribution of unemployed job seekers following the duration of search

	Europe 12	Europe 10		Belgium		Denmark	
	1989	1983	1989	1983	1989	1983	1989
Males							
Unemployment rates							
Total	7.3	7.7	6.7	8.1	5.3	9.2	7.5
14-24 years	15.2	18.4	13.8	19.3	11.4	18.1	10.7
Duration of search in percentage of unemployed							
6 months and more	69.8	69.7	69.9	81.1	84.5	53.4	43.9
12 months and more	53.7	47.2	53.9	60.0	74.5	27.3	21.4
24 months and more	36.8	23.9	37.3	34.9	62.2	10.6	7.6
Percentage of unemployed for more than 12 months							
14-24 years	45.2	41.1	43.9	46.4	50.7	15.8	(11.9)
25-49 years	55.1	49.8	55.3	65.6	81.3	32.8	23.5
50 years and more	66.5	55.8	69.4	72.0	85.0	36.0	(30.9)
Females							
Unemployment rates							
Total	12.0	10.7	10.8	17.8	13.0	10.4	8.9
14-24 years	20.2	21.1	17.4	28.9	20.2	19.8	12.4
Duration of search in percentage of unemployed							
6 months and more	72.6	70.6	70.4	86.2	88.9	65.3	52.8
12 months and more	55.3	46.0	52.3	70.3	76.9	37.4	27.7
24 months and more	36.1	23.0	33.1	49.3	63.2	14.2	10.7
Percentage of unemployed for more than 12 months							
14-24 years	53.3	42.3	49.2	53.1	61.1	27.2	(9.8)
25-49 years	55.8	47.9	52.6	79.8	81.7	43.1	32.3
50 years and more	60.4	56.3	61.0	87.0	87.9	41.9	43.3

	Germany		Greece		Spain	France	
	1983	1989	1983	1989	1989	1983	1989
Males							
Unemployment rates							
Total	5.8	4.5	5.8	4.6	13.1	6.1	7.3
14-24 years	10.2	5.2	17.0	16.9	27.5	16.0	16.2
Duration of search in percentage of unemployed							
6 months and more	65.8	68.1	51.3	63.1	70.4	62.8	64.2
12 months and more	40.7	52.3	24.6	42.2	53.5	39.4	45.9
24 months and more	16.7	35.2	8.3	18.9	36.2	17.6	29.7
Percentage of unemployed for more than 12 months							
14-24 years	29.7	26.5	20.3	36.4	50.2	26.3	26.1
25-49 years	44.0	50.2	27.2	46.3	54.9	39.8	48.0
50 years and more	49.6	74.1	(25.9)	48.6	57.0	67.4	71.5

continued

	Germany		Greece		Spain	France	
	1983	1989	1983	1989	1989	1983	1989

Females

Unemployment rates

	1983	1989	1983	1989	1989	1983	1989
Total	7.5	7.5	11.7	12.4	25.3	10.5	12.6
14-24 years	11.1	5.9	29.8	33.9	42.6	23.9	23.1

Duration of search in percentage of unemployed

	1983	1989	1983	1989	1989	1983	1989
6 months and more	63.7	65.5	69.2	79.9	81.8	70.7	70.4
12 months and more	37.7	46.0	44.6	58.7	67.3	44.9	49.8
24 months and more	14.2	27.4	16.9	30.4	48.7	20.9	28.2

Percentage of unemployed for more than 12 months

	1983	1989	1983	1989	1989	1983	1989
14-24 years	29.7	30.6	41.3	55.9	66.0	37.9	35.5
25-49 years	39.5	43.3	48.7	62.2	69.5	46.3	53.4
50 years and more	51.9	64.2	-	(49.5)	57.3	67.3	67.9

	Ireland		Italy		Luxembourg	
	1983	1989	1983	1989	1983	1989

Males

Unemployment rates

	1983	1989	1983	1989	1983	1989
Total	9.2	15.9	5.7	7.4	2.3	(1.1)
14-24 years	18.1	23.7	24.1	26.0	(5.5)	-

Duration of search in percentage of unemployed

	1983	1989	1983	1989	1983	1989
6 months and more	68.2	84.5	78.3	84.0	(60.6)	(68.8)
12 months and more	42.3	71.5	53.6	68.1	(36.8)	50.8
24 months and more	23.5	56.4	24.8	45.8	-	-

Percentage of unemployed for more than 12 months

	1983	1989	1983	1989	1983	1989
14-24 years	30.5	60.1	53.6	69.3	-	-
25-49 years	47.7	74.5	55.9	68.3	-	-
50 years and more	54.9	81.8	43.2	55.3	-	-

Females

Unemployment rates

	1983	1989	1983	1989	1983	1989
Total	10.4	16.5	14.4	17.4	5.0	(2.3)
14-24 years	19.8	19.6	35.3	38.7	(8.0)	-

Duration of search in percentage of unemployed

	1983	1989	1983	1989	1983	1989
6 months and more	54.6	75.8	83.2	86.4	(53.6)	(49.1)
12 months and more	24.8	57.4	58.4	71.7	(31.1)	-
24 months and more	14.6	35.6	31.7	49.9	-	-

Percentage of unemployed for more than 12 months

	1983	1989	1983	1989	1983	1989
14-24 years	22.5	49.5	57.5	72.0	-	-
25-49 years	25.9	61.9	61.6	72.5	-	-
50 years and more	-	(62.3)	32.1	50.4	-	-

continued

	Netherlands		Portugal	United Kingdom	
	1983	1989	1989	1983	1989
Males					
Unemployment rates					
Total	10.9	6.8	3.6	12.0	7.6
14-24 years	23.0	12.7	8.5	22.4	11.2
Duration of search in percentage of unemployed					
6 months and more	72.0	67.9	62.3	71.7	63.5
12 months and more	49.0	55.1	43.1	52.3	48.6
24 months and more	24.8	41.9	24.6	30.4	35.5
Percentage of unemployed for more than 12 months					
14-24 years	38.7	26.1	39.7	45.9	28.5
25-49 years	53.0	64.5	43.4	56.2	52.0
50 years and more	60.8	80.2	55.4	56.6	67.8
Females					
Unemployment rates					
Total	13.8	11.9	7.4	9.8	7.1
14-24 years	19.1	14.1	15.7	17.5	9.3
Duration of search in percentage of unemployed					
6 months and more	75.8	62.5	69.4	59.2	46.2
12 months and more	49.9	43.5	51.8	36.0	28.1
24 months and more	24.6	27.3	30.3	17.8	15.4
Percentage of unemployed for more than 12 months					
14-24 years	40.7	24.2	46.2	32.6	19.9
25-49 years	56.4	50.0	58.5	35.3	25.7
50 years and more	57.2	62.8	-	53.9	52.7

Source : Eurostat (1983c and 1989c), *Labour Force Survey.*

6 The ambiguous role of employment policies

The sudden increase in unemployment rates in 1974-75 caused all the European countries to devise and implement a series of initiatives designed to cope with imbalances on the labour market. Since then, employment policies have essentially consisted of initiatives designed to reduce unemployment and, because of this, they have rather overshadowed the traditional type of policy employed in the organization of the labour market. Two countries (Luxembourg and the United Kingdom) stand out for completely opposite reasons. In Luxembourg, the only worry concerning the imbalance between labour demand and labour supply is to ensure that there is an abundance of the latter. In the United Kingdom,

> ... the policy of the government has been to leave it to the market to provide jobs for the unemployed and the task of the government has been seen to be that of deregulating the labour market to allow people to price themselves back into work. To some extent the growth of low paid part-time work has been hailed as evidence of the success of the government's 'job creation' programme. Nigel Lawson when Chancellor of the Exchequer once argued that we needed to create 'no tech low wage' jobs to absorb the unemployed (Lawson, 1984, quoted by Humphries and Rubery, 1991, p. 73). Thus, the eighties saw a retreat from wage and job subsidies as a means of reducing unemployment; policies which encouraged firms to put workers onto short-time instead of declaring them redundant were ended; local authorities were restricted in their local development and job creation activities; and the only explicit job subsidy programme, the young workers scheme which operated in the mid-eighties, was aimed as much at cutting wages for young people (only firms which paid low wages to the young employees received the subsidy) as it was at reducing unemployment (Humphries and Rubery, 1991, pp. 73-4).

160

These employment policies - as many as they are varied - cover both macroeconomic and microeconomic aspects. A comprehensive catalogue and analysis of such policies would exceed the terms of reference of this survey. Our present task is twofold and takes in firstly the identification of provisions relating to women in the mass of general employment policies and the extent to which they have benefited from them and, secondly, the listing of policies with a specific bearing on female employment and the evaluation of their effectiveness. Thus, the only employment policies that will be looked at in this chapter are those for which information is available in the national monographs. We have opted for a typology which draws a distinction mainly between passive and active policies [1] as a means of facilitating a comparison between the policies adopted by the member states.

1. Women's poor representation in general employment policies

1.1 Passive policies

Policies covering early retirement and career breaks have certainly had the most widespread repercussions on labour supply. While the purpose of early retirement is evidently to reduce the numbers of registered unemployed by removing the older age groups from the labour market, career breaks have often been hailed as a potential way of assisting women to enter - and especially to re-enter - the labour market. Even if career breaks were not explicitly designed for women, available figures show that it is they who take career breaks and parenthood leave in the vast majority of cases.

The effect of parenthood leave is ambiguous. According to Bäcker et al. (1990, quoted by Quack, Figge and Schäfgen, 1991, p. 48), in Germany the switch from maternity to parenthood leave was intended to facilitate women's reintegration on the labour market by easing their return, yet only half the women took up the reins again after an eighteen-month break. The federal government's plan to extend parenthood leave to a maximum of three years could make the problem even worse.

One can also wonder to what extent these policies handicap the subsequent careers of their 'beneficiaries' by creating an increased vertical segregation which also affects their earnings.

It is hardly surprizing that the main 'beneficiaries' of early retirement are men since, in the majority of cases, it has been introduced in industrial sectors in difficulty. It obviously cannot be assumed that the underrepresentation of women in this category is the result of discrimination against the female element in the labour force. Whether for financial or for psychological reasons, early retirement is not always a positive experience, particularly for people in their early fifties.

1.2 Active policies

Three major classes of employment policy can be described as active, i.e. as initiatives which either provide direct or indirect encouragement to labour demand or aim at a better adequation between supply and demand. These three classes take in : employment grants, which involve not only direct job creation, but also different types of employment subsidies whether paid to employers or to employees; the reduction and allocation of working hours; and various training and requalification initiatives. Table 6.1 contains some figures on employment subsidies and training. In the case of general initiatives the percentages of women affected must be compared to the average unemployment rates for the groups for which the initiatives are intended.

The policies dealing with working arrangements show that governments have chosen to allocate available work to men and women on the basis of the former working full-time and the latter being encouraged to choose part-time work. The incentives take the form of premia when jobs are allocated or of extra unemployment benefits. One can only deplore the sexist effects of such an option, which has been preferred to a general policy of reducing working hours.

Training. Following OECD (1991b, p. 20) :

> The introduction of some form of 'training entitlement' could ensure a more even spread of further education and training opportunities. Training entitlements are consistent with lifelong learning. It can be argued that each individual has a right to a certain amount of education and training across the life cycle. This would enable those who received little initial education or vocational training - often middle aged and older women - to have a 'second chance' or to 'catch up' at some later point. It would also be instrumental in side stepping rigid eligibility criteria that have hitherto excluded women from opportunities for further learning. Entitlement models already exist in some OECD countries.

In the majority of cases training schemes are intended for lowly qualified workers or for workers whose qualifications and experience are out of date. However, during a brief period at the end of 1980s there was an insufficient supply of highly qualified labour in the United Kingdom and particular attention was consequently devoted to training schemes aiming at integrating inactive but highly qualified women on the labour market.

Horizontal segregation in employment - already discussed in general terms in Chapter 2 - once again emerges, this time in the context of training. Knudsen (1991) provides some figures (table 6.2) demonstrating that it still exists even though there has been a slight improvement. According to Humphries and Rubery (1991, p. 75), the traditional patterns of occupational segregation are strengthened rather than weakened by these training schemes. They undergo the twin influences of social conditioning and employer attitudes reinforced by government views that employers' views should prevail (Cockburn, 1987, quoted by Humphries and Rubery, 1991, p. 75). These training schemes are seen in a positive light, however, because they really do seem to facilitate the integration of those making use of them. The United Kingdom figures focus attention on a second area of occupational segregation, namely women's limited access to firms' internal training programmes.

In a number of countries training schemes are complemented by special arrangements for women so as to cause a break with stereotyped occupational choices.

The improvement observed in Denmark between 1983 and 1987 in the numbers of women participating in training resulted in part from the male

Table 6.1
Women's participation in employment policies

Specification	Country	Context	Specification	Arrangements for women	Women's participation	Reference years
Trainings	Germany	Law promoting employment	Vocational training	Existence of premia and subsidies granted to training organizations or female trainees; their purpose is to promote women's training with particular reference to typically male jobs	37 %	1989
			Redeployment		43 %	
			Beginners		32 %	
	France	Traineeships	Courses for 16-25 age group		62 %	
			Fonds national pour l'emploi / long term unemployed's courses (FNE/CLD)		62 %	
			Modular courses		69 %	
			Sandwich courses for returnees		65 %	
			Retraining courses		70 %	
			Updating courses		55 %	
			Fonds national pour l'emploi's courses for lone women	For women only	100 %	
			Conversion schemes		51 %	
	United Kingdom	Employment training			32 %	1987
		Youth training scheme			40 %	
	Netherlands		Centres for vocational practice and guidance		40 %	1988
			Vocational training centres		19 %	
			Set of regulations on training		43 %	

Table 6.1 continued

Specification	Country	Context	Specification	Arrangements for women	Women's participation	Reference years
	Nether-lands		Vocationally oriented training for adults		61 %	
	Denmark	Training for un-skilled workers	Temporary employment agencies		33 %	
				Male dominated occupations strategy	31 %	1987
	Ireland	National training and employment authority training schemes (CFAS)	Specific skills training		37 %	1990
			Skills foundation		43 %	
			Community workshops		47 %	
			Community youth training (CYTP)		15 %	
			Alternance		84 %	
			Community response		67 %	
			Enterprise		58 %	
			Apprenticeships		2 %	
	Italy	Employment cum training contracts		Young people and women with upper middle schooling	40 %	1987
Withdrawal from activity	France	Various arrangements			44 %	1989
	Belgium	Career breaks Early retirement			85 % 15 %	1989
Job subsidies	Germany	Law promoting employment	Subsidized pay when hard to place unemployed persons are recruited	Persons returning to the labour market after bringing up a child	32 % full-time 77 % part-time	

Country	Scheme type	Scheme	%	Year
France	Different types of assistance with job creation in commerce	Tax-free recruitement of the first employee	62 %	1989
		The setting up of an enterprise by an unemployed person	24 %	
		Article of apprenticeship	29 %	
		Training contracts leading to an occupational qualification	29 %	
		Vocational reorientation contracts	38 %	
		Work initiation courses (SIVP)	53 %	
		Returnees' contracts	44 %	
		Sandwich reintegration contracts	51 %	
	Different types of assistance with job creation outside commerce	Community work schemes (TUC)	67 %	
		Local integration programmes (PIL/AIG)	48 %	
		Local resettlement programmes for women (PLIF)	100%	
Belgium	Restrat schemes		57 %	1989
Netherlands	New worker scheme	Local authority youth employment schemes	70 %	
	New worker scheme	Youth employment project	40 %	1988
	New worker scheme	Scheme for the long-term unemployed	26 %	
Ireland		Enterprise	20 %	1990
		Teamwork	61 %	

Table 6.2
Women's rates for sectors where training is organized for unskilled workers
(Denmark 1983 and 1987)

	1983		1987	
	Women number	Women's rates in per cent	Women number	Women's rates in per cent
Clothing	2,678	99	3,631	92
Brewing	47	31	46	22
Building and civil engineering	933	7	758	6
Fishing	8	2	2	5
Floor coverings	109	36	69	19
Hotels and catering	976	81	898	73
Agriculture	762	17	786	18
Butchery	226	10	576	21
Transport	1,441	6	1,832	8
Metal	2,750	12	11,805	36
Plastics	9	5	101	18
Legal arbitration [a]	-	-	1,071	32
Cleaning	7,354	81	6,720	84
Stoneware, pottery and glass	165	32	98	39
Textiles [b]	700	74	-	-
Wood	156	14	560	35
Laundry	96	81	150	84
Others (in general)	63	14	825	38
Total	19,449	22	30,577	31

a. After 1984.
b. Some courses in 1983; listed under clothing after 1987.

Source : Volqvartz, 1989, quoted by Knudsen, 1991, p. 91.

dominated occupations strategies. In the Netherlands, women's vocational training centres have been set up at the instigation of the Netherlands trade union federation. They are mainly there to train women with low-level or out-dated training for occupations with an extremely low rate of female participation. Between 70 per cent and 80 per cent either obtain a job or continue their education. As part of its positive action programme the Irish national training and employment authority - which looks after Irish labour policy - has attempted to increase the number of women apprentices, traditionally few and far between in Ireland, but the programme's modest target (ninety such apprentices) has not been attained. The inclusion of women in training arrangements that orient them towards traditionally male occupations is another aspect of this programme. In Portugal, the employment authorities' share in training costs has been increased from 75 per cent to 100 per cent in cases where women offer themselves for training in traditionally male fields. The Spanish government has also adopted similar measures for the training of women in areas of employment where, traditionally, they are heavily underrepresented.

The various *Länder* of Germany also encourage the training of young women in typically male fields either through subsidies or through the launching of pilot schemes. However, Figge, Quack and Schäfgen (1991) emphasize that once a woman's training is complete it is her responsibility to find herself a suitable job.

Employment subsidies. The considerable number of schemes of this type involve either direct job creation by the public authorities or various subsidies and aids to recruitment. In this context equal opportunities policy operates around two main axes, i.e. the creation of jobs for certain target groups in the female workforce and extra subsidies when women are recruited.

Extra subsidies. In Denmark, women receive extra support under certain aid to employment schemes. In Portugal, these subsidies are 20 per cent above those generally granted under schemes fostering the creation and preservation of jobs in craft industry and providing assistance with the setting up of new businesses. In southern Italy the Italian authorities have attempted - with little success according to Altieri and Villa (1991, p. 122) - to encourage the recruitment of women to manufacturing industry by paying firms ex-post-facto subsidies in proportion to the length of the period of employment involved. The Netherlands opted for a different system, with 12 per cent of the funds devoted to job allocation being utilized for women returning to the labour market, but this arrangement disappeared with the regionalization of employment policy. What remains unchanged is that the level of mediation between women and regular employment must be at least equal to their percentage in the unemployment figures. This said, these new provisions could easily backfire since, at regional level, women are more often in a weaker position than men. Plantenga (1991) therefore suggests that there should be parity at the different levels of management in the regional employment offices as well as in the job placings that they carry out.

Aid to persons entering self-employment or setting up their own businesses can also be classified under the heading of active labour policy and bracketed together with employment subsidies. However, women are only affected to the extent that they belong to the groups so targeted, i.e. the long-term unemployed, workers undergoing redeployment and women returnees. These latter are sometimes seen as belonging to a special category and, in certain countries, benefit from job subsidies. Chagas Lopes, Ferreira and Perista (1991, p. 46) emphasize that the relative lack of success of self-employment policies has resulted in women returning to paid employment after trying their luck in self-employment or at the head of firms.

Target groups. Some arrangements for the provision of direct aid to employment include instructions and recommendations relating to certain clearly defined categories of women workers. This is so in the case of Italy and law no. 44/86 on young people's spirit of enterprise. Article I of this law makes explicit reference to initiatives fostered by cooperatives and companies with a mainly female composition. However, it does not seem that there are any explicit conditions or quotas attached to the granting of subsidies. Nor are there any figures available for these schemes. In Germany - and this includes the new *Länder* - persons returning to work after bringing up children are classified as a target group under schemes providing assistance with training and integration. Doubt has been expressed concerning the efficiency of the target group strategy, which only seems to function properly when it is backed up by coercion and supervision.

1.3 Women's place in general employment policies

The variable percentages that we have managed to collect show a general underrepresentation of women except in the case of some very special schemes. Apart from obstacles that could be described as traditional - occupational choices, for example - the conditions of eligibility for such schemes also constitute an impediment to women's participation. Barry (1991, p. 48) shows that eligibility is a real problem for unemployed women with children. The conditions of eligibility for certain key programmes form the greatest obstacle to women's taking part in government organized employment programmes. Eligibility is directly linked to formal registration as an unemployed person for clearly defined periods of between thirteen and fifty-two weeks. This criterion is not applicable to the school leavers' 'teamwork' programme. In cases where they have not recently lost their jobs or resigned, considerable numbers of women are given little incentive to 'sign on' if they are not actually prevented from doing so. This eliminates most women with children who have withdrawn from the labour market for a short period. The size of this obstacle and the need to overcome it are freely acknowledged by the national training and employment authority. The programme for social and economic progress recently agreed to and adopted by the various representative bodies also identifies this obstacle to women's participation in employment schemes. Even though certain of these training and reintegration policies may well be very necessary for the least privileged groups of women, these very women are prevented from benefiting from them.

This situation is not specifically Irish and the same obstacles are found in Germany.

> Women on social security are at a particular disadvantage since in the majority of cases they have no formal qualifications and/or are lone mothers. They cannot claim an allowance that would enable them to take part in redeployment schemes. The exception is a pilot scheme run in the Bremen employment office area. In this area steps have been taken in cooperation with local organizations to prepare women on social security for redeployment before redeployment actually takes place (Figge, Quack and Schäfgen, 1991, pp. 46-7).

The overall percentages at our disposal are unfortunately insufficient to provide a clear picture of the place occupied by women in general employment policies. With reference to training cum employment contracts the Italian report states that in the services sector these contracts have been of consistent benefit to the least qualified members of the female workforce. In 1989 women in Southern Italy only accounted for 8 per cent of these contracts even though it is agreed that they should receive preferential treatment. These points confirm what we emphasized in Chapter 2, i.e. the idea of the occupational segmentation of the female labour market and the need for the voluntary implementation of equal opportunities policies.

If it is left to the mercies of market forces, the labour market will inevitably fragment even more. As has already been shown by the regional and structural analysis of female employment and unemployment, this fragmentation will certainly take place not only along gender lines but also within the female labour force itself.

2. Employment policies specific to women or the major trends in equal opportunities over the decade

The initiatives which we have been looking at are of a general nature and were not devised with equal opportunities in mind. Even so, this aspect does show through either in the form of recommendations and extra support, or because such and such a scheme is intended for women workers only. The initiatives which we will now look at fall within the context of equal opportunities alone.

Whereas the earliest legal provisions in the field of equal opportunities dealt with pay, the big event of the decade was the inclusion of equal opportunities policy not only as a component of labour relations but also as an important part of labour market management - and not only in the context of the unemployed.

In our view, the situation in the Netherlands is interesting firstly because of the amount of pressure in favour of the development of an equal opportunities policy (the passages following make use of large extracts from the report by Plantenga, 1991, pp. 64-70) and secondly because the country's female activity rate is rather low (see Chapter 1).

> As far as labour and remuneration are concerned, the target of emancipation policy is the widest possible gender participation in paid employment. This option is related as much to a desire for a situation where every single person is entitled as of right to an income as it is to the fact that women's equal and unbiased participation in paid activity constitutes an emancipatory goal in itself.

One of the means by which the government wants to encourage participation in paid activity is the so-called '1990 initiative'. Before the introduction of this initiative cohabiting or married men who were unemployed or the victims of industrial disablement received supplementary benefit if their basic family allowances were below an acceptable minimum for their families and themselves. This changed with the 1990 initiative. Since 1990, supplementary benefit is no longer payable to eighteen year-olds. The female partner is required to find employment and only receives supplementary benefit if her attempts to do so are unsuccessful. However, if she has children under twelve she is not required to find a job and the supplementary benefit is maintained (Janswijer, 1989, pp. 365-6, quoted by Plantenga, 1991, p. 65). The women affected will probably be anything but prepared for employment since they are mainly in the lowest wage categories. And it would be necessary to take measures to help these women to find a job.

Women's activity rates are one of the topics covered in a recent survey carried out by the scientific council for government policy.[2] This survey, entitled *'Een Werkend Perspectief: Arbeidsparticipatie in Jaren '90's* (An active prospect : participation in activity in the nineties)', puts forward various proposals with a view to increasing these rates. As far as these low rates are concerned, it is not without significance that they are perpetuated, among other things, by the Netherlands system with its numerous provisions in support of the family. The scientific council for government's proposal is to undertake the progressive transformation of these provisions into direct support for households with children. The government can then adopt a more neutral attitude towards choices favouring certain lifestyles and of role sharing formulae. Direct support for parenthood can be realized as much by an increase in the family allowance as by an extension of child care facilities (Wetenschappelijke Raad voor het Regeringsbeleid, 1990, p. 199 and onwards, quoted by Plantenga, 1991, p. 66). The limited capacity of public child care facilities in the Netherlands is in fact a hindrance to women's activity on the labour market.

The government wants to expand existing facilities by 52,000 places over the 1990-94 period through the release of extra funds. Although the increase is substantial it can be assumed that only a minimum level of child care facilities will be obtained in this way. The government remains unenthusiastic about the scientific council for government's other proposals concerning greater income tax individualization because of the possible negative effect of such a move on the incomes of certain groups, and particularly on bread-winners whose incomes are just below the modal value. The disadvantages of greater individualization would exceed the advantages (Kamerstukken II, 1990-91, 21477, no. 13, p. 21, quoted by Plantenga, 1991, p. 67).

Attempts are being made to diminish the extent of horizontal and vertical segregation particularly through positive action and a policy of emancipation in education. In recent years this policy has consisted mainly of directing girls towards the exact sciences and away from their usual options. Thus, since 1987 most of the Ministry of Education and Science's budget has been devoted to 'the right choice', a publicity campaign aimed at influencing girls' choices.

In order to break away from the one-sided nature of an education-bound emancipation policy pressure has been brought to bear over recent years to have domestic science included in the 12-15 year-olds' core syllabus, a change that will become applicable after 1993. A new distribution of unpaid activity is in fact an important condition for women's increased participation in paid activity and so for their economic independence.

Government policy envisages positive action as an important means of catching up on the time lost by women over the years and of organizing corporate life in such a way that women can successfully hold all types of posts at all levels. Government action operates through a concomitant policy to be seen in particular in the regulations in force since May 1989 to stimulate positive action in favour of women. Thanks to these regulations firms can be compensated for costs incurred in the implementation of positive action programmes. A sum of two million florins per annum is earmarked in connection with these regulations. As at 1 July 1990, eighty-three profit making and non-profit making concerns had taken advantage of them. The greater part of the budget intended for the appointment of an organizational expert has been used for long-term projects in local authority areas and municipal establishments. Profit making concerns have mainly taken advantage of the chance to obtain subsidies for such things as externally carried out labour analyses, extra training for women employees and publicity campaigns to draw attention to internal positive action policies.

A preliminary evaluation of the policy to stimulate positive action demonstrates clearly that there is a vast difference between drawing up tables showing women's circumstances in their firms, working out plans for concrete action and implementing such plans.

Unfortunately, the number of collective agreements containing positive action clauses is still small, but then such clauses are no guarantee of effective policy. Thus, a study carried out in 1988 by the collective labour conditions inspectorate on a representative sample of eighty-five collective agreements in the private sector and the sector receiving premia and subsidies showed that only eight of these agreements contained clauses mentioning positive action. Generally speaking these clauses only referred to projects and good intentions rather than to agreements on the implementation of any plans.

Two royal decrees of significance to women have been issued in Belgium in recent years (Meulders and Vander Stricht, 1991, pp. 113-4).

The royal decree of 14 July 1987 concerning initiatives for the promotion of gender based equality of opportunity in the private sector found an echo in the greater response to women's demands in the interprofessional agreement of 18 November 1988. Apart from the setting up in 1989 of a positive action group for the purpose of assisting negotiators to work out positive action plans, this led to the introduction of an employer's contribution of 0.18 per cent of the total wage bill to an employment fund in support of groups at risk. Exemption is possible in cases where an equivalent effort is made at sectoral or corporate level in support of these groups which include returnees (mainly women) and the long-term unemployed. The fund thus serves as a means of financing positive action. On 30 April 1990 a collective agreement was signed in the sectors covering department stores and food distribution chains and also on the equal representation subcommission representing white collar workers and employees in the steel industry, hosiery savings banks and large retail stores. The interprofessional agreement of 27 November 1990 maintains the compulsory nature of the effort in support of the training and employment of groups at risk, but the employers' contribution now stands at 0.25 per cent of the wage bill.

The royal decree of 27 February 1990 concerning initiatives for the promotion of gender based equality of opportunity in the public services, makes it incumbent upon all public services to pursue a policy of positive action; this contrasts with the private sector, where positive action is on a voluntary basis only.

This policy has two stages, namely : a) the preparation of an analytical report; b) the preparation of the actual plan.

The *Secrétariat d'Etat à l'Emancipation Sociale* has also campaigned for the diversification of professional choice.

Concerning Italy, the interesting point in law no. 125 is its reversal of the *onus probandi*. Unlike in earlier legislation, a women worker is no longer obliged to assume the burden of proof for any discrimination of which she may be the victim. This burden falls on the person allegedly initiating the discrimination, i.e. the employer. In addition, this law invests trade union negotiations with a more enhanced value because it accords priority to agreements between the representative bodies in matters connected with the financing of positive action. Another important aspect of this law is that it lays down that the aim of positive action is to eliminate the factual inequality from which women still suffer at school and during training. Training is thus allocated an important role and specific finance is earmarked to this end. Because of its recent enforcement it has not been possible to evaluate the effects of this law. At all events, it must be borne in mind that it not only closes the gap between Italy and the other European countries with respect to female labour legislation, but also responds to the desires expressed on numerous occasions by the Council of the European Community through its directives and recommendations. Course guidance and occupational training procedures are a constant in countries where positive action exists. This has already been emphasized in our study of general employment and training policies.

In Denmark, 'employment policy specifically aims at improving the position of women. Certain schemes have been launched for the exclusive benefit of women, and women have profited from extra support' (Knudsen, 1991, pp. 88-91) amongst other things.

The public authorities have been focusing on a so-called 'male dominated occupations strategy' since the middle of the 1980s. The aim of this strategy is to motivate women to seek training and employment in one or another of the sections of the labour market where, generally speaking, only men are employed. Whereas in its conception the male dominated occupations strategy was one of equality, in its implementation it has become one of job creation. In accordance with their own forecasts the employers and labour authorities saw the need to transfer workers from sectors badly hit by unemployment to those suffering from labour shortages. A chance was thus perceived to do something in favour of equality by improving the training and employment chances of many women in areas of employment that were new to them. The egalitarian philosophy of the male dominated occupations strategy is that women should not be excluded from large sections of the labour market simply because they are women.

The male dominated occupations strategy has attracted most attention in the context of technical training. The efforts undertaken for the benefit of unqualified women have been on a larger scale but have not attracted the same publicity. While some surveys intimate that the male dominated occupations strategy has not been successful in obtaining employment for women, others show that it has had positive repercussions in that it has been successful in bringing about the recruitment of women in non-traditional areas of employment. Even though the male dominated occupations strategy has not been successful in eliminating gender segregation, the strategy of equality in labour policy has not been without success. Equality lies at the heart of all policy throughout the training system.

A number of laws on equal opportunity, in the public sector, have just been passed in certain of the five new *Länder* of Germany. In the case of Berlin, for example, a law stipulates that public institutions will have to take measures in favour of the professional training and recruitment of women until half of the posts in any given category are held by women.

As far as recruitment is concerned, the law provides for the following :
- 50 per cent of the applicants for any given post and of which invite for interview must be women;
- if only a few women apply (less than 50 per cent of all the applicants), all the women must be invited for interview;
- staff recruitment boards must include 50 per cent of women;

- if a female and a male applicant have the same qualifications (*gleichwertige Qualifikation*), the woman must be chosen;
- all public institutions are invited to develop plans promoting women's employment.

We consider it extremely important to highlight the failure of these training initiatives which tend to see vertical and horizontal segregation as having their roots in the maladjustment of female labour supply and not in stereotyped behaviour patterns provoked by the labour requirements of public and private enterprise. Once training is complete, the next step is to obtain the right kind of job.

3. Employment policies in the new *Länder* of Germany

These five new *Länder* naturally occupy a unique position on the Community labour market scene. However great the investment, the steps taken to cope with both unemployment and the labour market seem to be wholly derisory. The prospects traced out by Figge, Quack and Schäfgen (1991, pp. 49-51; the following pages are taken directly from the report) and their analysis of the situation are not at all encouraging for female employment in the region.

The local employment offices are completely swamped by the unexpected size of the wave of unemployment. Admittedly the federal government has just made billions of DM available for job promotion, further training and redeployment, but the implementation of such qualification and job initiatives can hardly keep abreast of the increase in unemployment.

3.1 Job creation and placements (Arbeitsbeschaffungsmabnahmen) in the five new Länder

Women seem to be handicapped with respect to job placements, and particularly with respect to *Arbeitsbeschaffungsmabnahmen* jobs. Trends are emerging which indicate that their return to work is not being made easy and that even though they are relatively more affected by unemployment than men, their placement in jobs is on a much smaller scale. Another problem is caused by the serial collapse of large numbers of enterprises and institutions. Their demise means their loss as a context for *Arbeitsbeschaffungsmabnahmen* jobs and this in turn means that funds available for such jobs remain unused.

3.2 Initial, further training and redeployment schemes in the five new Länder

Faced with the enormous size and recent nature of the unemployment problem in the ex-German Democratic Republic, employment policy has not yet been modified to cope. Centres (*Frauenladen*) and projects run by women cannot at present offer anything in the way of job oriented further training and redeployment. All they can do is to run general courses in such things as data processing and foreign languages - courses which can only be of minor assistance in enhancing women's employment chances. But whereas local authority equal opportunities officers (*Gleichstellungsbeauftragte*) and women's affairs officers in the unions and associations for the unemployed

173

align themselves on an employment policy biased particularly towards women, [3] they cannot do anything apart from legal counselling to combat female unemployment and are obliged to work hand in glove with local employment offices.

One problem is posed by the fact that these initiatives are devoid of any point of reference. Since it is impossible to foretell what firms and sectors will manage to make the switch to a market economy and what industries will move into the ex-German Democratic Republic, it is also impossible to know what areas of employment will result and what qualifications will be required. As the figures on job placements and women affected (relatively more frequently) by unemployment show, the trend emerging in the new *Länder* is towards an increasing rejection of economic activity on the part of women and a curb on their return to active life. This is all the more serious since, as the country's high rate of female employment shows, occupational activity was an integral part of women's lives in the ex-German Democratic Republic. Such activity enabled women to be economically independent even if they were less favoured than men in terms of income and promotion. When all comes to all, what can be said is that the unification of the two German states must be seen as having a retrograde effect as far as women's position on the labour market is concerned.

4. Conclusions

Women have been relatively less favoured by general employment policies than men. Measures taken to encourage career breaks and parenthood leave have only affected women and have jeopardized their return to the labour market and their later promotion.

General training policies often duplicate employment segregation, which they tend to reinforce.

Several countries have undertaken specific policies aiming at greater equality of opportunity in various directions and with various degrees of success.

Regarding these policies, the emphasis should not focus mainly on training which assumes that segregations have their roots in the maladjustment of female labour supply and not in the behaviour of labour demand.

Notes

1. This typology was used by Deimezis, Freese, Guillaume, Meulders and Plasman (1988) and Plasman (1989).
2. Scientific council for government policy = *Wetenschappelijke Raad voor de Regeringsbeleid* (WRR).
3. A social policy taking particular account of 'lone' women, for example.

7 Conclusions

On the eve of the third programme, the position of women on the labour market is the sum total of the development of three sets of factors. The first, which is of a sociological nature, is related to women's ability and desire to take part in economic activity, and is measured in terms of labour supply and the levels and structure of training. The second, which is of an economic nature, stands in relation to the quantitative and qualitative development of the demand for labour which, in its turn, depends on structural and cyclical fluctuations in economic activity and the cost of labour with the increased prospect of competition and a search for competitiveness due to the final implementation of the single market. The third, which is of a political nature, groups together the employment policies in the widest sense of the term implemented by the different levels of government and Community institutions with respect to working hours, social security coverage, training etc.

Trends observed in recent years in the supply of female labour point to an increase in women's activity rates and either a decrease or the stabilization of men's. These trends should be consolidated. This development in male activity rates can be explained by the reduction in men's activity at both ends of the age spectrum. On the one hand there has been an increase in the requirement for education, either voluntarily or as the result of government intervention, while on the other there is a tendency in a number of countries (Belgium, the Netherlands, France, Denmark, the United Kingdom and Italy) for people in the 50-64 age group to leave the labour market, often encouraged by provisions for early retirement. These phenomena have also affected women to the extent that the increase in female activity rates is mainly due to the growth of the activity of women in the 25-50 age group.

In comparison with the North of Europe, the countries in the South (with the exception of Portugal) are characterized by their low levels of female activity. However, the dynamism in the growth observed in southern countries in the 1980s leads us to expect that this North-South divide will disappear.

These different levels of activity reflect differentiated profiles corresponding to life cycles. The high activity rates observed in Denmark, the five new *Länder* and France have a profile in inverted U. There is a movement towards this type of model on the part of the other countries which currently exhibit bimodal or flat topped models. Of all the factors weighing on the level and structure of women's activity by age, family responsibilities have weighted most heavily on their behaviour patterns. This inverse relationship between family responsibilities and activity can be seen to different degrees in all the countries except Denmark, where the activity rates are not influenced by family circumstances, their influence is decreasing. Mothers' activity rates increased in all the countries of the Community and motherhood often occurs later.

Another factor found in a number of countries is that the rate of activity for women in their thirties is higher than the rate for young women with children of a given age. At the root of this observation is the level of training and the job experience acquired, both of which form a positive correlation with the pursuit of occupational activity. In the case of women there is a much more marked relationship between rates of activity and levels of training than in the case of men. Highly qualified women are more likely to be economically active than less qualified ones.

Education levels also influence activity cycles. Highly qualified women more often pursue an uninterrupted career and more frequently take up the reins again should an interruption occur. It seems that in the countries of southern Europe (Spain and southern Italy) with relatively low activity rates, the differences in these rates increase in proportion to educational attainment. This means that the rates for highly educated women exhibit fewer differences from country to country than in the case of poorly qualified women.

However, it seems that even if training can be placed on an equal level for either sex, there is every reason to believe that differences in career options will survive, and that these differences might turn out to be handicaps on the labour market. This means that equal opportunities policies must come into play in girls' full-time training so as to eliminate segregation in their career options.

Women's employment increased in all the countries between 1983 and 1989 and behaved better than men's. This growth was not reflected in a corresponding decline of unemployment because the new jobs were taken up by young women arriving on the labour market and women returners.

The growth in employment was mainly due to the growth in employment in the tertiary sector and, more particularly, to the employment of women in banking and finance, insurance, business and renting, and 'other services'. However, what must not be lost from sight is the extreme heterogeneity of the services sector which includes public and private service organizations alongside highly productive advanced technology concerns and unproductive low technology ones; the conditions of employment and remuneration that they offer are very heterogeneous, too. The distribution and growth by region and country of women's employment in these different areas of the services sector leads to a segmentation of the structure of female employment. The high proportion of women in sectors likely to be faced with job losses increases the risk of segmentation even more.

Women's employment remained concentrated in traditionally female sectors in 1989, even if horizontal segregation has slightly declined in most of the member states, the national experts are much less optimistic about vertical segregation and its concomitant lack of equality in corporate hierarchies and in matters pertaining to qualifications at both corporate and sectoral level. The problem of segregation is not only associated with job preferences and training, i.e. with female labour supply patterns. Demand patterns emanating from public and private enterprises seem to be just as important from the point of view of vertical segregation. Apart from levels to which recruitment is made, vertical segregation is also determined by internal promotion opportunities.

The decrease in agricultural employment and its part in employment as a whole is neither surprising nor recent. It does, however, pose a problem for the female labour market in countries where agriculture accounted for a large part of female employment. Whereas in 1983 agriculture accounted for between 10 per cent and 40 per cent of total female employment in Italy, Spain, Portugal and Greece, over the 1983-89 period the numbers of women working in agriculture dropped by between 9 per cent and 25 per cent. The need for these countries or regions (southern Italy, for example) is to absorb this supply of female labour - often badly prepared for industry or the services - by means of a demand for labour that the still relatively under-developed services are hardly able to furnish for new women entrants.

A regional breakdown provides a hint of differentiation in developments inside the female labour force, or at least as far as the United Kingdom and Italy are concerned. These developments are characterized by the level of demand for labour in addition to its content. Thus, in the case of women, the employment difficulties associated with declining regions are coupled with mobility problems, and particularly when the spouse has a job in the region. Active regional labour policies seem necessary if such polarization is to be avoided.

The public sector has made a positive contribution to the increase in the employment of women throughout the European Community. This said, female employment has not been immune to modifications in the general conditions of employment in the public sector - modifications which have resulted from changes in direction in the policies of most European governments during the 1980s. While variations in public employment remained part of contracyclical policy in the 1970s, in the 1980s these variations in employment and the associated reward packages were used to reduce public expenditures and budget deficits. Hence the slowdown, the stagnation and even the regression in public employment, the prolongation of the temporary contracts of persons occupying posts on an unestablished basis or awaiting appointment as established civil servants, and the generalization of part-time appointments. Moreover, while all the governments have now been obliged to enact equal opportunities legislation, gender segregation - particularly from the career distribution point of view - does not differ to any great extent to what obtains in the private sector.

Earlier studies by the European network of experts on the situation of women in the labour market have showed the preponderance of women in atypical employment. Developments and the numbers of women implicated vary from country to country, and it often happens that no community-wide trend is discernible at all. The only constant in employment outside the wage system lies in a decrease in the numbers of family workers, who are overrepresented among women. In contrast, the number of women employers - weakly represented in female employment - remains stable. There are contrasting developments in self-employment and we have echoed the discussion concerning the quality of this type of employment which, for women, is often a matter of second best.

Whereas part-time working remains the exponent *par excellence* of the flexibility of female employment, as far as women are concerned its relative growth seems to have come to a standstill in both Denmark and the United Kingdom and it concerns now a slightly larger number of young men reconciling studies and work. In France, the Netherlands, the United Kingdom, Ireland and Germany, the growth of female employment between 1983 and 1989 is largely attributable to the growth of part-time employment. In this connection the differences with respect to the countries of the South of Europe is striking since the proportion of part-time employment is low and has not increased significantly since 1983. Its concentration in already very closed sectors, its non-optional nature, its insecurity and its awkward working hours make part-time employment a form of employment that is of very little personal value for women even if in the United Kingdom a majority of women part-timers declare that they do not want to work full-time. In Belgium, unemployment benefits combined with part-time employment prevent a switch from part-time to full-time employment in the case of low wage earners.

While women remain overrepresented in temporary employment, developments differ from one country to another. Some considerable increases have been recorded in France and Spain, where temporary employment often characterizes entry onto the labour market and serves as a means of probation. Once entry has been gained, however, the percentage of temporary employment remains higher for women than for men, and this type of employment includes a large amount of part-time working.

Generally speaking, it seems that while the situation relative to these different forms of employment did not degenerate between 1983 and 1989, it did not improve, either. Women remain overrepresented in these forms of employment and are fair game as far as policies aiming for flexibility are concerned.

The extent of female atypical employment provides one of the explanations for average gender pay differentials. Job structure and definition, hierarchical structures, and reward package conditions and components are so many details which contribute to the fact that in all the countries the average women's wage is below men's, even in the countries where women's activity rates are very close to men's (Denmark and the ex-German Democratic Republic).

Hierarchical structures and job composition are the factors which, in one way or another, indirectly determine wage discrimination. Other sources of wage discrimination noted in the national surveys are more interesting and would seem to merit special studies either of individual cases or on the basis of data from firms or sectors.

In the countries where wages are determined by sector by means of job analysis, the grid used often gives greater weight to certain features characteristic of male jobs and plays things down in the case of women.

The composition of the reward package may also be a source of gender discrimination. Overtime seems to be more frequently made available to, and worked by, men while part-timers are used to cover any extra hours in the case of women employed in the services. Permanency of employment and seniority are also criteria for the granting of premia and fringe benefits, but these criteria may not be satisfied as the result of career breaks.

The methods employed to determine wages are of vital importance. Labour market flexibility in the United Kingdom is characterized by a shift in wage determination firstly towards the corporate level, and then towards more individualized arrangements. This shift has increased gender pay disparities in marked contrast to the situation prevalent in countries where collective bargaining remains more centralized. In this context we can do no better than to quote Rubery's (1991) conclusions on wage differentials where she says that in place of concentrating on equal pay directives, wage equality would be more easily attainable via Community directives, recommendations and policies ensuring the basic universal rights that feature, at least to some extent, in documents dealing with part-time and temporary employment and hours of work.

Women have done relatively less well out of the reduction in European unemployment rates. Except in the United Kingdom, women's unemployment rates remain well in excess of men's, and were even on the increase between 1983 and 1989. Three points stand out from the point of view of the structure of female unemployment.

Firstly, the advantages of a high level of education are fewer for women than for men. Male unemployment is more concentrated among the unskilled and poorly educated than in the case of women. So it is not at all evident that the training of unemployed women is necessarily the best or, indeed, the only way of reabsorbing them. Then, in addition to the problems caused by a lack of congruence between labour demand and certain types of training there is the attitude adopted by the employers, who often prefer to recruit men rather than women in cases of equal qualifications.

Secondly, women are also at a disadvantage when it comes to unemployment benefit since they are compensated less frequently or receive lower benefits. As in the case of wages, what is involved here is not direct discrimination but rather the criteria governing the granting of benefits. Both the insurance and the assistance formulae come under this heading.

Finally, as was emphasized in our examination of regional employment distribution, in certain countries the regional composition of unemployment is of extreme importance because it highlights cracks within the female labour force itself. While the cases of the United Kingdom and Italy were mentioned, it is also clear that in the five new *Länder* of Germany there is a danger that the position of the female unemployed will deteriorate very rapidly in terms of unemployment rates, job access, and a return to inactivity.

All these points naturally bring us to employment policy. What employment policies have had a specific effect, either direct or indirect, on the female labour market ? What directions should be taken by national and Community employment policies with a view to establishing gender equality ?

Faced with enduringly high unemployment rates the public authorities have focused their labour policies on the reabsorption of the unemployed, and women are, in the main, given their weight of numbers in their ranks. They have been affected by passive policies intended to force them out of the active population. Thus parenthood leave and career breaks jeopardize their return to the labour market and their occupational advancement. Their rate of participation in the other general programmes promoting employment and combating unemployment is low in relation to their position on the unemployment scene.

As most of the national reports show, training and education schemes often duplicate traditional gender based orientations. However, in most of the European countries where these programmes exist, efforts have been made to diversify the vocational guidance given to unemployed women and to provide them with training to enable them to carry out traditionally male jobs. Even when the training is successful, the most perilous step seems to be into actual employment. In fact, there is no guarantee that women trained to do men's jobs will be offered appropriate employment. So it would be useful to undertake a study at a European level of the impact of this type of training on the possibility of unemployed women and female returnees finding jobs. It cannot therefore be claimed that general employment policies have done anything towards rectifying the inequalities and discrimination to which women are subject whether they are employed, unemployed or inactive.

Equal opportunities policy has been developed round three axes, namely initiatives connected with women's participation in economic activity, the redirection of academic and job preferences and the inclusion of equal opportunities in the system of collective labour relations.

The redirection of academic and job preferences is a constant in equal opportunities policies, at least in the countries where such policies exist. While it is a necessary condition, it nevertheless falls short of the mark since offer does not necessarily create demand.

Active policies are necessary if discrimination in recruitment and personnel management are to disappear. Therefore the effort should not focus mainly on training policies postulating that the segregation in employment and unemployment has its roots in the maladjustment of female labour supply while the behaviour of labour demand is just as responsible, if not more.

The inclusion of equal opportunities in collective agreements at corporate, sectoral and intersectoral level is essential in this respect. However, it is only too frequent that equal opportunities clauses limit themselves to declarations of intent. If the limited number of collective agreements mentioning equal opportunities is also taken into account, it will become clear that there is still a long way to go.

Active equal opportunities policies on the labour market, the enhanced participation of women in general programmes, the redirection of academic and job preferences, the abolition of material barriers and barriers caused by direct taxation and additional levies, the adoption at Community, national and regional levels of directives and initiatives ensuring basic rights and guarantees for all workers - all these will be more necessary than ever if we want to prevent the inevitable increase in women's activity from going hand in hand with increased inequality not only between the sexes, but also inside the female labour force itself - a development which can be seen in the countries where the functioning of the labour market has been left to 'market laws'.

Bibliography

Abbate, C. (1989), 'Relazione tra Tasso di Disoccupazione e Variabili Demografiche, Sociali ed Economiche', *Economia e Lavoro*, no. 2.

Abel, V. and Wolfson, L. (eds) (1989), *Ka' Kvinder Arbejde ?*, Equality Council, København.

Aburrà, L. (1989), *L'Occupazione Femminile dal Declino alla Crescita. Problemi Risolti, Soluzioni Problematiche*, IRES, Piemonte, giugno.

Aburrà, L. and Marcenaro, P. (1986), *Le Ore e i Giorni. L'Orario di Lavoro tra Contrattazione e Orientamenti dei Lavoratori. Un'Indagine nel Gruppo Fiat*, Edizione Lavoro.

Administration de l'Emploi (1991), *Indication sur la Situation de la Femme sur le Marché du Travail au Grand-Duché de Luxembourg*, Luxembourg.

Alcobendas Tirado, M.P. (1982), *L'Emploi des Femmes en Espagne*, Commission des Communautés Européennes.

Alcobendas Tirado, M.P. (1983), *Datos Sobre el Trabajo de la Mujer en Espana*, CIS, Madrid.

Alcobendas Tirado, M.P. (1991), *La Position des Femmes sur le Marché du Travail en Espagne, Evolution entre 1983 et 1989*, Report for the Equal Opportunities Unit of the European Communities, Brussels.

Alessi, T. (1990), 'Scuola e Mercato del Lavoro in Italia : il Caso dei Laureati e delle Alte Professionalità', in Ministero del Lavoro e della Previdenza Sociale (ed.), *Lavoro e Politiche della Occupazione in Italia*, Rapporto '89, Roma, pp. 162-87.

Altieri, G. and Meghnagi, S. (1986), 'Dequalificare con il Lavoro', *Politica ed Economia*, no. 10, October, pp. 75-6.

Altieri, G. and Pugliese, E. (1990), 'Tre Italie, Due Disoccupazioni', *Inchiesta*, no. 88-89, April-September, pp. 26-37.

181

Altieri, G. and Villa, P. (1991), *La Position des Femmes sur le Marché du Travail en Italie, Evolution entre 1983 et 1989*, Report for the Equal Opportunities Unit of the European Communities, Brussels.

Ambos, I., Gertner, S. and Schiersmann, C. (1989), 'Zur Situation von Berufsrückkehrerinnen', *Frauenforschung*, no. 1-2, pp. 5-26.

Andersen, B.H. (1991), 'Bornefamiliernes Hverdag', Report 91 : 6, Social-forskningsinstituttet, København.

Aumüller-Roske, U. and Pollvogt, R. (eds) (1989), *Frauenerwerbslosigkeit in Osnabrück*, Lang, Frankfurt a.M..

Axhausen, S. (1990), 'Hintergründe der Wachsenden Armut von Frauen', *Frauenforschung*, no. 1-2, pp. 15-24.

Bach, H.U. and Brinkmann, C. (1986), 'Erwerbsbeteiligung von Frauen im Internationalen Vergleich', *MittAB*, no.3, pp. 356-61.

Bach, H.U. and Reyher, L. (1985), 'Strukturen und Entwicklung der Erwerbstätigkeit, Frauen auf dem Arbeitsmarkt', *MittAB*, no.1, pp. 11-19.

Bäcker, G., Bispinck, R., Hofemann, K. and Naegele (1989), *Sozialpolitik und Soziale Lage in der Bundesrepublik Deutschland, Band 1 und 2, Zweite Überabeitete, Auflage*, Bund, Köln.

Bäcker, G. and Stolz-Willig, B. (1990), 'Kindererziehung, Arbeitszeiten und Soziale Sicherung', *WSI-Arbeitsmaterialien*, no. 26, Düsseldorf.

Baisier, L., Humblet, P. and Van Haegendoren, M. (1990), *Travail de Nuit des Femmes*, Secrétariat d'Etat à l'Emancipation Sociale, Brussels.

Barbano, F. (ed.) (1987), *L'Ombra del Lavoro*, Angeli, Milano.

Barbero, G. and Marotta, G. (1987), *Il Mercato del Lavoro Agricolo Negli Anni Ottanta. Strutture e Aspetti Emergenti*, INEA, Il Mulino, Bologna.

Barca, F. and Magnani, M. (1989), *L'Industria fra Capitale e Lavoro, Piccole Imprese e Grandi Imprese dall'Autunno Caldo alla Ristrutturazione*, Il Mulino, Bologna.

Barile, G. and Stefanizzi, S. (1990), *Donne, Lavoro e Condizione Familiare. Confronto tra due Indagini Empiriche*, Irer, Milano.

Barile, G. and Zanusso, L. (eds) (1980), *Lavoro Femminile e Condizione Familiare*, Angeli, Milano.

Barry, U. (1991), *La Position des Femmes sur le Marché du Travail en Irlande, Evolution entre 1983 et 1989*, Report for the Equal Opportunities Unit of the European Communities, Brussels.

Becchi Collidà, A. (1987), 'Lavoro e Mezzogiorno : Il Castello delle Possi-bilità è Crollato', *Politiche del Lavoro*, no. 4.

Begg, I., Blake, A. and Deakin, B. (1991), 'YTS and the Labour Market', *British Journal of Industrial Relations*.

Belloni, M.C. (1984), *Il Tempo della Città*, Angeli, Milano.

Berg, C. (1990), 'Existenzgründung - Frauen als Selbständige', in Lucke, D. and Berghahn, S. (eds), *Rechtsratgeber Frauen. Unter Mitarbeit von Anke Scheiber*, Hamburg, pp. 166-84.

Bergmann, T. (1990), 'Socioeconomic Situation and Perspectives of the Individual Peasant', *Sociologica Ruralis*, no. 1, pp. 48-61.

Bessy, P. and Lheritier, J.L. (1990), 'Les Salaires en 1989 : le Secteur Privé', *INSEE Résultats, Série Emploi-Revenus*, no. 19, August.

Bettio, F. (1985), 'The Secular Decrease of Sex Linked Wage Differentials : a Case of Non-Competition', *Economia e Lavoro*, no. 3.

Bettio, F. (1987), 'Segregation Versus Substitution. Cyclical and Secular Trends in Women's Employment in Italy', in Rubery, J. (ed.), *Women and Recession*, Routledge and Kegan Paul, London.

Biagioli, M. (1987), 'Sanità : Chi Guadagna di Piu e Perché', *Politica Economica*, no. 4.

Bimbi, F. and Pristinger, F. (eds) (1985), *Profili Sovrapposti*, Angeli, Milano.

Blackwell, J. (1986), *Women in the Labour Force*, Employment Equality Agency, Dublin.

Blackwell, J. (1989), *Women in the Labour Force*, Employment Equality Agency, Dublin.

BMFJ (1990), 'Frauen in den Neuen Bundesländern im Prozeß der Deutschen Einigung', *Materializen zu Frauenpolitik 11/1991* - Ergebnisse einer Reprasentativen Umfrage des Instituts für Angewandte Sozialwissenschaft Bad Godesberg.

BMJFFG (eds) (1989), *Frauen in der Bundesrepublik Deutschland*, Bundesministerium für Jugend, Familie, Frauen und Gesundheit, Bonn.

Boolsen, M.W. and Mærkedahl, I. (1990), *Jeg Vil Være Min Egen Chef*, Report 90 : 13, Socialforskningsintituttet, København.

Bore, C., Perreaux, P. and Pietri, A. (1988), 'Les Mouvements de Main-d'Oeuvre en 1987', *Le Bilan de l'Emploi*, no. 43-44, October.

Born, C. and Vollmer, C. (1984), *Familienfreundliche Gestaltung des Arbeitslebens*, Band 135, Schriftenreihe des Bundesministeriums für Jugend, Familie und Gesundheit, Stuttgart.

Bosch, G., Gabriel, H., Seifert, H. and Welsch, J. (1987), 'Beschäftigungspolitik in der Region', WSI (eds), *Studie zur Wirtschafts- und Sozialforschung*, no. 61, Köln.

Bosman, E. (1989), 'De Incompatibiliteit van Buitenshuisarbeid van de Vrouw en de Ouderschap : Historische Situering en Begripsbepaling', *Bevolking en Gezin*, no. 2, pp. 103-33.

Bouillaguet-Bernard, P., Gauvin, A. and Prokovas, N. (1985), *L'Evolution de l'Activité et de l'Emploi des Femmes dans la Communauté Economique Européenne*, V/1252/86-Fr, Report for the Equal Opportunities Unit of the European Communities, 197 p.

Bracalente, B. and Marbach, G. (1989), *Il Part-Time nel Mercato Italiano del Lavoro*, Angeli, Milano.

Brandes, W., Buttler, F. *et al.* (1990), *Der Staat als Arbeitgeber*, Frankfurt/Main.

Breidenstein, W. (1990), 'Frauen im Öffentlichen Dienst', *Wirtschaft und Statistik*, no. 5, pp. 323-9.

Brinkmann, C., Klauder, W., Reyher, L. and Tohn, M. (1987), 'Methodische und Inhaltliche Aspekte der Stillen Reserve', *MittAB*, no.4, pp. 387-409.

Brown, W. and Rowthorm, R. (1990), *Pay in the Public Services*, Fabian Pamphlet.

Bruni, M. and Franciosi, F. (1981), 'Una Interpretazione in Termini di Flusso della Dinamica delle Forze Lavoro in Italia', *Economia e Lavoro*, no. 2.

Büchel, F. and Weißhuhn, G. (1990), 'Zur Stabilität der Wiederbeschäftigung nach Arbeitslosigkeit', *MittAB*, no. 2, pp. 263-83.

Büchtemann, C.F. and Gout, M. (1988), *Développement et Structure du Travail 'Indépendant' en RFA*, Report prepared for the European Economic Commission and the French Commissariat du Plan, Berlin, mimeo.

Büchtemann, C.F. and Höland, A. (1989), *Befristete Arbeitsverträge nach dem Beschäftigungsförderungsgesetz*, BeschFG 1985, Berlin.

Büchtemann, C.F. and Schupp, J. (1986), *Socio-Economic Aspects of Part-Time Employment in the Federal Republic of Germany*, Discussion paper, no. FS I, 88-6, Wissenschaftszentrum Berlin, Berlin.

Büchtemann, C.F. and Quack, S. (1989), *'Bridges' or 'Traps' ? Non-Standard Forms of Employment in the Federal Republic of Germany. The Case of Part-Time and Temporary Work*, Discussion paper, no. FS I, 89-6, Wissenschaftszentrum Berlin, Berlin.

Bue, J. and Cristofari, M.F. (1986), 'Contraintes et Rythmes des Salariés à Temps Partiel', *Travail et Emploi*, no. 27, March.

Bulletin des Communautés Européennes (1986), supplément 3, 'Egalité des Chances pour les Femmes - Programme Communautaire à Moyen Terme (1986-1990)'.

Bulletin des Communautés Européennes (1990), 'Egalité des Chances pour les Femmes et les Hommes - Le Troisième Programme Communautaire à Moyen Terme (1991-1995)', doc. COM(90)449 final.

Burchell, B. and Rubery, J. (1990), 'An Empirical Investigation into the Segmentation of the Labour Supply', *Work, Employment and Society*, December.

Burkhard, G., Fietze, B. and Kohli, M. (1989), *Liebe, Ehe, Elternschaft. Materialien zur Bevölkerungswissenschaft*, Heft 60, Bundesinstitut für Bevölkerungswissenschaft, Wiesbaden.

Cavouriaris, M. (1991a), *La Position des Femmes sur le Marché du Travail en Grèce, Evolution entre 1983 et 1989*, Report for the Equal Opportunities Unit of the European Communities, Brussels.

Cavouriaris, M. (1991b), *Emploi et Chômage dans les Régions en Retard de Développement*, PerItaca, Rome.

Central Statistics Office (1988), *Industrial Employment, Earnings and Hours Worked Updated Series 1980-1986*, Dublin, January.

Chaberny, A. and Zeller, K. (1989), 'Neue Arbeitsplätze für Frauen', *MaiAB*, no. 4, pp. 1-13.

Chagas Lopes, M., Ferreira, C. and Perista, H. (1991), *La Position des Femmes sur le Marché du Travail au Portugal, Evolution entre 1983 et 1989*, Report for the Equal Opportunities Unit of the European Communities, Brussels.

Chiesi, A. (1988), 'I Lavoratori Emergenti del Terziario Arretrato', *Prospettiva Sindicale*, September, pp. 23-36.

Chiesi, A. (1989), *Sincronismi Sociali*, il Mulino, Bologna.

Chiesi, A. (1990), 'Nuove Forme di Lavoro e di Rappresentanza. Un Quadro di Riferimento Concettuale', *Democrazia e Diritto*, January, February, Roma.

Christoffersen, M.N. (1987), *Familien under Forvandling*, Report no. 168, Socialforskningsinstituttet, København.

Clarke, K. (forthcoming), *Women and Training : a Review of Recent Research and Policy*, Equal Opportunities Commission, Manchester.

Cockburn, C. (1987), *Two-Track Training*, Macmillan, London.

Cornetz, W. (1986), 'Theorie und Empirie des Arbeitskraftangebots', *MittAB*, no. 3, pp. 422-38.

Commission of the European Communities (1990), *Employment in Europe*, Office for Official Publications of the European Communities, Luxembourg.

Commission of the European Communities (1991), *Employment in Europe*, Office for Official Publications of the European Communities, Luxembourg.

Curran, J. and Burrows, R. (1989), 'National Profiles of the Self-Employed', *Employment Gazette*, July.

Dahlerup, D. (1989), 'Køn Sorterer - Det Nordiske BRYT-Projekt', *Serien Nord*, no. 1, Nordisk Ministerräd.

Dal Co, M. (1986), *Ristrutturazione dell'Occupazione e Relazioni Industriali*, Il Mulino, Bologna.

Daniel, W.W. (1990), *The Unemployed Flow*, PSI, London.

D'Antonio, M. (1985), 'Mezzogiorno : Tra Sviluppo Dipendente e Sviluppo Autocentralo', *Delta*, no. 14, January-February.

De Bruijn, J. (1988), 'Functiewaardering en Sekse', *Tijdschrift voor Arbeidsvraagstukken*, pp. 75-83.

De Bruijn, J. (1991), 'Functiewaardering en Beloning van Vrouwenwerk', *Tijdschrift voor Vrouwenstudies*, pp. 19-31.

Degen, B. and Möller, C. (1990), 'Teilzeitarbeit und Andere Varianten Ungeschützter Arbeitsverhältnisse', in Lucke, D. and Berghahn, S. (eds), *Rechtsratgeber Frauen. Unter Mitarbeit von Anke Scheiber*, Hamburg, pp. 124-48.

Degimbe, N. (1991), 'Evolution de la Réglementation et Mesure Statistique du Chômage', *Revue du Travail*, January-February-March.

Deimezis, N., Freeze, V., Guillaume, Y., Meulders, D. and Plasman, R. (1987), 'Politiques d'Emploi : Une Analyse Comparée pour Différents Pays de la CEE', *Stratégies Internationales et Intégration Européenne, Actes du Colloque de l'AFSE*, Paris, 21-22 September 1987, Nathan, Paris.

Del Boca, D. (1982), 'Strategie Familiari Interessi Individuali', in Martinotti, G. (ed.), *La Città Difficile*, Angeli, Milano, pp. 183-260.

Del Boca, A. and Rota, P. (1989), *La Cassa Integrazione Straordinaria a Milano, Risultati di un'Indagine Microeconomica*, IRES, Milano.

Demazy, S. (1991), *Le Poverty Trap en Belgique*, a final year graduation paper at the Université Libre de Bruxelles, Brussels.

Deneve, C. (1991), 'Le Travail à Temps Partiel pour Echapper au Chômage', *Revue du Travail*, January-February-March, pp. 69-72.

Department of Labour (1991), *Economic Status of School Leavers 1989*, Department of Labour, Dublin.

Dequan, J. (1991), 'L'Indisponibilité et la Garantie de Revenu dans le Cadre de l'Article 143', *Revue du Travail*, January-February-March, pp. 65-8.

Desplanques, G., Raton, I. and Thave, S. (1991), 'L'Activité Féminine', *INSEE Résultats*, no. 10.

Dessens, J., van Doorne-Huiskes, J. and Mertens, E. (1990), *Arbeidsmarkt en Gezin*, OSA-Werkdocument W 72, April.

Dex, S. (1987), *Women's Labour Supply and the Demand for Childcare Provision in the Women and Employment Survey*, Report to the Equal Opportunities Commission.

185

Dex, S. and Shaw, L. (1986), *British and American Women at Work*, Macmillan, London.

Dex, S. and Walters, P. (1989), 'Women's Occupational Status in Britain, France and the USA : Explaining the Difference', *Industrial Relations Journal*, Autumn.

Dienst Collectieve Arbeidsvoorwaarden (DCA) (1988), *Aspecten van Emancipatie in CAO's*, Ministerie van Sociale Zaken en Werkgelegenheid, Den Haag.

DIW (1990), Erwerbstätigkeit und Einkomment von Frauen in der DDR', *DIW-Wochenbericht*, no. 19, pp. 263-7.

Drohsel, P. (1986), *Die Lohndiskriminierung der Frauen*, SP-Verlag, Marburg.

Eisfeld, G. (1988-89), 'Berufliche Weiterbildung für Arbeitslose Frauen - Erfahrungen aus einer Laufenden Modellversuchsreihe', *Frauenforschung*, no. 3/88, pp. 57-80 and *Frauenforschung*, no. 1-2/89, pp. 57-80.

Elfring, T. and Kloosterman, R.C. (1989), 'De Nederlandse 'Job Machine'', *Economisch-Statistische Berichten*, pp. 736-40.

Emancipatieraad (1989), *Emancipatiebeleid in Macro-Economisch Perspectief*, Den Haag, 1989.

Employment Gazette (1981), Historical Supplement, no. 1, April.

Employment Gazette (1991), April.

Engelbrech, G. (1987), 'Erwerbsverhalten und Berufsverlauf von Frauen : Ergebnisse Neuerer Untersuchungen im Überblick', *MittAB*, no.2, pp. 181-96.

Engelbrech, G. (1989a), 'Erfahrungen von Frauen an der 'Dritten Schewelle', Schwierigkeiten bei der Beruflichen Wiedereingliederung aus der Sicht der Frauen', *MittAB*, no. 1, pp. 100-13.

Engelbrech, G. (1989b), 'Frauen an der Dritten Schwelle', *Frauenforschung*, no. 1-2, pp. 35-47.

Equal Opportunities Commission (EOC) (1987), *Women and Men in Britain*, HMSO.

Eurostat (1983a-1989a), *Employment and Unemployment*, Theme 3, Series C, Luxembourg.

Eurostat (1983b), *Hourly Earnings - Hours of Work*, Theme 3, Series B, Luxembourg.

Eurostat (1983c-1989c), *Labour Force Survey*, Theme 3, Series C, Luxembourg.

Eurostat (1985), *Yearbook of Regional Statistics*, Luxembourg.

Eurostat (1990a), *Rapid Reports, Régions*, no. 1, Luxembourg.

Eurostat (1990b-1991b), *Unemployment*, Theme 3, Series B, monthly, Luxembourg.

Eurostat (1990c), *Earnings, Industry and Services*, Luxembourg.

Eurostat (1991c), *Demographic Statistics*, Theme 3, Series C, Luxembourg.

Fadiga Zanatta, A.L. (1988), 'Donne e Lavoro', *Immagini della Società Italiana*, Istat, Roma, pp. 281-303.

Feltrin, P. and La Mendola, S. (1988), 'I Lavori Manuali Non Operai : Il Caso delle Donne delle Pulizie', *Prospettiva Sindicale*, no. 69.

Fernandez Mendez de Andes (1985), *La Participacion Laboral de la Mujer*, Ministerio de Trabajo, Madrid.

Fey-Hoffmann, S. (1990), 'Berufswahl und Rechte bei der Berufsaus-bildung', in Lucke, D. and Berghahn, S. (eds), *Rechtsratgeber Frauen. Unter Mitarbeit von Anke Scheiber*, Rowohlt, Hamburg, pp. 59-79.

Fiedler, A. and Regenhard, U. (1983), 'Wieso Gibt es Frauenlöhne ? Ein Beitrag zur Einkommensdiskriminierung als Monetärer Ausdruck von Frauendiskriminierung auf dem Arbeitsmarkt', in ZE Frauenforschung (eds), *Zentraleinrichtung zur Förderung von Frauenstudien und Frauen-forschung an der FU Berlin*, Vortragsreihe zur Frauenforschung SoSe 82 - WS 82/83, Berlin (West), pp. 115-39.

Fiedler, A. and Regenhard, U. (1987), *Das Arbeitseinkommen der Frauen. Analysen zur Diskriminierung auf dem Arbeitsmarkt*, Berlin Verlag Arno Spitz, Berlin.

Figge, K., Quack, S. and Schäfgen, K. (1991), *La Position des Femmes sur le Marché du Travail en Allemagne, Evolution entre 1983 et 1989*, Report for the Equal Opportunities Unit of the European Communities, Brussels.

Foster, H. (1989), 'Der Stellenwert von Umschulung für den Wiedereinstieg von Frauen ins Erwebsleben', *Frauenforschung*, no. 1-2, pp. 59-83.

Franchi, M. (1988), *Nuove Imprese - Nuovi Impreditori*, Essegi, Ravenna.

Fransen, G. (1991), 'De l'Indemnisation Chômage aux Politiques du Marché du Travail', *Revue du Travail*, January-February-March, pp. 30-4.

Frey, L. (1989), 'Le Politiche del Lavoro e dell'Occupazione', in Ministero del Lavoro e della Previdenza Sociale (ed.), *Lavoro e Politiche della Occu-pazione in Italia*, Rapporto '89, Roma, pp. 401-26.

Fricke, W. (ed.) (1987), *Jahrbuch Arbeit und Technik in Nordrhein-West-falen 1987*, Dietz, Bonn.

Friedmann, P. and Pfau, B. (1985), 'Frauenarbeit in der Krise - Frauenarbeit trotz Krise ? Korrekturversuch an einem Arbeitsmarkttheoretischen Allge-meinplatz', *Leviathan*, no.2.

Garonna, P. (1984), *L'Economia della Cassa Integrazione Guadagni*, Fac. di Soc. DD.AA., Padova, October.

Gasbarrone, M. (1990), 'L'Offerta di Lavoro delle Donne : Il Peso delle Variabili Non Economiche', in Nassisi, A.M. (ed.), *Il Lavoro Femminile in Italia tra Produzione e Riproduzione*, Primo Rapporto, Fondazione Gramsci, Roma.

Gauvin, A. and Silvera, R. (1991), *La Position des Femmes sur le Marché du Travail en France, Evolution entre 1983 et 1989*, Report for the Equal Opportunities Unit of the European Communities, Brussels.

Gerhard, U., Schwarzer, A. and Slupik, V. (1987), *Auf Kosten der Frauen. Frauenrechte im Sozialstaat*, Beltz, Weinheim/Basel.

Giannini, M. (1989), 'Donne e Contratti di Formazione e Lavoro', *Politiche del Lavoro*, no. 8, Angeli, pp. 179-91.

Gierse, M. (1990), 'Kursfristige Arbeitsmarktwirkungen des Zustroms van Aus- und Übersiedlern', *RWI-Mitteilungen*, Jg. 41, pp. 153-67.

Gil Calvo, E. (1989), 'Participacion Laboral de la Mujer, Natalidad y Tamano de Cohortes', *REIS*, no. 47, July-September, pp. 137-75.

Goldmann, M. (1990), 'Berufsrückkehr nach einer Familienbedingten Unter-brechung', in Lucke, D. and Berghahn, S. (eds), *Rechtsratgeber Frauen. Unter Mitarbeit von Anke Scheiber*, Rowohlt, Hamburg, pp. 462-77.

Gottschall, K. (1986), 'Frauen auf dem Arbeitsmarkt : Verdrängung Statt Integration ?', *WSI-Mitteilungen*, no. 8, pp. 514-21.

Gottschall, K. (1987), *Arbeitsmarktpolitik für Frauen ? Zur Teilhabe Erwerbsloser Frauen en Arbeitsmarktbeschaffungsmaßnahmen*, in Rudolph, H. (ed.),*Ungeschützte Arbeitsverhältnisse. Frauen zwischen Risiko und Neuer Lebensqualität*, Hamburg, pp. 42-52.

Green, A. (1991), 'Spatial Aspects of the Single European Market Scenarios', paper presented at the IER/EOC Conference on the Implications of the Single European Market of the Employment of Women and Men in Great Britain, Warwick, March.

Gregg, P. (1990), 'The Evolution of Special Employment Measures', *National Institute Economic Review*, May.

Groot, L.F.M., Schippers, J.J. and Siegers, J.J. (1988), 'The Effects of Interruptions and Part-Time Work on Women's Wage Rate : A Test of the Variable-Intensity Model', *Economist*, pp. 36-54.

Grüning, M. (1986), 'Alles nur Zahlen... ? Vom Erkenntnileitendent Umgang mit Amtlichen Statistiken über Erwerbslove Frauen', *Frauenforschung*, no. 1-2, pp. 29-53.

Hakim, C. (1987), *Home-Based Work in Britain*, Research paper, no. 60, Department of Employment, London.

Hakim, C. (1988), 'Self-Employment in Britain : Recent Trends and Current Issues', *Work, Employment and Society*, December.

Hansen, P.V. (1982), *Lønforskelle, Lønpolitik og Beskæftigelse i 1970' Erne*, Socialforskningsintituttet, Publikation 111, København.

Hecq, C. and Meulders, D. (1990), 'Effets Sectoriels de l'Achèvement du Marché Intérieur sur l'Emploi Féminin en Belgique', Report for the Secrétariat d'Etat à l'Europe 1992, DULBEA, Brussels, July.

Heiligers, P. (1990), 'Toekomstige Herintreedsters, een Gevarieerd Aanbod aan Capaciteiten', *Tijdschrift voor Vrouwenstudies*, pp. 39-50.

Hellmann, U. and Schiersmann, C. (1990), 'Der Prozeß des Berufsübergangs und Berufliche Perspektiven Technisch Ausgebildeter Frauen', *Frauenforschung*, no.1-2, pp. 49-67.

Heran-Le Roy, O., Hiriart-Durruty, M. and Poinat, F. (1989), 'L'Activité Féminine dans les Régions', *INSEE Résultats, Série Emploi-Revenus*, no. 1.

Hlawaty, P. (1987), 'Empirische Untersuchungen über die Wirkungen des Bechäftigungsförderungsgesetzes', *Die Mitbestimmung*, no. 10, pp. 602-4.

Hofbauer, H. and Nagel, E. (1987), 'Mobilität nach Abschluß der Betrieblichen Berufsausbildung', *MittAB*, no.1, pp. 45-73.

Horrell, S. and Rubery, J. (1991), *Employer's Working-Time Policies and Women's Employment*, Equal Opportunities Commission, Research Series, HMSO.

Huinink, J. and Lauterbach, W. (1990), *Bedingungen des Erwerbsangebots Verheirateter Frauen, Vortrag für das IAB-Kontaktseminar zum Thema 'Erwerbstätigkeit- und Arbeitslosigkeitsanalyse auf Basis von Paneldaten' in Berlin*, mimeo, Berlin.

Humblet, P. (1989), 'Accueil des Enfants et Egalité des Chances : Un Programme des Communautés Européennes', *Revue du Travail*, January-February-March, pp. 17-28.

Humphries, J. (1983), 'The 'Emancipation' of Women in the 1970s and 1980s : From the Latent to the Floating', *Capital and Class*, no. 20, Summer.

Humphries, J. (1988), 'Women's Employment in Restructuring America : The Changing Experience of Women in Three Recessions', in Rubery, J. (ed.), *Women and Recession*, Routledge and Kegan Paul, London and New York..

Humphries, J. and Rubery, J. (1984), 'The Reconstitution of the Supply Side of the Labour Market : The Relative Autonomy of Social Reproduction', *Cambridge Journal of Economics*, vol. 8, December.

Humphries, J. and Rubery, J. (1991), *La Position des Femmes sur le Marché du Travail au Royaume Uni, Evolution entre 1983 et 1989*, Report for the Equal Opportunities Unit of the European Communities, Brussels.

Industrial Relations Services / Equal Opportunities Commission (IRS/EOC), (1991), *Pay and Gender in Britain*, IRS, London.

Ingram, P. and Cahill, J. (1989), 'Pay Determination in Private Manufacturing', *Employment Gazette*, June.

Institut National de Statistique (1990), *Recensement de la Population et des Logements au 1er mars 1981*, tome 8, Population Active.

International Labour Office (1989), *World Labour Report*, no.4.

Irish Times Supplement (1991), *Working and Living*, Dublin, 10 May.

Jäckel, S. and Kirner, E. (1987), 'Immer mehr Frauen im Beruf', *DIW-Wochenbericht*, no. 29, pp. 393-402.

Jahn, S., Reissert, B. and Schmid, G. (1989), *Mehr Arbeitsplätze durch Dienstleistungen ? - Ein Vergleich der Beschäftigungsentwicklung in den Ballungsregionen der Bundesrepublik Deutschland*, Discussion paper, no. FS I, 89-4, Wissenschaftzentrum Berlin, Berlin.

Janswijer, R. (1989), '1990 Begint Nog Lang Niet', *Jeugd en Samenleving*, pp. 360-72.

Jaspers, A.Ph.C.M. and Riphagen, J. (1991), *Schets van het Sociaal Zekerheidsrecht*, Deventer.

Jochmann-Döll, A. (1990), *Gleiber Lohn für Gleichwertige Arbeit. Ausländische und Deutsche Konzepte und Erfahrungen*. Hampp, München/Mering.

Jortay, F., Meulders, D. and Plasman, R. (1990), *An Evaluation of the Impact of the Implementation of the Single Market on the Employment of Women in Banking*, Report for the Equal Opportunities Unit of the European Communities, Brussels.

Judisch, M., Meine, H., Schwitzer, H. and Stamm, S. (1990), 'Wider die Lohndiskriminierung von Frauen - Konfliktlinien und Perspektiven in der Metalindustrie', *WSI-Mitteilungen*, no. 9, pp. 581-90.

Kamerstukken II (1990-91), 21 477, no. 13, Regeringsstandpunt ten aanzien van het rapport van de Wetenschappelijke Raad voor het Regeringsbeleid 'Een werkend perspectief'.

Kamerstukken II (1990-91), 21 800 XV, no. 53, Regeringsstandpunt inzake de positie van vrouwen in de arbeid.

Knudsen, R. (1989), 'Lønudviklingen for kvinder og mænd, i : Uden Ligeløn - Ingen Ligestilling', in Abel, V. and Wolfson, L. (eds), *Ka' Kvinder Arbejde ?*, Equality Council, København.

Knudsen, R. (1991), *La Position des Femmes sur le Marché du Travail au*

Danemark, Evolution entre 1983 et 1989, Report for the Equal Opportunities Unit of the European Communities, Brussels.

Krais, B. and Trommer, L. (1988), 'Studentenberg, Akademikerschäftigung', *WSI-Mitteilungen*, no.12, pp.712-30.

Kristensen, N.B. (1990), 'The Development of the Wage Structure for Salaried Employees in Denmark 1965-1988', paper presented at the EALE conference, Lund, 20-21 September.

Kurz-Sherf, I. (1986), 'Von der Emanzipation des Brunnenmädchens in Heilbädern - Frauendiskriminierung, Frauenförderung durch Tarifvertrag und Tarifpolitik', *WSI-Mitteilungen*, no. 8.

Landenberger, M. (1990), *Wirkungen des Erziehungsurlaubs auf Arbeitsmarktchancen und soziale Sicherung von Frauen,* Discussion paper, no. FS I 90-7, Wissenschaftszentrum Berlin, Berlin.

Lawson, N. (1984), 'The British Experiment', *Public Money*, September.

Lehmann, A. (1985), 'Le Travail à Temps Partiel de 1978 à 1983. Pratiques des Employeurs et Conditions d'Emploi des Salariés', *Travail et Emploi*, no. 26, December.

Le Monde (1991), 22 May.

Linne, G. and Vosswinkel, S. (1989), 'Befristete Arbeitsverträge : Aspekte eines Arbeitsverhältnisses ohne Bestandsschutz', *Arbeitspapier*, no. 5 des Arbeitskreises SAMF, Paderborn.

Lippman, C. (1989), 'Die Bedeutung der Betriebsvereinbarungen aus Arbeinehmerinnensicht', *Frauenforschung*, no. 1-2, pp. 121-30.

Livraghi, R. (1989), 'La Problematica del Lavoro Femminile e le Azioni Positive in Italia', in Ministero del Lavoro e della Previdenza Sociale (ed.), *Lavoro e Politiche della Occupazione in Italia,* Rapporto '89, Roma, pp. 436-47.

Lollivier, S. (1988), 'Activité et Arrêt d'Activité Féminine, le Diplôme et la Famille', *Economie et Statistiques*, no. 212, July-August.

Loontechnische Dienst (1978), *Verslag van de Loontechnische Dienst met Betrekking tot de Uitgeoefende Begeleidingstaak Inzake de Wet Gelijk Loon voor Vrouwen en Mannen over het Jaar 1977,* 's-Gravenhage.

Loontechnische Dienst (1987), *Functiewaardering in Nederland 1984', Ministerie van Sociale Zaken en Werkgelegenheid,* Den Haag.

Loontechnische Dienst (1988a), *De Positie van Mannen en Vrouwen in het Arbeidsproces', Ministerie van Sociale Zaken en Werkgelegenheid,* Den Haag.

Loontechnische Dienst (1988b), *Toepassing Bedrijfstakgebonden Functiewaarderingsregelingen in Nederland,* Ministerie van Sociale Zaken en Werkgelegenheid, Den Haag.

Loontechnische Dienst (1989), *Toepassing van de Functiewaarderingsregeling bij de Nederlandse Rijksoverheid,* Ministerie van Sociale Zaken en Werkgelegenheid, Den Haag.

Lörcher, K. (1982), 'Die Verbreitung von Zeitverträgen im Öffentlichen Dienst', *MittAB*, no.1, pp. 58-68.

Lucke, D. and Berghahn, S. (eds) (1990), *Rechtsratgeber Frauen. Unter Mitarbeit von Anke Scheiber*, Rowohlt, Hamburg.

MacLennan, E. and Weitzel, R. (1984), 'Labour Market Policy in Four Countries : Are Women Adequately Represented ?', in Schmid, G. and Weitzel, R. (eds), *Sex Discrimination and Equal Opportunity. The Labour*

Market and Employment Policy, Gower, Aldershot, pp. 202-48.

Maerkedahl, I. (1989), 'Knowledge but no Work', in Abel, V. and Wolfson, L. (eds), *Ka' Kvinder Arbejde ?*, Equality Council, København.

Marsh, C. (1991), *Hours of Work of Men and Women in Britain*, Equal Opportunities Commission, Research Series, HMSO.

Martin, J. and Roberts, C. (1984), 'Women's Employment in the 1980s : Evidence from the Women and Employment Survey', *Employment Gazette*, May.

Martin Pliego *et al.* (1990), *Politica Regional. Paro e Inflacion : El Caso de Espana*, Instituto de Estudios Fiscales, Madrid.

Martin, R. and Tyler, P. (1990), 'Local Disparities in Unemployment and Real Wages in Great Britain', *Cambridge Regional Economic Review*.

Martinez, E. and Vanheerswynghels, A. (1991), 'Estimation du Travail à Temps Partiel : Entre l'INAMI et l'INS ?', *Lettre d'Information, Point d'Appui Travail Emploi Formation*, February.

Martinotti, G. (ed.) (1982), *La Città Difficile*, Angeli, Milano,

Maruani, A. and Nicole, C. (1989), *Au Labeur des Dames, Métiers Masculins, Emplois Féminins*, Syros, Paris.

Maugeri, C. (1988), *I Lavoratori in CIGS e le Forme della Cassa Integrazione*, Angeli, Milano.

Mayer, C. (1987), 'Zum Spannungsverhältnis von Beruflicher Selbständigkeit von Frauen und Eigenständiger Existenzsicherung', in Rudolph, H. (ed.), *Ungeschützte Arbeitsverhältnisse. Frauen zwischen Risiko und Neuer Lebensqualität*, Hamburg, pp. 59-69.

Meiners, B. (1991), 'Die Liebe in der Moderne : Zum Verhältnis von Ökonomischer Umstrukturierung der Frauenerwerbsarbeit und Veränderten Lebensweisen von Frauen', *Beiträge zur Feministischen Theorie und Praxis*, no. 29, pp. 125-33.

Merelli, M. et al. (1985), *Giochi di Equilibrio*, Angeli, Milano.

Metcalf, H. and Leighton, P. (1989), *The Under-Utilization of Women in the Labour Market*, Institute of Manpower Studies, Report no. 172.

Metz-Göckel, S. and Müller, U. (1986), *Der Mann*, Dortmund.

Meulders, D. and Plasman, R. (1989a), 'Women in Atypical Employment', EEC, V/1426/89, Report for the Equal Opportunities Unit of the European Communities, 205 p.

Meulders, D. and Plasman, R. (1989b), 'Pouvoirs Publics et Nouvelles Formes d'Emploi', *Revue Française des Affaires Sociales*, Special Issue, November.

Meulders, D. and Plasman, O. (1991), 'The Impact of Single Market on Women's Employment in the Textile and Clothing Industry', *Social Europe*, Supplement, no. 2.

Meulders, D. and Vander Stricht, V. (1991), *La Position des Femmes sur le Marché du Travail en Belgique, Evolution entre 1983 et 1989*, Report for the Equal Opportunities Unit of the European Communities, Brussels.

Mingione, E. (1991), *Fragmented Societies*, Basil Blackwell, Oxford.

Ministère de la Présidence du Conseil (1990), *Bulletin Statistique sur le Personnel du Secteur Public*, Athens.

Ministère de l'Emploi et du Travail (1990a), *La Négociation des Plans d'Actions Positives dans les Entreprises Privées*, Ministère de l'Emploi et du Travail, Brussels.

Ministère de l'Emploi et du Travail (1990b), *Le Marché du Travail en Belgique*, Ministère de l'Emploi et du Travail, Brussels.

Ministère de l'Emploi et du Travail (1991a), *Femmes au Foyer à la Recherche d'un Emploi*, Ministère de l'Emploi et du Travail, Brussels.

Ministère de l'Emploi et du Travail (1991b), *Les Aides à l'Embauche : Réductions des Charges Sociales*, Ministère de l'Emploi et du Travail, Brussels.

Ministère du Travail (1990), *Rapport d'Activité, 1989*, Grand-Duché de Luxembourg.

Ministère du Travail (1991), *Rapport d'Activité, 1990*, Grand-Duché de Luxembourg.

Ministerie van Binnenlandse Zaken (1983-87), *Emancipatie in Cijfers, 1983-87*, Den Haag.

Ministerie van Sociale Zaken en Werkgelegenheid (1988a, 1989, 1990), *Rapportage Arbeidsmarkt 1988, 1989, 1990*, 's-Gravenhage.

Ministerie van Sociale Zaken en Werkgelegenheid (1988b), *Vrouwen en Nachtarbeid, Onderzoek naar Nachtarbeid door Vrouwen in de Industrie*, 's-Gravenhage.

Ministero del Lavoro e della Previdenza Sociale (ed.) (1990), *Lavoro e Politiche della Occupazione in Italia*, Rapporto '89, Roma.

Miscione, M. (1989), 'Qualificazione del Contratto di Formazione e Lavoro', in Neri, F. (ed.), *Le Politiche del Lavoro degli Anno '80*, Angeli, Milano, pp. 205-24.

Mitter, S. (1986), 'Industrial Restructuring and Manufacturing Homework : Immigrant Women in the UK Clothing Industry', *Capital and Class*, no. 27.

Mogensen, G.V. (eds) (1990), *Time and Consumption. Time Use and Consumption in Denmark in the Last Decades*, Danmarks Statistik, København.

Möller, C. (1991), 'Über das Brot, das Euch in der Küche Fehlt, Wird Nicht in der Küche Entschieden', *Beiträge zur Feministischen Theorie und Praxis*, no. 29, pp. 7-24.

Moss, P. (1990), 'Childcare in the European Communities', *Women of Europe, Suplements*, no. 31, August.

Mottura, G. and Pugliese, E. (1975), *Agricoltura Mezzogiorno e Mercato del Lavoro*, Il Mulino, Bologna.

Nassisi, A.M. (ed.) (1990), *Il Lavoro Femminile in Italia tra Produzione e Riproduzione*, Primo Rapporto, Fondazione Gramsci, Roma.

Neri, F. (ed.) (1989), *Le Politiche del Lavoro degli Anno '80*, Angeli, Milano.

Neubauer, E. (1988), 'Alleinerziehende Mütter und Väter - Eine Analyse der Gemastsituation', *Schriftenreihe des BMJFFG*, Band 219, Stuttgart.

Nouws, J. and Meijs-Appels, M. (1989), *Doorwerken rond de Bevalling. Een Onderzoek naar Zwangerschaps- en Bevallingsverlof voor Zelfstandige en Meewerkende Vrouwen in het MKB*, Economisch Instituut voor het Midden en Kleinbedrijf, Zoetermeer.

Office National de l'Emploi (ONEM) (1989), *Les Chômeurs Complets Indemnisés, Sondage au 30 juin 1989*, Office National de l'Emploi, Brussels.

Office National de l'Emploi (ONEM) (1990), 'Les Mesures de Résorption du Chômage', *Bulletin Mensuel de l'ONEM*, July, pp. 5.1-5.69.

Office Régional Bruxellois de l'Emploi (ORBEM) (1990), *Les Aides à l'Emploi*, ORBEM, Brussels.

Oosterhaven, J. (1991), *Het Noorden in Europees Perspectief : Regionale Economie in de Praktijk, Oratie*, Groningen.

Organisme pour l'Emploi de la Force de Travail (OAED) (1991a), *Le Phénomène du Chômage de Longue Durée en Grèce*, Athens.

Organisme pour l'Emploi de la Force de Travail (OAED) (1991b), *Promotion de l'Emploi et de la Formation Professionnelle des Femmes*, Athens.

Organization for Economic Cooperation and Development (OECD) (1988, 1989 and 1991a), *Employment Outlook*, OECD, Paris.

Organization for Economic Cooperation and Development (OECD) (1991b), *Shaping Structural Change, The Role of Women*, Report by a high-level group of experts to the Secretary General, Paris.

Ostendorf, H. (1987), 'Arbeitsbeschaffungsmaßnahmen für Frauen ? Die Unzulänglichkeit des Wichtigsten Arbeitsmarktpolitischen Instruments', in Rudolph, H. (ed.), *Ungeschützte Arbeitsverhältnisse. Frauen zwischen Risiko und neuer Lebensqualität*, Hamburg, pp. 29-41.

Ouziel, J. (1991), 'Quinze Ans de Lutte contre le Chômage : Entre Gestion Sociale et Intervention Economique', *Revue de Travail*, January-February-March.

Paci, M. (ed.) (1985), *Famiglia e Mercato del Lavoro in un'Economia Periferica*, Angeli, Milano.

Papo, M. (1989), 'L'Evoluzione dell'Offerta e della Domanda di Lavoro nel Periodo 1985-1989', in Ministero del Lavoro e della Previdenza Sociale (ed.), *Lavoro e Politiche della Occupazione in Italia*, Rapporto '89, Roma, pp. 93-115.

Payne, J. (1990), 'Adult Off-the-Job Skills Training : An Evaluation Study, PSI', *The Training Agency Research and Development Report*, no. 57, Sheffield.

Pedersen, L. and Plougth, N. (1991), *Løntilskudsordninger*, Report 91 : 3, Socialforskningsintituttet, København.

Peinado Lopez, A. (1988), *La Discriminacion de la Mujer en el Mercado de Trabajo Espanol*, Ministerio de Trabajo, Madrid.

Perulli, P. (1988), 'Il Lavoro Manuale non Operaio nelle Società Avanzate. Stati Uniti, Gran Bretagna, Italia', *Prospettiva Sindicale*, no. 69.

Pfarr, H. (1988), *Quoten und Grundgesetz. Notwendigkeit und Verfassungsmäßigkeit von Frauenförderung*, unter Mitarbeit von Fuchsloch, C., Nomos, Baden-Baden.

Pfarr, H. and Bertelsmann, K. (1981), *Lohngleichheit. Zur Rechtsssprechung bei Geschlechtsspezifischer Entgeltdiskriminierung*, Stuttgart.

Phizacklea, A. (1990), *Unpacking the Fashion Industry : Gender, Racism and Class in Production*, Routledge.

Plantenga, J. (1991), *La Position des Femmes sur le Marché du Travail aux Pays-Bas, Evolution entre 1983 et 1989*, Report for the Equal Opportunities Unit of the European Communities, Brussels.

Plantenga, J., Schippers, J.J. and Siegers, J.J. (1990), 'Een Afwijkend Patroon ? Een Vergelijkend Onderzoek naar Participatie en Segregatie op de Arbeidsmarkt in Nederland en de Bondsrepubliek Duitsland, 1960-1985', *Mens en Maatschappij*, pp. 337-54.

Plasman, O. and Plasman, R. (1991), *La Position des Femmes sur le Marché du Travail au Luxembourg, Evolution entre 1983 et 1989*, Report for the Equal Opportunities Unit of the European Communities, Brussels.

Plasman, R. (1989), 'Les Politiques d'Emploi en Belgique : Analyse et Estimation de leur Impact Macroéconomique', *Cahiers Economiques de Bruxelles*, no. 122.

Platz, M. (1988), *Arbejdstid*, Report 88 : 8, Socialforsk-ningsintituttet, København.

Pontarollo, E. (1982), *Tendenze della Nuova Imprenditorio nel Mezzogiorno degli Anni '70*, Angeli, Milano.

Postler, J. (1987), 'Arbeitslose Frauen und Berufliche Weiterbildung nach dem Arbeitsförderungsgesetz', *Frauenforschung*, no. 4, pp. 55-76.

Rabe-Kleberg, U. (1987), *Frauenberufe - Zur Segmentierung der Berufswelt*, Bielefed.

Regini, M. (ed.) (1988), *La Sfida della Flessibilità*, Angeli, Milano.

Regini, M. and Sabel, C.F. (1989), *Strategie di Raggiungimento Industriale*, Il Mulino, Bologna.

Rella, P. (1990), 'Le Donne nel Pubblico Impiego', in Nassisi, A.M. (ed.), *Il Lavoro Femminile in Italia tra Produzione e Riproduzione*, Primo Rapporto, Fondazione Gramsci, Roma, pp. 101-52.

Robijns, M. and Volman, M. (1990), 'Zorgzelfstandigheid', *Tijdschrift voor Onderwijs en Opvoeding*, pp. 40-1.

Rosti, L. (1987), 'L'Occupazione Indipendente in Italia : Stock e Flussi', *Economia e Lavoro*, no. 4, pp. 15-27.

Rubery, J. (ed.) (1988), *Women and Recession*, Routledge and Kegan Paul, London and New York.

Rubery, J. (1991), *Equal Pay and Institutional Systems of Pay Determination : A Comparative Study*, Study for the Commission of the European Communities, Contract no. 900547, January.

Rubery, J., Horrell, S. and Burchell, B. (1990), 'Part-Time Work and Gender Inequality in the Labour Market', paper presented to the International Working Party on Labour Market Segmentation conference, Trento, July, and forthcoming in Scott, A. (ed.), *Gender Segregation in British Labour Markets*, OUP.

Rubery, J., Earnshaw, J. and Burchell, B. (1991), *New Forms and Patterns of Employment : the Role of Self-employment in Britain*, Report of the Zentrum fur Europaisches Rechtspolitik, Bremen.

Rudolph, H. (1987a), 'Befristete Beschäftigung - ein Überblick', *MittAB*, no. 2, pp. 257-70.

Rudolph, H. (ed.) (1987b), *Ungeschützte Arbeitsverhältnisse. Frauen zwischen Risiko und Neuer Lebensqualität*, Hamburg.

Samek, L.M. (1987), 'L'Evoluzione della Struttura Industriale e il Ruolo della Piccola Impresa Meridionale : 1981-1985', *Rassegna Economica*, no.1 January, February.

Saraceno C. (ed.) (1980), *Il Lavoro Maldiviso*, De Donato, Bari.

Schippers, J.J. (1989), *Beloningsverschillen tussen Mannen en Vrouwen*, Groningen.

Schmid, G. and Weitzel, R. (1984), *Sex Discrimination and Equal Opportunity. The Labour Market and Employment Policy*, Gower, Aldershot.

Schwarze, J. (1988), Nebenerwerbstätigkeit in der BRD, Dissertation, Berlin.

Scicchitano, M. (1985), *Cassa Integrazione e Discoccupazione Involontaria, Prestazioni e Procedure*, Edizione Lavoro, Roma.

Segura, J., Duran, M., Toharia, L. and Bentolila, A. (1991), *Analisis de la Contratacion Temporal en Espana*, Ministerio de Trabajo y Seg. Social, Madrid.

Semenza, R. and Ichino, A. (1987), *Riduzione dell'Occupazione Industriale e Mobilita di Lavoro*, IRES, Lombardia.

Serdjenian, E. (1988), *12 Programmes Européens pour l'Egalité Professionnelle*, V/1483/90-FR, Commission des Communautés Européennes, Brussels.

Sgritta, G.B. (eds) (1988), *Percorsi Femminili : Lavoro, Formazione e Famiglia nella Regione Lazio*, Angeli, Milano.

Simon, A. (1991), 'De l'Indemnisation aux Politiques du Marché du Travail', *Revue du Travail*, January-February-March.

Singh, A. (1977), 'UK Industy and the World Economy : a Case of De-Industrialisation ?', *Cambridge Journal of Economics*, June.

Singh, A. (1989), 'Third World Competition and De-Industrialisation in Advanced Countries', *Cambridge Journal of Economics*, March.

Sirati, A. (1987), 'Differenze Retributive e Segregazione Occupazionale per Sesso nell'Industria Manifatturiera', *Economia e Lavoro*, July-September.

Skinhøj, K. (1989), *Kvinder og Mænd i Mandefag*, Report 89 : 15, Socialforskningsintituttet, København.

Smith, N. (1990), *Male-Female Differentials in Denmark - In Nordic Labour Market Policies and Labour Market Research*, Nordic Council of Ministers, NORD 1990 : 117.

Smith, N. and Westergaard-Nielsen, N. (1988), 'Wage Differential Due to Gender', *Population Economics*, no. 3.

Sormano, A. (1988), *L'Espulsione Tutelata, Processi di Riconversione Socio-Lavorativa degli ex Dipendenti delle Granci Fabbriche*, IRES, Torino.

Steedman, H. and Wagner, K. (1989), 'Productivity, Machinery and Skills : Clothing Manufacture in Britain and Germany', *National Institute Economic Review*, May.

Stiftung F.E. (1985), *Rationalisierung, Intensivierung und 'Arbeitsmarkt' in der DDR*, Bonn.

Strauss, J. and Jablonka, P. (1984), *Strukturen und Entwicklungen der Ausbildung und Beschäftigung Junger Frauen in NRW*, im Auftrag des Bundesministers für Arbeit, Gesundheit und Soziales des Landes NRW, Dortmund.

Sullerot, E. (1988), *Diversification des Choix Profesionnels des Filles et des Femmes*, V/111734/90-FR, Commission des Communautés Européennes, Brussels.

Tölke, Angelika (1989), Lebensverläufe von Frauen. München.

Tollet, R. and Vandewalle, J. (1987), *L'Emploi à Temps Partiel de 1973-1985*, Bureau du Plan, Brussels.

Tollet, R. and Vandewalle, J. (1989), *L'Emploi à Temps Partiel de 1983-1987*, Bureau du Plan, Brussels.

van Amstel, R. and van den Berg, T. (1991), *Evaluatie Stimuleringsregeling Positieve Actie voor Vrouwen*, Ministerie van Sociale Zaken en Werkgelegenheid, 's-Gravenhage.

195

van der Laan, L. and van den Bout, E. (1991), 'Een Analyse van de Regionale Verschillen in de Participatie van Vrouwen op de Arbeidsmarkt in Nederland', *Tijdschrift voor Politieke Economie*, pp. 43-53.

van der Laan, L. and Scholten, H. (1989), 'Regionale Aspecten van de Arbeidsmarktparticipatie in Nederland', *Mens en Maatschappij*, pp. 405-23.

van Paridon, K. (1989), 'De Werkgelegenheid in Nederland : Duidelijkheid Gewenst !', *Economisch-Statistische Berichten*, pp. 1031-2.

Van Regemortel, T. and Vandeloo, R. (1990), *Femmes Rentrantes, un Groupe à Risques pas comme les Autres*, Hoger Instituut voor de Arbeid, Leuven.

Veldman, A.G. (1989), 'Arbeid van Gelijke Waarde', *Gedrag en Organisatie*, pp. 20-36.

Veldman, A.G.and Wittink, R. (1990), *De Kans van Slagen; Invloeden van Culturen en Regels op de Loopbanen van Vrouwen*, Leiden.

Vlemickx, M. (1991), 'Participation des Femmes au Marché du Travail : Oui mais pas n'Importe Comment !', *Aperçu Economique Trimestriel*, Ministère des Affaires Economiques, Brussels, pp. 117-35.

Vogel-Polsky, E. and Vogel, J. (1991), *L'Europe Sociale 1993 : Illusion, Alibi ou Réalité ?*, Editions de l'Université Libre de Bruxelles, Brussels.

Vollmer, C. (1987), 'Frauenpolitik und Arbeitspolitik', in Fricke, W. (ed.), *Jahrbuch Arbeit und Technik in Nordrhein-Westfalen*, Dietz, Bonn, pp. 143-52.

Volman, M. (1991), 'Leren voor Gelijkheid; Kanttekeningen bij het Onderwijsemancipatiebeleid', *Tijdschrift voor Vrouwenstudies*, pp. 47-60.

Volqvartz, S. (1989), 'Equality in Occupational Training', in Abel, V. and Wolfson, L. (eds), *Ka' Kvinder Arbejde ?,* Equality Council, København.

von Lübke, K. (1989), *Das Arbeitsförderungsgesetz als Instrument zur Bekämpfung der Frauenarbeitslosigkeit*, in Aumüller-Roske, U. and Pollvogt, R. (eds), *Frauenerwerbslosigkeit in Osnabrück*, Lang, Frankfurt/Main, pp. 189-207.

Walsh, J. and Brown, W. (1990), *Regional Earnings and Pays Flexibility*, Working paper, no. 9008, Department of Applied Economics, University of Cambridge.

Weggelaar, M., Trommel, W. and Molenaar, F. (1986), *Doorstroming van Vrouwen in het Bedrijfsleven; Feiten en Visies*, Ministerie van Sociale Zaken en Werkgelegenheid, Den Haag.

Wentholt, K. (1990), 'Emancipatiebeleid Dringt niet door in de Nieuwe Arbeidstijdenwet', *Sociaal Maandblad Arbeid*, pp. 444-55.

Wetenschappelijke Raad voor het Regeringsbeleid (1990), *Een Werkend Perspectief : Arbeidsparticipatie in de Jaren '90*, 's-Gravenhage.

Winkler, G. (ed.) (1990a), *Sozialreport DDR 1990*, Stuttgart/München/Landsberg.

Winkler, G. (ed.) (1990b), *Frauenreport' 90*, im Auftrag der Beauftragten des Ministerrates für die Gliechstellung von Frauen und Männern, Dr. Marina Beyer, Berlin.

Winkler, U. (1990), 'Leistungen nach dem Arbeitsförderungsgesetz bei Arbeitslosigkeit', in Lucke, D. and Berghahn, S. (eds), *Rechtsratgeber Frauen. Unter Mitarbeit von Anke Scheiber*, Rowohlt, Hamburg, pp. 185-213.

Wloch, E. and Ambos, I. (1986), 'Erschlißung Neuer Beruflicher Arbeitsfelder und Tätigkeiten für Frauen - Frauen als Gelbständige', *Frauenforschung*, no. 3, pp. 1-33.

Wunn, C. (1983), 'Kein Fortschritt für Frauen - Zu den Novellierungen des Arbeitsförderungsgesetzes', *Frauenforschun*, no. 3-4, pp. 92-102.

Wunn, C. (1989), 'Rechtliche Rahmenbedingungen und Förderungsmöglichkeiten der Beruflichen Wiedereingliederung', *Frauenforschung*, no.1-2, pp. 109-20.

Youth Employment Agency (1985), *Transition from School to Work*, Youth Employment Agency, Dublin.

Zander, M. (1991), 'Konservative Familienpolitik als Investition in die Zukunft', *Beiträge zur feministischen Theorie und Praxis*, no. 29, pp. 95-104.

ZE Frauenforschung (eds.) (1983), *Zentraleinrichtung zur Förderung von Frauenstudien und Frauenforschung an der FU Berlin,* Vortragsreihe zur Frauenforschung SoSe 82 - WS 82/83, Berlin West.